THE CRUEL RADIANCE

RON POWERS

THE CRUEL RADIANCE

Notes of a Prosewriter
in a Visual Age

Middlebury College Press

Published by University Press of New England
Hanover and London

PN
4775
P645
1994

Middlebury College Press
Published by University Press of New England,
Hanover, NH 03755
© 1994 by Ron Powers
Printed in the United States of America
5 4 3 2 1
CIP data appear at the end of the book

FOR RICHARD HAWLEY,

BREAD LOAF COMRADE

AND TEACHER

CONTENTS

PREFACE

The pieces in this collection are the work of a journalist who has tried to advance his craft into the reaches of . . . what? I started to type out "literary nonfiction," but was dizzied by a rush of such intense nausea that it could have been induced only by an oversurge of Type A Jargon Antibodies or the shade of my old Hannibal confederate, Samuel L. Clemens. "High and fine literature is wine," he wrote to someone once, "and mine is water; but everybody likes water."

On the other hand, Clemens actually committed some high and fine literature; and he had an alias to cover him as well; so all of that is easy for *him* to say. Let me begin again:

The pieces in this collection are the work of a journalist who has heard of "literary nonfiction" and tried feverishly to . . .

No nausea this time, but that somehow doesn't sound exactly right either. Give me a moment to get in touch with my Inner Thesaurus, and I will give it one more try.

The pieces in this collection are the work of a journalist, mostly unscathed by his education in the Midwest and mostly innocent of aesthetic, who, in newspaper city rooms in St. Louis and Chicago, grew bedazzled by the daily demonstration that relatively unknown men and women in shirtsleeves and sensible shoes—people within an arm's reach or a burning cigarette's range—could conjure brilliant universes on the printed page, via narrative and critical analysis formed out of vivid observation and direct experience.

That's enough dependent clauses to send Henry James himself reeling out of the room. It seems we're getting somewhere, somewhere . . . literary. Let's build on it:

. . . And has tried to advance this craft beyond dailiness into the reaches of that-which-endures—what James Agee called "the cruel radiance of what is." Has tried to do so by enlisting those charged elements—narrative and critical analysis, formed out of vivid observation and direct experience—in the service of themes that matter to him. Paramount among them, the location and affirmation of human community.

* * *

Why does this precision of origin and purpose matter? I think because both the origin and the purpose I have described (and lived) are currently imperiled—at least as they relate to "serious" writing and the writerly consciousness. That is to say, both "journalism" and "community" as they are now understood have been transmuted—reduced—from replenishing elements of a stable society to the marginalized, often synthetic vestiges of a convulsive one.

The newspapering life as literary seedbed-in-the-rough has been a long-standing, if underappreciated, dynamic of American intellectual life. Shelly Fisher Fishkin has pointed out that "American writers have continually struggled to wrest art from the raw material of life as if no one had ever done so before."[1] She has traced this impulse—the core of a "distinctively American aesthetic"—to the newspaper and periodical apprenticeships served by a bibliography of American *literati* whose breadth might astonish the unsuspecting: Whitman and Twain and Hemingway, of course; but also John Greenleaf Whittier, and Willa Cather, and Katherine Anne Porter, and Eugene O'Neill, and Robert Frost, and Eudora Welty, and Carl Sandburg, and Frank Norris—among many others.

Since the end of World War II, newspapers and magazines have still occasionally attracted the novelist- or essayist-in-chrysalis—the former *Washington Post* reporter Tim O'Brien and the ex-*Vogue Magazine* ad copywriter Joan Didion, and James Agee himself come quickly to mind—but this connection, so bountiful for a century, atrophies with each passing year. The death of dailies, the shrinking size of the survivors, the abolition of narrative copy in favor of TV-analogous charts, graphics, and crunched verbiage; the emerging folk literature of grievance and aggression; and the magazine world's collective gaudy loss of soul, have guaranteed that.

Newspaper journalists even of my recent era, the 1970s, in certain ways would have less in common with the Gannetized fact-processors of 1994 than they had with reporters of Mark Twain's day. "I had been dropped willy-nilly into a world that

---

1. Shelley Fisher Fishkin, *From Fact to Fiction: Journalism and Imaginative Writing in America* (New York: Oxford University Press, 1985), p. 6.

fitted me as water fits a fish," wrote one of them, Ben Hecht, of his introduction to the Chicago newspapering life in 1910, a few months before Twain died. "It was a world that offered no discipline, that demanded no alteration in me. It bade me go out and look at life, devour it, enjoy it, report it. There were no responsibilities beyond enthusiasm."[2] I knew that world, or one almost exactly like it, in the same city sixty years later.

No responsibilities, perhaps (and certainly no "literary nonfiction," either!), but a saving ecstasy of perception that supplied all the motivation. "I was a newspaper reporter, playwright, novelist, short-story writer, propagandist, publisher and crony of wild hearts and fabulous gullets," exulted Hecht in his memoir. "I haunted streets, whore houses, police stations, courtrooms, theater stages, jails, saloons, slums, mad houses, fires, murders, riots, banquet halls and bookshops."[3] He savored, through his recall, "The walls of the city, the buildings that slid off into space; the rooftops of houses like a tangle of decks of ships at anchor; the smoke of chimneys making awning stripes across the sky . . ."[4]

This overflowing consciousness of Hecht's not only projected its momentum forward six decades, to the shirtsleeve poets of my newspaper era in Chicago; it radiated backward in time as well, and conjoined with what was perhaps its own formative voice: "The blab of the pave . . . the tires of carts and sluff of boot-soles and talk of the promenaders, The heavy omnibus, the driver with his interrogating thumb . . . Arrests of criminals, slights, adulterous offers made, acceptances, rejections with convex lips/I mind them or the resonance of them . . . I come again and again."[5] This is Whitman, the poet, recalling the world of Whitman the young editor of the New York *Aurora*. Form from facts, as Emerson instructed.

But in an age of managerial editing-by-market-research, when facts are industrially processed into factoids, when ecstasy is

---

2. Ben Hecht, *A Child of the Century* (New York: Primus/Donald Fine, 1985), p. 119.

3. Ibid., p. 113.

4. Ibid., p. 112.

5. Walt Whitman, from *Walt Whitman's Leaves of Grass: Authoritative Texts, Prefaces, Whitman on His Art, Criticism* (New York: W. W. Norton & Co., 1973), p. 36.

tamed into the ironic smirk, and when the richness of narrative development is jettisoned under television's impatient competitive glare and replaced with the robotically punning headline, the imaginations of those supplying the "content"—the stories—cannot but wither. At this writing, my friend the Princeton scholar and elegant prose stylist Anne Matthews ("Where the Buffalo Roam") is developing an essay on "the problem of observation in reporting, or observation as the great neglected reporter's art." Her quest is timely. With a few exceptions, it's not a place in the literary pantheon, but a regular spot on the Capital Gang, that beckons the Hechts and Whitmans of our time.

As for "community," the pages of our factoid newspapers unscroll its daily obituary. Religious and racial/ethnic street-battles in the cities; the ongoing suburbanization and security-gate privatization of American living space; the institutional abandonment of the mentally ill and the homeless; the great public turning-away from financing public education; the growing popularity of "grievance" and "personal therapy" books and cults; the annihilation of Main Street by the interstate-accessible Superstore; government opinion polls and factionalized voting blocs; shock radio; ideological warfare and rising intolerance on college campuses.

My point in yoking these two seemingly unrelated concepts—expansive, narrative journalism-as-storytelling, and beloved community—is that the former has always helped create the latter. More accurately, each creates the other: In telling the people of a certain place the elemental tales about themselves and their place, the teller creates the common consciousness necessary for community. Likewise, the common consciousness of a community at once enhances the need for a teller—as honest broker of local history, ritual and myth—and serves as a sort of moral regulator; it assures, by the critical attention it pays, that the broker remains honest.

Wendell Berry established this affinity most gorgeously in his unforgettable image of the battered galvanized bucket hanging from a fencepost on Kentucky land that had been his grandfather's farm. Over many autumns, the bucket had filled with leaves; and also rain and snow, and nuts carried by squirrels, and animal droppings, and dead insects, and the feathers and droppings of birds. "This slow work of growth and death, gravity and decay, which is the chief work of the world, has by now produced in the bottom of the bucket several inches of black humus,"[6] writes Berry, who sees metaphor inside there as well. "It is one of the signs by which I know my country and myself," he goes on. "It collects stories, too, as they fall through time . . . It is doing in a passive way what a human community must do actively and thoughtfully . . . collect leaves and stories, and turn them into account. It must build soil, and build that memory of itself . . . that will be its culture."[7]

That is the idea—preservation of the human community, and preservation of it particularly through storytelling—that compels me the most as a writer. It is the common thread that binds together the work I have done as a television critic (corporatized television being one of the most powerful anticommunitarian forces ever created, although the technology itself offers many resources, mostly untapped, for collecting local stories and turning them into account); as a novelist and in my present pursuit, as a writer of nonfiction books.

And that idea contains the reason why I cannot, with a straight face, talk about my writing in terms of "literary nonfiction"— though there are many days when I secretly wish I could.

I am not, you see, dammit anyway, one of those fortunate and admirable writers who can proceed from the conscious intention of exhibiting a certain elegant design, or structure, or unified field of technique—what writing instructors call *form*. (Ask me to write a short story in the first person demonstrating the efficacy of the Unreliable Narrator and you're likely to induce a catatonic trance.) Passion—often some complicated stew of anger, laughter, and regret—is my igniting force, and my "methodology" is to make a headlong rush into as many facts, personal observations, and sensory impressions as time and energy permit me, and then

6. "The Work of Local Culture," in *What Are People For? Essays by Wendell Berry*, (San Francisco: North Point Press, 1990), p. 153.

7. Ibid., p. 154.

sift compulsively through them until, somewhat Zenlike I suppose, some intrinsic pattern of order finds its way to *me*.

On those feverish terms, I must own up that I have drawn my inspiration from a source fierier even than my fellow townsman Sam Clemens, with his pen warmed up in Hell: that other enflamed fugitive son of a mid-Southern river town, the late Mr. James Agee of Knoxville, Tennessee.

I came upon Agee's work while I was still a feckless newspaperman in Chicago. Came crashing down upon it, in fact; and in this case I was worse than feckless. I encountered Agee as the kind of reader he always suspected he was stuck with.

I had written a television column in which I had tossed in a trope on the phrase, "Let us now praise famous men." A few days later an angry reader wrote to tell me I lacked the depth and the moral intelligence to deal so flippiantly with the title of James Agee's great book, a book that I probably had never read. I fired back a letter assuring the woman that *of course* I had read the book; I practically knew it by heart and she had obviously missed the subtle allusion that I had intended. Then I ran out to a bookstore on Michigan Avenue and bought the damned thing, so that I could quote some passages to her if she dared keep the argument going.

Many and strange are the paths to enlightenment. When I felt Agee's hands reach out from the pages of that vast tormented feat of human witnessing and clutch me by the throat as his stridulent voice demanded, *"Who are you who will read these words and study these photographs, and through what cause, by what chance and for what purpose, and by what right do you qualify to . . . ?"* I was at once celestially rebuked for my ignoramus vanity and released from its constrictions for all time.

"For in the immediate world, everything is discerned, for him who can discern it . . . with the whole of consciousness," Agee wrote, thrashing out his luminous obsession with those sharecropper families in Alabama in the summer of 1936,[8] ". . . and all of consciousness is shifted from the imagined, the revisive, to the effort to perceive simply the cruel radiance of what is."

---

8. I dwell on this passage, and Agee, at greater length in the Bread Loaf lecture, "Don't Think of It as Art: Nonfiction and the Inflected Voice."

The cruel radiance of what is. More than twenty years after I first gaped at those words, they have not left me alone. They, and the monumental, flawed, great beating heart of a book that they ushered me into, have answered so many questions in my writing life: questions involving money, publicity, and comfort; questions involving the acceptance of one's chosen demons and the value of pretension toward Art; questions involving the existence or nonexistence of Truth and whether it matters to pursue ordinary truthfulness even if its apotheosis must forever remain a mystery. *The cruel radiance of what is.* Reason enough to fashion a writing life, however ambiguous its ultimate yield; and that is what I have done, and that is why.

Middlebury, Vermont,
February 23, 1994

THE CRUEL RADIANCE

Part One

FIVE BREAD LOAF LECTURES

These essays owe their existence and whatever value they may possess to Robert Pack, who directed the Bread Loaf Writers Conference from 1973 until his retirement in August 1994. I first attended Bread Loaf in 1979, as a fellow in fiction. It was Pack, I learned years later, who took the long view regarding my humid first novel and decided to let me in. Thank goodness he was not in the mood for affirming limits. The precision and the sublime inquiry of Robert Pack's own poetic odysseys, as they have revealed themselves to me over the years, cause me to wonder what he might have seen in that fervid work, "half autobiographical, half successful," that he pulled from the submissions pile that year.

How hard it is, now, to recover a memory of what I, the wary Midwestern interloper two years removed from the *Chicago Sun-Times* features department, expected. My mind's eye has preserved a real or conjured anticipatory image, something like a grainy black-and-white newsprint flash-photograph: several pale and baleful Authors, their talons dug into plastic winecups garlanded by soggy napkins, who seem to be vaporizing into the Vermont night upon the capacity of hyperpluralism in art to destroy the possibility of eponymy, as seen from the perspective of a Weimar burgher. Or something like that.

But I will never forget my first flood of actual impressions: an impossible nineteenth-century aerie in a rounded meadow eight winding mountain miles off the scuffed surface of America, which seemed even to occupy its separate season—sodden August giving way to crisp autumn in a matter of rapidly elevating minutes. A blue-gray wall of higher mountains in the distance, tendrils of cloud curling into their crevices; and here, filling my view as I unfold myself from the car, the campus virtually as it looked in 1882: a phalanx of upright three-story cottages with stacked porches, yellow clapboards and green Mansard roofs; and, anchoring them, similarly trimmed in yellow and green, the triumphal Victorian vessel known as the Bread Loaf Inn.[1]

My enduring regret, as I have returned to Bread Loaf over the intervening summers, has been that I can vaguely recall, but can never relive, that first transition from the quotidian to the charmed; from the

1. For a more sumptuous rendering of the Bread Loaf ambience, see "Whose Woods These Are: A History of the Bread Loaf Writers Conference 1926–1992," by David Haward Bain (Hopewell, N.J.: Ecco Press, 1993).

world as we have accepted it to a chamber of the world as we might dream it.

Words and sentences spoken in this charged New England enclave, I would soon learn, took on a verdurous intensity—dangerous, almost, to absorb in sustained quantities—that they seemed to draw from the ambient light and air. This was especially true of words and sentences spoken from the battered wooden podium to the audience in the Little Theatre, where lectures and readings took place. Such shaped, such *right*, words and sentences; hearing them gave the tantalizing illusion that, of course, *that* was the way to do it; *that* was how to write—an illusion that would not evaporate until many days later, when one's own fingers descended malletlike on one's own keyboard again.

Frost, McCullers, Stegner, Toni Morrison had leaned their elbows on the slanted surface of that old upright crate. And John Gardner, one night before my initiate-eyes, with the theater in utter darkness except for a lone spotlight setting his platinum hair ablaze. Populating the night with his monsters and saints.

The responsibility of speaking from that knocked-together podium was unimaginable to me—privelege and terror in equal quantities. Not that there was much danger of my ever being thrown in harm's way. Or even setting foot on these grounds again.

Two summers later I stood at the podium with what seemed to be a Bread Loaf lecture clutched in my fists. This was my third trip to the Mountain—Bob Pack had asked me at the last minute, the summer before, to fill a vacancy as a staff association in nonfiction—and my first as a senior staff member. I had not begun working on this lecture until several days after Pack's invitation, in September 1980; and I'd finished revising it at least eight or ten minutes before its scheduled delivery.

It was hardly a conventional Bread Loaf talk, if there is such a thing; certainly it was not "literary." In it, I had clung closely to the shore of the world I knew—the world of mass communications, particularly television, with its behaviorist techniques for sampling and quantifying the public's receptivity to ideas and information and its marketing techniques for appeasing the public's preferences. My point was that serious writers were inescapably affected by this new craft of manipulating and merchandising the perception of truth.

It got me through the hour without being hissed or stoned.

In succeeding summers Robert Pack continued to invite me back, always to my surprise—it was fully five years before I could steady myself to have a sustained conversation with his formidable eminence in the faculty hospitality bungalow—and each summer I continued to push a little farther away from that safe shore. My talks gathered more and more of their critical weight from the realm of American prose writing, its lineage and its moral accountability to its readers, and less and less from the narrow perspective of information packaging in a TV-dominated culture.

And yet I never let that shore slip entirely from my view. I had discovered a concern that linked the coarsened popcult world I'd come to know as a journalist and the more rarefied concerns of this new writing community: the concern that "serious" writers remain in touch with, and morally accountable to, their host culture—that they locate their true *community* inside it, rather than simply among one another.

I said at the outset that these lectures owe their existence and value, if any, to Robert Pack. I mean that exactly. Had this fierce and gallant man not called on me to perform a task far beyond any previous level that had been expected of me, I would not have probed my consciousness or conscience, nor would I have extended my own critical reading and my synthesizing explorations, to produce the arguments presented here.

One measure of a truly great teacher, it has been said, is his capacity to enhance the quality of a student's question by the quality of his answer. Another is his capacity to confer intellectual prowess on a student by the act of presuming such prowess.

By each measure—as I can personally attest—Robert Pack is a great teacher as well as a distinguished poet.

As for learning to have a sustained conversation with his formidable eminence, that skill is simple once you understand it. You make him laugh.

Tilting at What Is Not There: The Journey into Nonfiction

Most of the literary ideas that you will hear expressed at writers' conferences deal—and quite properly so—with writing as observed from inside the craft.

As Michael Arlen once put it at the Bread Loaf Writers Conference, we're here to find out the hunting secrets of the elders.

And the fact is that the elders tend to be quite generous with their secrets. The authors and the poets who speak here typically invite us to step into rather sacred territory: into the private chambers of their life's calling. And they invite us to look around.

And as our greedy eyes become accustomed to the dimness—and as we start to memorize the brand names on all the equipment—we gradually begin to make a rather breathtaking, almost Egyptian discovery.

It occurs to us that the writers' chambers are in fact connected to an infinitely receding series of chambers that extend backward in time; back through the centuries of the written word—and that these connective chambers serve as a conduit for the accumulating comprehension of the writer's peculiar calling.

This conduit is useful to us. It is our good fortune that the best writers are usually custodians as well as constant reinventors of their craft. That's why this conference can be so powerful—because it gives a rare chance to step back from the dailiness of writing and dwell for a while on those imperatives of literature that seem almost to stand outside the changes of the world: the imperatives of character and plot and meter and metaphor and clarity and honesty. These imperatives are redefined not so much by the whims of behavior and politics and culture as by writers themselves, as they continue their watch on the human heart in conflict with itself.

But this pleasant continuum I've described is presently subjected to a certain level of danger. This majestic slow cadence of change in the writer's craft is under assault—an assault from outside the self-contained universe of literary aesthetics. It is grounded in the hypertemporal and ever-expanding empire of broadcasting and now the computerized data technologies.

The disturbing truth is that writers and poets can no longer afford to sift exclusively through the assembled legacy of their art for guidance as to how to advance their voices. The reason is that writers, and readers, have been encircled by a rival communications system: more accurately, by an overlapping sequence of systems that amount to the first unified rival claim on printed thought since the Renaissance.

This abrupt new electronic rival is no less appalling to writers for the fact that it has no particular political or pedagogic axe to grind against print. It has no value system of its own, and it is in fact infuriatingly neutral. It colonizes indifferently, independent of human passion.

Nor is it necessary to caricature the electronic revolution, to portray it in some reductive extreme, in order to make the case that it is radically redefining the universe of print.

Television will not make people illiterate. Video display terminals will not render libraries extinct—not for a while yet—and it is true that broadcasting is in many ways responsible for an increase in what might broadly be described as "reading."

The fact remains that this convulsive transformation from a purely visual to a multisensory culture of communication is affecting writers, readers and, God knows, editors and publishers, in ways perhaps too subtle to be isolated and analyzed by people day by day.

The effects stem from two diametrically opposing but equally destructive impulses. On the one hand there is the impulse that's embedded in the more commercial and mass-directed branches of print: in newspapers and magazines, but also in a widening sector of hardcover and paperback publishing houses; and even in the strategies, the techniques, of many writers who have come of age since the mid-'60s. This is the impulse to imitate broadcasting: to somehow transfer its kinetic, immediate, and visceral impact to the page of linear type.

The second and opposite impulse, equally futile and perhaps even tragic, seems to afflict the most sensitive and gifted young writers. These artists cast a cold and measured eye across the battlefield of electronics and print, and then they lift their gaze to take in the society that seems to have rushed out drunkenly to embrace the invader. And then these writers turn away. They reject this fickle culture as having grown too profane, too promiscuous to be worthy of a serious literary investment, or offering. They begin to write in a narrow and increasingly codified language for what they imagine as a small surviving garrison of kindred spirits: academics and fellow writers.

Academics and fellow writers quite soon become the subjects and the content of this exquisite, ever-more-abstracted and solipsistic writing. And then the writing itself becomes its own referent.

There is no doubt that this emerging literary aesthetic has been triggered by many forces and ideas that have gathered in our century and that have nothing to do with broadcasting, nor that at its best this writing offers a brilliant critique of modernist values. It has produced great literature.

But when this mode of writing is embraced out of nothing more than anger and contempt for a bankrupt culture, and when it coalesces as the only serious alternative to a mass communications system that itself makes no distinctions between print and broadcast values—then something has gone terribly wrong. A gulf of ideas has opened up in the middle of our society—a gulf that leaves what you might call "ordinary" people either exploited or ignored. The language atrophies, and along with it, people's capacity to analyze, to make distinctions, to intervene in a life beyond the personal life—even the capacity to become indignant about continually being had.

These, I think, are the results of those two opposing impulses that have arisen from the colonization of broadcasting.

More specifically, these impulses take shape in the following ways:

—First, by the replacement of "truth" as a goal of expression with a quality that has come to be popularly known as "perceptions."

—Second, the devaluation of intuition, spontaneity, and personal insight as the wellsprings of writing by a kind of over-wrought awareness of what the people (or the market, as they are now collectively called) wants to hear. This awareness is objectively, impersonally harvested from the behaviorist sciences, most typically from market research.

—And finally, as I wrote a moment ago, the despair among good writers of ever reaching the victims of all this manipulation, and even a tendency, as so often happens, to blame those victims.

Before I go further into the specifics of how I think the electronic imperative has affected truth, and spontaneity, and the writer's connection with the reader, I'd like to offer some more general thoughts on what it is about good prose that's worth saving from the onslaught.

I will be speaking mainly about nonfiction. There are many novelists whose work is accessible to general readers. But in the last generation or so, the novel as a form has veered sharply away from its old function of rendering the world in terms that everyone can understand. It tends to require a more or less specialized readership that is somewhat more educated and more wise to the rules of the game than the general population.

As for poets—well, nobody ever made a TV movie out of a poem.

That leaves nonfiction as the form perhaps most naturally suited to filling that gulf of ideas that I mentioned—for satisfying people's intrinsic hunger for the real, without condescension and without sacrificing the highest fidelity to language and form that constitutes literature.

One of the characteristics of American prose that has always appealed to me has involved a sense of motion. The writer is off on a journey and he has invited you to come along. At its best, this is both an empirical journey and a journey of ideas, or a spiritual "journey of discovery," in which there is both an expository and a psychological level of movement. These two levels are constantly informing and reinforcing each other.

Perhaps the most eloquent example in recent years has been Peter Matthiessen's *The Snow Leopard*, in which Matthiessen travels to the Crystal Mountain on the Tibetan Plateau in the company of a zoologist friend. Their stated purpose is to find and study an animal known as the Himalayan blue sheep, and perhaps to catch a glimpse of a rare snow leopard. If Matthiessen had set out to do nothing more than render terrain, or to describe the hardships of trekking over frigid mountain peaks and observing wildlife, he would have written a superior travel book.

But almost from the first sentence, it is obvious that Matthiessen is up to more than that. There is an inner journey to be made as well, and its terrain spiritually parallels the remote and forbidding peaks of the Himalayas.

Matthiessen is a man grieving of death and obsessed by time. He has tried to overcome these wounds of the spirit by immersing himself in the teachings of Zen Buddhism, a religion whose origins lie in the same unyielding part of the world over which he is now struggling.

Matthiessen's great artistry in this book is his ability to superimpose his spiritual journey, what he called his "journey of the heart," his ultimately failed quest toward the timeless center of that religion—to superimpose that journey upon the actual physical trek across the mountains of Tibet. He does it in such a way that the two journeys become fused in the reader's mind; their successions of logic and revealed truth, and their symbols, become wondrously interlinked.

Another useful example of this multilevel journey may be found in the railroad books of Paul Theroux. In *The Old Patagonian Express*, Theroux wakes up one winter morning in a Boston suburb and boards a subway train. When he finally finishes riding the rails eight months later, he is on the great Plateau of Patagonia, at the southern tip of Argentina.

Again, this is an excellent travel book. But it is also a consistent, progressive journey into a man's social consciousness, his accumulating criticisms of politics and wealth and poverty and manners and national self-images. Theroux builds his case before the reader's eyes. His methodology is always out in the open. He earns rather than assumes your trust in his vision.

Near the beginning of *The Old Patagonian Express*, Paul Theroux sets down a few thoughts on the art of traveling—as distinct from the expedient of getting there. With few changes, these ideas could be adapted to a meditation on the approach to communication by print as distinct from the approach by electronics.

Theroux writes: "The literature of travel has become measly; the standard opening, that farcical nose-against-the-porthole view from the plane's tilted fuselage . . . that straining for effect . . . how does it go? 'Below us lay the tropical green, the flooded valley, the patchwork quilt of farms, and as we emerged from the clouds I saw the stately palms, the people like ants, the colorful . . .'"

And Theroux goes on to ask:

> Meanwhile, what of the journey itself? Perhaps there is nothing to say. There is not much to say about most airplane journeys. Anything remarkable must be disastrous, so you define a good flight by negatives: you didn't get hijacked, you didn't crash, you didn't throw up, you weren't nauseated by the food. So you are grateful. The gratitude brings such relief, your mind goes blank, which is appropriate, for the airline passenger is a time traveler. Time is truncated, or in any sense warped: he leaves one time zone and emerges in another . . . time is brilliantly blinded, there is nothing to see . . .

I'm letting Mr. Theroux grouse on like this because as I say, while he may not know it, he is almost perfectly describing the difference in receiving intelligence through narrative prose and through broadcast data—or writing that has been victimized by the imperatives of broadcast data.

But to let him complete his own thought: "What interests me is the waking up in the morning, the progress from the familiar to the slightly odd, to the rather strange, to the totally foreign, and finally to the outlandish.

"The journey, not the arrival matters; the voyage, not the landing." Exactly so.

There is one other currently celebrated example of the nonfiction idea developed as a journey: the book called *Blue Highways*, in which the writer William Least Heat Moon, suffering from reverses in his life, sets out in his pickup truck for a journey around the backroads of America. (The motivating factor of spiritual suffering at the start of these books is a recurring theme.)

Least Heat Moon's enlistment in these parallel journeys—of passage through space and time that becomes a metaphor of the writer's movement through the interior of being—reminds us that the "American" roots of this impulse lie very deep indeed.

Least Heat Moon is descended partly from the Sioux Indians. In Cedar City, Utah, a few thousand miles into his trip, Moon runs into a young Hopi college student who shows him the ancient symbol for the Hopi concept of emergence. This in fact is the symbol that Moon uses as the typographical design that begins each section of his book.

The interwoven lines within the symbol represent the course a person follows on his "road of life"—the Hopi, along with most other Indian societies, see human existence as essentially a series of journeys—and the emergence symbol itself is a kind of map of the wandering soul, an image of a process.

Like Theroux, Least Heat Moon is concerned with the distinction between authentic and false journeys, as when he writes:

"A car whipped past, the driver eating and a passenger clicking a camera. Moving without going anywhere, taking a trip instead of making one . . . rolling effortlessly along, turning the windshield into a movie screen in which the viewer did the moving while the subject held still."

All right: the American narrative as a journey. Joan Didion in California; Jack Kerouac on the road; John Steinbeck traveling with Charlie; James Agee headed for those sharecropper cabins in Alabama—all these and many others, stretching back to the fiction and the journals of Mark Twain, floating on the Mississippi's current or trudging through Egypt with his fellow American pilgrims.

It is almost as though this inclination to incorporate motion into narrative prose were an American impulse that springs from deeper wells even than each writer's subconscious. I think that is in fact true, and in a minute I'll explain why I think so. But all these works that I've mentioned share at least a few characteristics that are extremely compelling—and also that tend to get sacrificed very quickly when writing tries to imitate the fashionable broadcast mode.

Recall what Theroux said about "the progress from the familiar to the slightly odd, to the rather strange, to the totally foreign, and finally to the outlandish." That's the route that narrative should lead the reader in the psychological sense. If you don't like "outlandish," substitute "mystical" or "undiscovered" or "uncontemplated"—somewhere, in the realm of authentic ideas or wisdom or point of view, where the reader is not likely to have journeyed on his own—but starting with the familiar: the neighborhood subway station, the pickup truck—the known universe.

An openness of method, an inclusionary spirit, illuminates the narrative journey. The writer's methods are not submerged or concealed. They are transparent: "Let's go exploring." "What I shall assume, you shall assume." We move into the unexpected along with the writer. We share his risks. And at the end, if the final point has been worth the assembling, and if we are attentive readers, we can feel the satisfaction of having collaborated in making it.

I don't want to overstate the scale of this particular approach to writing. It's not the only way. You don't have to take a trip to write a book. I'm really talking about the interior movement in a book, this quality of an open quest for whatever idea you're driving at, this sense of allowing the reader to look through your glass as you gather evidence. This, I think, is a powerful and reliable way of establishing your claim to the reader's trust.

Obviously, Americans did not invent this journeying, this almost improvisational approach to expository prose. A Frenchman named de Tocqueville wrote the Great American non-novel. The form is characteristic of the classic British travel journal. And if you haven't read the essays of George Orwell from the 1920s and '30s, especially such works as "Down and Out in Paris and London" and "The Road to Wigan Pier," you have missed some of the defining work that freed nonfiction as a literary form from any derived allegiance to the novel.

But somehow Americans have made this approach their own. It has suited the national temperament, which has always been shaped by the conquest of frontiers and with the restless reinvention of the self. Thomas Wolfe, a man who knew the power of a train whistle, understood this as he wrote, "For we are all so lost, so naked and so lonely in America. Immense and cruel skies bend over us, and all of us are driven on forever and we have no home."

I think it's worth reviewing for a moment just why this kind of writing became so intertwined with American culture, so that when we start to discuss the forces that are threatening it, we'll have some appreciation of exactly what is in danger of being reduced, or lost.

In about the middle of the nineteenth century, Americans were still taking abuse from European intellectuals on the issue of whether American had any culture or not—if you can imagine that. The Europeans said they didn't think we had any. Matthew Arnold was particularly starchy on the subject. Arnold said that even if we did have a culture, it was an "uninteresting" one, and how did we like them apples.

Arnold's definition of culture, a definition that generally held throughout western Europe, consisted in one's knowing the best that had been thought and written in the world: particularly the Latin and Greek classical texts. The cultural life, according to this view, amounted to an immersion in finished things. Calcified ideas, settled scores. Celebrating an aesthetic that, as the American critic Van Wyck Brooks put it, repeated its message over and over: "Stay put."

For a long time this critique made Americans feel well and truly put in their place. But among those who were not cowed by it were a couple of pretty formidable savages, Ralph Waldo Emerson and, later, Walt Whitman. It seemed to these thinkers that culture was *not*—at least not in the New World—some fait accompli of received standards and fossilized ideas, but was instead a matter of constant spiritual rebirth, an organic process that required a willingness to explore and experience new, even threatening terrain. As Emerson insisted: "The effect of culture on the man will not be like the trimming and turfing of gardens, but the educating of the eye to the true harmony of the unshorn landscape, with horrid thickets, wide morasses, bald mountains, and the balance of land and sea."

In other words, culture in the new world amounted to a kind of enlightened trusting of one's own experience—or, by extension, the experience of authentic writers who stand as one's "representatives" on the quest. This, I think, is the historic backbone of our mandate today: our threatened mandate to satisfy the reader's legitimate hunger for the real.

Walt Whitman, 1867: "I feel, with dejection and amazement, that among our geniuses and talented writers or speakers, few or none have yet really spoken to this people, or absorbed the central spirit and idiosyncracies which are theirs, and which, thus, in the highest ranges, so far remain entirely uncelebrated, unexpressed . . . I say," Whitman continued, "I have not seen one single writer, artist, lecturer, or whatnot, that has confronted the voiceless but ever erect and active, pervading, underlying will and typic aspiration of the land, in a spirit kindred to itself."

But Whitman's wish was soon fulfilled. Eighteen years later, Mark Twain, writing in heretical dialect and following the quotidian flow of the Mississippi River, published a sojourning work that left Matthew Arnold sputtering, but which forever ratified that "central spirit" as the wellspring of our literature.

So it seems clear that the impulse to create prose that parallels a pushing out of boundaries, an open testing of frontiers, is almost inseparable from the organizing motives of the American culture itself.

And so it strikes one as piquant, to say nothing of critical in its claim on our ability to understand it, that this prose is being assaulted, if not overwhelmed, by another expression of our culture—which is in itself a great if not sublime achievement: that expression being the idiom of electronic broadcasting, and more recently electronic data transmission.

Broadcast information tends to bring the classic narrative journey of ideas to a halt. That may not be an intrinsic effect of broadcasting, but it certainly is a function of the commercial imperatives that generally govern the use of airwaves in this country. Ideas (and I'm not talking just about formal newscasts, but about ideas in every form, most especially including advertising) are compressed: compressed into a kind of bulletin mode that preempts any degree of complexity or illumination or argument-building of any kind. Broadcast ideas have a prere-solved quality about them; their claim is authoritarian rather than empiric.

The same is true of prose that is written under the thrall of broadcasting's thrilling, imperious immediacy.

One of the most influential books within the circles of broadcast executives these days is *Megatrends*, the big best-seller about what our economic and technological future is going to be like. *Megatrends* is very much a book of the Television Age.

Its prose suggests a data read-out quality. A series of presettled conclusions, nonsequential and noncumulative, is issued. Statistical data are cited to buttress the conclusions. The weight of just about any section of *Megatrends* is about the same as that of any other section. Never, for one moment in *Megatrends*, does a distinct "voice"—the voice of the book—break through into the reader's awareness and draw the reader into a progressive journey of the intellect, a shared quest with the author, wherein the reader can reason and analyze along with his host and guide.

Megatrends is a collage of atomized data, condensed to its most reducible elements and offered as a quick, referential guide. It makes no attempt to enlist the power of narrative language to give shape and unity to its basic argument.

That description fits broadcast information exactly.

Just by coincidence, another book has emerged this summer, one that I think is driving at essentially the same thing *Megatrends* is after: a sense of who we are as a people and where we're headed. This book is *Modern Times*, by the British author Paul Johnson.

Superficially, the two books have absolutely nothing in common—which is my point. They are as different as print and broadcasting.

Modern Times is a massively detailed and dense history of Western societies from about the 1920s through time present. It argues that the "Modern" era began precisely on May 29, 1919, when photographs of a solar eclipse, documenting the degree to which light is bent, confirmed Einstein's Theory of Relativity. Johnson proceeds to construct a progressive sequence of interlocking dislocations in Western life: dislocations in psychiatric and economic theory (Freud and Marx), in warfare, in the rise of totalitarian regimes, in the origins of social engineering, in the rise of superpower states, in the Vietnam era, in the explosion of science.

In every important episode of Western life through six decades, Paul Johnson is building a case of cause and effect. Or a lot
of cases, really. Among the dominant ones is that Western man, as
a result of these dislocations and also of certain key misinterpre-
tations of Einstein and Freud, has become utterly separated from
any notion of personal accountability of his moral actions and
choices, with discernably catastrophic results.

One may disagree with Paul Johnson; many reviewers have.
His own rather regressive politics are revealed in his interpreta-
tions of history.

But so are his methods. So is his reasoning process. And so is
the evidence from which he built his theory. At the end of *Modern
Times* one may, indeed, reject Johnson's vision of Western history
in the twentieth century; but one has reasoned and imagined and
argued along with him; one has been required to *earn* one's point
of view, as Johnson has earned his.

An interesting side benefit may well be that one will discover
a rather clear and well-informed set of notions as to how things
are likely to flow forward from time present—which is the overt
intent of *Megatrends*, which, by contrast, manages to be simultaneously authoritarian and unauthoritative.

The two books yield yet another singular difference. Johnson's
history, as mentioned, makes a firm point about how modern
man has been separated from any belief in personal accountability for his actions. As far as I can discover, that point is not taken
up in *Megatrends*, a book very much within the broadcast mode of
thought.

I think there's a reason for this. Personal accountability is
anathema to the success of broadcast communications. The test
of an idea on the airways (generally speaking) is not how
passionately the broadcaster *believes* in the idea. The test is in how
fervently the audience wishes to *receive* the idea, as revealed by
saturated, behaviorist-inspired market research.

You ask a television executive whether he is comfortable with
the content of the programming that he is unleashing on this
society, and you get a blank expression—or else a reflexive
defense of the broadcaster's "free speech rights." He genuinely
does not grasp the question. His personal tastes, his own convictions, if he has any, simply aren't part of the equation. He has

discovered a tool that has leapfrogged past such messy, subjective matters. The tool is market research, and it ends up, invariably, in *giving the people what they want.*

This brings us to what I think is the most corrosive, insidious effect of broadcasting's influence on the world of writers. In separating ideas from any test of their authenticity other than how well they go over with a sample fragment of the mass audience, broadcasters are perhaps unwittingly rearranging the terms of truth.

This is not the same as to propose that they are lying. What I mean is that the broadcast idiom has separated the concept of truthfulness from a sense of why truthfulness matters. And I assure you that this separation has become well entrenched in the print world. The point of entry has been the daily newspaper (although the imperative has spread into magazines and book publishing as well).

Consider the new Gannett newspaper *USA Today*, which may be viewed as the first successful attempt to clone the broadcast electrode. Here is a newspaper that is dispensed from a vending machine designed to look exactly like a TV set. It is a paper that routinely fills its multicolored front page with such rigorously accurate and statistically impeccable nuggets of fact as the annual per capita rate of popcorn consumption in the United States. It is a paper that has abolished the defining pleasures of American newspaper prose: verbal color, wit, nuance, editorial passion, the attempt to render visceral experience, and replaced these qualities with the uninflected, minimalist drone of the broadcaster. Voice, giving way to voice-over.

This kind of writing, and the broadcasting from which it derives, are atrophying our grand, unruly American vernacular. In the process, Gannettspeak is advancing the paralysis of people's capacity to analyze, to make distinctions, and finally to intervene in a life beyond the personal life. Or to become indignant about continually being had.

There has arisen a codified rationale for why the broadcast mode enjoys a kind of diplomatic immunity from the obligations of truth. It has been developed by an auditory theorist named Tony Schwartz. In a seminal book first published in 1974, called *The Responsive Chord*, Schwartz assured the broadcast industry that it did not have to waste any time agonizing over whether its content was truthful or not. Because truth did not matter on the airwaves.

Schwartz's reasoning went as follows:

"Truth, as a social value, is a product of print. The question of truth is largely irrelevant when dealing with electronic media content."

The idea here is that sound, as well as the rapidly shifting dots on a cathode TV screen, act upon the central nervous system in a way that breaks down the critical process and places the viewer, or the listener, in a sort of emotionally collaborative fugue state with the broadcaster—a state antithetical to the active and analytical process of decoding print.

Schwartz offers another maxim that bears heavily on the way broadcast ideas operate. He writes: "In communicating at electronic speed, we no longer direct information into an audience . . . but try to evoke stored information out of them, in a patterned way."

Thus, market research. And the programming that flows from market research. And now, in our present moment, periodicals and books that seek to imitate the competitive success of market-researched ideas, not to mention a publishing industry that has rapidly adjusted itself to reward writers who can most closely approximate the idioms of the electronic colonizer.

The distinguished writers of nonfiction that I mentioned earlier, and many others of their stature, are but a small part of a publishing universe that generates more than 50 thousand titles a year. Most of those titles are not *The Snow Leopard*. An increasing percentage of these books speak the hybrid language and advance the hybrid truths and take refuge in the political and moral and spiritual indifference that the broadcast era has helped elevate to a signature of the national character.

I suggest that if you are a writer who has avoided this prototype, you have done so by a deliberate and ongoing act of will, because the prototype is as ubiquitous as those wall-sized television screens in George Orwell's *1984*. It has pervaded our news and our entertainment and our advertising and our movies and our music and our political discourse and even our public-school classrooms. It is echoed in the clothes we wear and in the food we eat and in the games we watch and in the wars we fight.

This is because the prototype takes the form not only of compressed data and a staccato style of antinarrative and a market-researched volition that replaces spontaneity and a suspension of moral judgment and a tinkering around with the terms of truth. It takes on the almost physical attributes of an obsession with personality over idea, of affectation over passion, of gratification over denial, of "winning" over solving or mediating.

I further suggest that even if you have managed to will your conscious and unconscious responses away from this all-pervading standard brand of communication; even if you can resist its seductive uniformities and conveniences—even if you have determined to pursue your most personal literary voice and informing vision—even then, you have won only half the battle.

Because then you become vulnerable to that second, perhaps even more futile and tragic alternative that I mentioned at the beginning of this talk: an angry, despairing rejection of the society you live in, based on a conviction that this society has grown so intellectually bankrupt that your only meaningful readership is that small surviving garrison of your fellow writers.

I find this alternative almost inexpressibly sad. Perhaps this is due to no reason more profound than that I believe my own life has been immeasurably enriched, by slow degrees, by serious and purposeful writers willing to turn their voices outward to the secular, working-class culture in which I grew up, and to fill me with a sense of a life beyond the immediate and the personal. This is nothing more than the shared affinity that Whitman cried out for a hundred years ago, voicing his dejection and amazement at the dearth of voices that had spoken to the central spirit of the common people.

I think it's terribly important—for the writer as well as the reader—for us to preserve a literature that assumes the interest and the passionate response of the common man. Market research shouts at us that this is impossible; that people cannot be reached except at the lowest common denominator, with formulas that have proven themselves in the past. That the only thing we can expect as "communicators" is to "evoke stored information out of them, in a patterned way."

This is a lie. The lie is revealed in that even market research needs someone else's idea, however hackneyed or debased, to measure. What market research cannot measure is the mystical fact that a writer creates his own audience even as he creates his work—because any writing worthy of the name is about the pushing back of frontiers, the reinvention of a point of view, the confrontation with mystery that no one could have guessed was possible until the writer made the pilgrimage.

Once you have established in your mind and heart that you are going to overcome the deadening, conforming effects of this synthetic hybrid language we live with, and also that you do not intent to further punish its victims by turning your back on them, it may even be desirable to examine this colonizing broadcast imperative with a detached eye, to see whether there is indeed anything useful to be learned from it.

It is undeniable that artists throughout this century of dislocation have strengthened their craft by a shrewd and selective borrowing from technology. The Cubist painters of the 1920s who changed the direction of art were interpreting a new, mass, urban, photographic culture. Christopher Isherwood, in 1930, spoke for a new generation of writers who came of age with the movies when he proclaimed: "I am a camera, with it shutter open, quite passive, not thinking."

Similarly, the new inconography of broadcast idiom must contain some inspiration, some prospect of renewal, for a writer who is alert enough not to surrender the craft's own legitimate properties in return. The essayist Michael Arlen has compared his own writing to the eye of a camera, and speaks admiringly of writers who employ "rapid motion . . . attempts to translate the paraphernalia of photography—the zoom lens, film-cutting . . . disconnection."

I think that our response to the colonizing imperatives of broadcast language can derive strength from considering the work of Arlen, as well as writers such as Matthiessen and Theroux and the others I've mentioned.

Our best response is one that lies within the possibilities of traditional English prose, and that has always resided there. It is a response that spares the writer the indignity of sacrificing narrative flow for immediacy, or truthfulness for the sake of "effects"—because it celebrates the great historic capacity of written English to achieve all these things, without compromising the essential legitimacy of an idea.

Writers need, in short, to get back what is their own, and they need to get it back on their own terms. Writers need to conquer both their deference to the colonizers from the electronic world, and their contempt for the great public culture that has been its victim.

Writers need to reestablish their traditional ties with this culture, and they need to do that by offering it a literature, and a poetry, that is honest, and clear; that is faithful to its own rules and distinctions, yet offers a constant renewal and mystery and a pushing outward of frontiers.

Writers need to get angry over the fact that they have temporarily surrendered their language to a ruling force that does not love language, nor trust it, nor betray any interest in it beyond its capacity to sell goods.

Writers need to get it back.

Flannery O'Connor seems to have foreseen this coming showdown between the spontaneous voice and the collective orthodoxy more than 20 years ago; and she certainly predicted the kind of writer that would be necessary to engage it.

"Such a writer," wrote O'Connor, "will be interested in what we don't understand rather than in what we do. He will be interested in possibility rather than in probability. He will be interested in characters who are forced to meet evil and grace and who act on a trust beyond themselves, whether they know very clearly what it is they act on or not. To the modern mind, this kind of character, and his creator, are typical Don Quixotes, tilting at what is not there."

It's there.

On Memory as Destiny:
My Rediscovery of Hannibal

The 1985 session of Bread Loaf was convened in a spirit of honoring the conference's sixty-year history. This is as it should be. Bread Loaf's history is glorious; it deserves all the ceremony and all the costumed croquet matches that we, the inheritors, can possibly bestow.

But these anniversary ceremonies are good for a larger reason as well: a reason that we writers should consider very closely. In honoring Bread Loaf's history we have an opportunity to honor the notion of history itself, in a modest way. We have an opportunity to affirm the idea of cultural memory as something that enriches us and that exacts legitimate obligations from us.

It happens that these values—of history and ceremony and cultural memory—are not exactly paramount concerns in this time-present age of ours, this age in which the culture seems preoccupied with disassembling its accumulated heritage, stone by stone, and reassembling it, mall by mall.

We live and write in an age that is distinctive partly for its withering sense of historical time. In the view of critics such as Christopher Lasch, it's an age of indifference, if not active hostility and rejection, toward the past as a political and psychological treasury from which we draw the reserves that we need to cope with the future.

Lasch, of course, is the American historian who has been brooding about the Culture of Narcissism and the age of the Minimal Self for several years. But he is hardly a lone voice anymore, if indeed he ever was. His warnings about this loss of interest in context, this loss of faith in continuity, were ratified earlier this spring. A group of Berkeley sociologists led by Robert Bellah interviewed several hundred Americans on the interesting topic of the right way to live: What is important to you? What is the meaning of freedom? How do you exercise moral choice? Do you care about the larger world, the public world, and how do you intervene in it?

The answers to these questions were collated as case studies and published in a book called *Habits of the Heart*—a phrase that Tocqueville used to describe the pattern of choices that Americans made that formed their character. The book's conclusions were pretty bleak. Americans don't feel very much connection to a wider community, or curiosity about the past, or shared obligation toward the future. Americans don't have much interest in any obligation that cannot be justified in terms of utilitarian self-interest.

In other words, the authors found that a kind of radical individualism has taken hold in current American life. The deep irony of this is that it's a historical continuation of the same individualism that helped America to make its cultural break from Europe a century and a half ago and begin to form its own character. That is, the unlimited sense of self that was instilled in America's new consciousness by those heroic poets and prophets of God-intoxicated invention, such as Emerson and Whitman and Thoreau.

It's pretty clear from any reading of those men that the newly liberated American self was meant to find its highest function not in Self-Improvement or Winning Through Intimidation or Power Diets, but through the process of creating art and bestowing it lovingly upon the culture.

Emerson put it best when he wrote:

"The maker of a sentence, like the other artist, launches out into the infinite and builds a road into Chaos and Old Night, and is followed by those who hear him with something of a wild, creative delight."

Times have changed. These days the maker of a sentence launches out toward those who read with moving lips, or better still await the videocassette, and get the gist of what is stored on microchips.

As for individualism, Robert Bellah and his *Habits of the Heart* co-writers conclude that it has long since parted company with any sense of obligation to art, or to anything else other than that

Great Scarlet Styrofoam Finger in the Sky eternally proclaiming, "We're No. 1."

Or to put it in slightly more pedagogic terms, Ballah's terms: "That very individualism may have grown cancerous—and may be destroying those social integuments that modify its capacities for destruction."

The American individual is suspended in "a glorious but terrifying isolation." For all our notorious glibness at explaining our lives and our decisions in various brands of jargon—the managerial jargon of the corporate technician, or the therapeutic jargon of the "human-potential" movement, or the studied anti-jargon of punk, or even the neobiblical jargon of television evangelists—despite all these strains of packaged fluency, we tend to fall silent when asked to explain what seem to be the real *commitments* that define our lives. We tend, in sum, to lack a moral language.

It's my strong belief that writers are among the people most directly affected by this atomized climate of the isolated, diminished self—isolated from history and diminished by the withering of cultural partnership, shared goals, the hope and even the wish that one might make a public difference.

I also believe that the form of writing most damaged by the trivializing rust of this climate is nonfiction—precisely because nonfiction is the most democratic of the writerly forms. By and large, it is the most approachable. Nonfiction, almost by definition, invokes a mandate to the general reader, the unspecialized reader, even at its highest and most deliberately "literary" levels.

We all know that novelists and poets (along with painters and musicians and sculptors) have reacted to the upheavals of this century, the technologies and the wars and the general loss of optimism, by drawing away from a "representational" plane of expression. Many novelists and poets have responded to the century's radical changes by radically *changing* expression—in some cases, by changing the function and the meaning of language itself. Our literature, since the time of Theodore Dreiser and Henry Adams, has veered off toward the theoretical, the self-referential, the highly codified, the abstract. That literature self-evidently requires a reader who is trained in the theory, the abstractions and the code: a specialized reader.

There is nothing inherently wrong with that trend, at least nothing that I can coherently argue in this context. The point is that it has left an enormous vacuum of *acknowledged obligation*: the obligation by writers to write on behalf of unspecialized readers who are nonetheless educated and eager to intervene in a life beyond the personal and the private—an obligation to satisfy, in the apt phrase of Michael Arlen, those readers' *legitimate hunger for the real.*

Much of the grandeur of twentieth-century writing has devolved from the acceptance of that obligation.

George Orwell in Britain in 1937, describing the impact of the Depression at the level of an English coal-mining town. James Agee in America at the same time, describing the same effects from the viewpoint of Alabama sharecroppers. John Hersey rendering the effects of the atomic bomb explosion at Hiroshima in the pages of the *New Yorker* magazine. These writers were among the greatest pioneers of a new lineage: a lineage of essayists and journalists and scholars and assorted misfits of no inherited literary pedigree—but men and women who prowled the fringes and the precincts and the dark alleys of society like Melville's "Isolato," full of passionate curiosity and a willingness to believe the evidence of their own eyes and ears, as opposed to the received and "official" truth of the sheriff and the bureaucrat and the governor—and who recorded that evidence in the clear common language of cultural memory.

There is no doubt that these writers, and the later writers whose work they made possible, believed along with Henry Adams that history becomes a memory of the race. Adams of course was the last of the great nineteenth-century mandarin historians. He was also an instinctive prophet whose misfortune it was to foresee the long-range implications of technology upon his native culture.

But Henry Adams did not offer his insights for common consumption. He wrote history from the high vantage point of social inheritance and privilege. He was related to Presidents; he was a diplomatic-political insider. He personified a tradition of interpreting the currents of politics and diplomacy in the grand manner.

The exact opposite was true of the new proletarian writer who arose a generation or so after Adams. This twentieth-century pioneer came of age with the movies and the single-lens reflex camera—and he brought a photographic kind of realism and intimacy to prose writing that Henry Adams would never have comprehended.

Nor was this new "camera eye" a mere technological crutch, or a withdrawal from active consciousness. It became a metaphor for a certain way of preserving history. It was a way of infusing the essay, the scholarly argument, the historical record, with a terrific new blast of urgency, and personal passion, and advocacy of proletarian interests: the legitimate concerns of the common man.

These writers seized possession of the novel's vanishing function as a transmitter of information and commentary about the real world. They made photographic use of the novel's narrative line and its focus on character and its intense colorings of detail and place and vernacular language. They took up the novel's fascination with values as they are contested and revealed— not in abstracted philosophy but in the particular moral conflicts of particular human beings.

Their legitimacy is still very much alive in these diminished times: this age of the withering historical sense and of individualism run rampant. It has managed to survive in this age of relentless, undifferentiated data and disconnected images that wash over us from the airwaves and from magazines and newspapers that cling to survival by imitating the data-drenched idiom of the airwaves. This age, in which the camera, electronic now and omnipresent, has served to eradicate history and create upon history's ruins a culture in the camera's own self-referencing image: a culture of the eternal time-present.

The best nonfiction writing of our time resists this kind of chaos. It resists this onslaught of data without scale, without value, without context or point of view. The best nonfiction writing continues to perform the diligent and loving task that Emerson called for when he and his friends liberated American writing from European standards: it organizes the chaos of the world into experience, and it invites the reader into an ever-widening sphere of understanding, founded on a trust in the writer.

Recall that manifesto from Emerson: "The maker of a sentence . . . launches out into the infinite and builds a road into Chaos and Old Night . . ."

Exactly.

The best nonfiction writing honors that ancient process of discovery. It preserves a passionate commitment to history and the discovery of truth, both internal and external to the story at hand. One can marvel at how this literature is accomplished partly by a generous and highly translucent style of writing: an unconcealed gathering of evidence, a democratic sort of invitation to the reader to come along and share the quest, share the discovery.

I'm going to give you, now, an example of the corrosion that is forming around the foundations of nonfiction writing, and separating it from its old agreements with the culture. Periodicals have been a wellspring of serious American prose writing. Shelly Fisher Fishkin and others argue that the journalistic backgrounds of many American *literati* (Whitman worked for newspapers for 25 years) helped produced the "distinctive American aesthetic," usefully defined by Philip Rahv as "the urge toward and immersion in experience."

In our time, however, "experience" is giving way to voyeurism.

This is from the cover story in *New York Magazine*, dated July 22, 1985. Its title is "The Comeback Kids—From Prison to the Paladium." Its subjects, displayed in a winsome cover photograph, are Steve Rubell and Ian Schrager, the founders of Studio 54 who went to prison in 1979 after being convicted of evading $800,000 in taxes.

The helicopter clattered over the dark waters of the harbor, and Calvin Klein asked the pilot to make a slight detour for his two guests. Steve Rubell and Ian Schrager watched the Plexiglas windshield fill with the gleaming towers of the New York skyline.

On this clear night last December, there seemed no greater
spectacle on earth.

"I mean, what's the Grand Canyon?" Ian says.

Well. This turns out to be the inspirational tale of how a couple
of boyish, likeable and newly sprung white-collar criminals
persuade their celebrity friends to help them get back on their
feet and finance another multimillion-dollar celebrity disco. It is
told in about nine thousand luxury words, many of them brand
names. It is in every conceivable way a paradigm of nonfiction's
increasingly contaminated covenant with its readers.

The author of the piece is a young journalist who was fired a
few years ago from a New York newspaper after it was discovered that he had been making up quotes from British soldiers
while on assignment to Northern Ireland. He is now writing in
his natural habitat—for a national magazine that celebrates the
artificial, and that receives its sensibilities most gladly and coldly
from the idiom of broadcasting: trend-oriented, data-rich, value-
free, antihistorical, and utterly insulated from the very world that
it is pleased to regard as a "market." This same magazine, and
others like it, reinforce the broadcast idiom, and amplify it, and
send it even deeper into the culture, so that it takes root not only
in slick magazines and full-color daily newspapers, but also in
the books that are written by the alumnae of this process, then
edited and published by the corporations that also embrace its
logic.

In 1936 James Agee, late of *Fortune Magazine*, was capable of
the following passage:

"If I could do it I'd do no writing at all here. It would be
photographs; the rest would be fragments of cloth, bits of cotton,
lumps of earth, records of speech, pieces of wood and iron, phials
of odors, plates of food and excrement."

In 1985 *New York Magazine* was capable of the following
passage:

"On the third night, the waitresses were serving champagne
with aplomb and the bartenders were jumping at the sight of a
famous face. Steve took Halston and Baby Jane Holzer on a tour
of the club. He started with Kenny Scharf's basement lounges.

" 'What a nice toilet,' Halston said."

* * *

A few years ago the writer George W. S. Trow dwelt on this obliteration of scale in a famous essay called "Within the Context of No Context."

Trow argued that, thanks largely to television, there remained only two "operative grids" in American society: the Grid of Intimacy and the Grid of Two Hundred Million.

The middle distance—the connective tissue—had fallen away, Trow claimed, because television's sensibility has raised up the trivial toward power and lowered the powerful toward the trivial.

In this absence of proportionate values, Trow wrote, "the preferences of a child carried as much weight as the preferences of an adult. In the place where this scale has its home, childish agreements can be arrived at and enforced effectively—childish agreements, and agreements wearing the mask of childhood."

As for the distance between the national life and the intimate life, Trow wrote, "the distance was very frightening. People did not want to measure it. People began to lose a sense of what the distance was and of what the usefulness of the distance might be."

I've said a couple of times now that writers are among the victims of this climate. But that isn't the worst news. The worst news is that we collaborate. We learn to survive by adding fuel to the energy force that is well on its way toward overwhelming our craft.

Sometimes we collaborate in the full knowledge of what we are doing; and I read you some examples of what that collaboration sounds like.

But perhaps more often we collaborate without exactly meaning to. We collaborate numbly, out of the pressure to meet deadlines and earn the living we need to write the "serious stuff." And the time of our writing lives tends to get spent earning the living we need to write "the serious stuff."

We learn, in daily increments, to think along with our kindly colonizers: those nice people from the magazines and the networks who supply us not only with assignments, but also with a point of view and even a ready-made language.

We learn to think in terms of trends, not the flow of history; of the typical, not the unique; of style, not character; of brand names, not fragments of cloth or bits of cotton; of the recombinant, not the mysterious or the strange. We learn to separate ourselves from the one inner resource that is uniquely ours—the memory that fuels our intuition—and replace it with a sort of public databank of pretested stimulus and response. We learn how fashionable it is, and how safe, to regard the use of memory with contempt. We learn to equate memory with "nostalgia," which is a "feminine" quality, as distinct from the "masculine" quality of hard data, gleaned from market research.

And as we master these silken and rewarding new skills, we find one day that we have tasted a new and sulfurous circle of the writer's hell. Instead of that familiar horror—writing something that seems perfectly brilliant one day only to realize the next that it's pretty damned awful—we now experience the horror of writing a formulaic passage under the pressure of a looming deadline, only to realize through the fog of our self-loathing that it's pretty damned glib.

The main problem for many writers thus becomes one of trying to keep in touch with whatever it was that led them into the craft in the first place—and then summoning the will to believe in those first instincts against the overwhelming evidence of what is now being published.

My analysis of the nonfiction writer's struggle against these powerful forces of orthodoxy—and the unevenness of that struggle—is based partly on personal experience. I have been a professional journalist for more than twenty years. For about half that time I have written *about* journalism: about the ways in which information is transmitted on the airwaves, and about how the nature of airwave transmission has changed the nature of information.

I had published a few books in that time span. But like so many people who make their living in journalism, I seldom found it necessary to think about the relationship of my work to any historical process or values. The very dailiness of it all served

to screen out any sense of urgency about confronting my sense of
the past.

About a year ago I began doing research for a book of nonfiction
about an American town in a decisive year of its existence. I
began writing this book earlier this summer.
The town is Hannibal, Missouri, where I was born and lived
until I was seventeen. As far as I know, there is no marketing
evidence of any overwhelming national consumer trend toward
wanting to know anything whatsoever about Hannibal. In fact,
the town is so remote and insignificant that only one other writer
has ever been able to do anything at all with it in terms of
packaging its ambience.
But I thought I'd try anyway. There are certain things that I
remember about Hannibal—or to be more accurate, there are
certain things that I cannot stop remembering. Although I could
never locate any specific use for these memories, at least in terms
I'd been conditioned to judge commercially exploitable, I could
not ever quite extinguish the conviction that the memories were
worth recording: if for no other reason, because they were part of
the way people lived and talked and thought and worked and
dreamed in a town in America at a certain time in history.
So far, that isn't much to go on; it certainly isn't very much to
build a book on. Everyone carries around a lot of highly charged
memories from childhood: memories of the way one's Fuller-
Brushman father would step back exactly two steps on the
customer's front porch after ringing the doorbell so as to reassure
the lady of the house that she would not be harmed; or of the way
the inside of an old drugstore used to reek of clove; or the way
one could feel a river's awful weight if one stared at it long
enough on a summer evening; or the way a table radio glowed in
the livingroom darkness when the tubes were hot; or the illicit
release one could experience by stepping out into the middle of
the town's Main Street during Fall Festival and not worry about
traffic because the street was a Midway.
But these are only fragments of images—fleeting, uncon-
nected, without any specific intensity or meaning. They don't add
up. They are the random images of the camera lens.
I could widen the lens now, and capture the more public town

in its time-present typicalness: the cluster of white-painted commerce at the riverfront; the plate-glass windows with merchants' names painted in semicircles; the main street that is too wide for its traffic like a Sunday suit on an old man. I could record the concrete grandstand at the baseball park with it sublime geological stink of Schlitz. I could focus tightly on the triangular notches on the short sleeves of the shirts of Hannibal businessmen as they open café doors festooned with stickers that say, "PUSH for the Pirates" on one side and "PULL for the Pirates" on the other. And I could zoom back all the way to the exact spot on Cardiff Hill below the lighthouse where you can stand and experience the perfect stereophonic progression of a freight train as it loops around the town—the noise echoing off Lover's Leap on one side of the Mississippi and Illinois on the other.

But we still don't have a book. We have some potentially interesting scraps that a novelist or a poet might use as the materials for delineating "place" or character or imposing a larger, organizing design. But this is nonfiction. No manipulation of empiric truth is allowable here. My intuition has told me that an *intrinsic* narrative lies concealed somewhere within these scraps and images: a narrative that will derive its power from its authenticity. My task is to discover it, not create or impose it—to discover that one clear, central, unifying idea that binds these image-fragments together, current and ancient, public and private.

If I can manage that discovery, the metaphors of my book will be natural, inherent metaphors, and more powerful for that. They will lead me toward the story's natural order and logic. If I succumb to the temptation to impose symbols, or to invent scenes or characters or dialogue for the sake of artistic design, then I will have violated the essense of what I'm after. I will have struck another blow against history, and memory.

But the fascinating thing about writing is that when you get deeply enough into it, you discover that the paranoid's deepest phobia is in fact true: *everything* is connected.

I had left Hannibal with my family when I was seventeen years old, in 1959. That was twenty-five years before I began going back there to try and discover the story I knew was there.

What I discovered, symmetrically enough, was that Hannibal in 1984 and 1985 was a town at war with its own history. Like so many small, isolated towns in the late twentieth century, Hannibal was struggling for its survival. And in that struggle, Hannibal was in the humiliating process of disassembling its authentic past and repackaging it as entertainment for tourists.

I'll summarize the process as briefly as I can.

Hannibal is famous around the world as the Boyhood Home of Mark Twain. It has always had a mythic attraction to outsiders for that reason. It's also attractive because it is a remote river town almost frozen in time. Most of its present downtown storefronts were in place when Samuel Clemens was writing *Huckleberry Finn*. A rare and fragile authenticity hangs about Hannibal; not only in its streets and much of its architecture, but in its civic character and its politics and its class system and its notions of honor and justice and a lot of other things. This civic character is not always noble by any means, but it is Hannibal's own; it has been passed along through the generations, and in many important senses it borrows little from the dispensed mass culture of the late twentieth century.

Now: 1985 is the 150th anniversary of Mark Twain's birth. Hannibal, beneath its romantic reputation, has paid a price for its authenticity. It is a gasping little town mostly bypassed by economic improvement. And lately it has been further depleted by the farm-belt depression around it.

And thus, on the 150th anniversary of Mark Twain's birth, Hannibal decided to join the twentieth century. To promote its "Mark Twain Sesquicentennial," Hannibal opened itself up to the artifices of mass marketing and consumer research and demographic strategies: the same forces I had been assailing for years as a media critic. These forces had now entered my turf. The sacred and mythic ground, not only of my personal memory, but of the American culture's memory. The memory of town life and of Mark Twain and what he meant to literature in this country.

I said a minute ago, echoing John Irving, that when you're writing, everything is connected. This is what I meant.

Now I have a context. Now there is a thematic link, a continuum, between Hannibal's past as I remember it, and Hannibal's destiny as it is being decided this very year, this very summer. When I decided to write the Hannibal book I had only the haziest idea that these events were taking place. But now that I understand them, and have witnessed them, I can see that they provide my original premise a wholeness that it would not have had otherwise.

This time-present "theme parking" of Hannibal allows—no, it requires—me to summon my personal memories of the town as *context*. Their function will be to allow the reader to "inhabit" the town as I knew it, and perhaps to feel some personal stake in its desecration.

Now, in case you poets think this is all pretty turgid stuff, you should know that a fellow named John Ciardi once wrote this same story, with a lot more economy and precision, in a poem he called "Centennial":

> This official bicentennial arts person programming
> state-wide culturals for the up and coming
> year-long Fourth of July, made an appointment,
> and came, and I said I would (what I could),
> and she said, "Are there any other New Jersey
> poets we should mention?" And I said,
> "Well, William Carlos Williams to start." And she:
> "Has he published books?"
>   And I saw hall on hall
> of stone glass buildings, a million offices
> with labels on glass doors. And at the first desk
> in every office, nothing. And beyond, in the inner
> office, nothing. And a lost wind going, and doors
> all swinging bang in the wind and swinging bang.
> And at the end of every corridor
> a wall of buttons blinking data dead

Well. If I can summarize a bit:

In deciding to write a book about Hannibal, I have tried to step outside the nonfiction formulas that derive from the idiom of broadcast technology and the tendency of print publishers to imitate that idiom.

In trying to free myself from those formulas, I have staked part of my success on the validity of memory, both personal and cultural. I have used the power that this memory has on my imagination as a starting point: I've used it as the impetus for exploring Hannibal in search of a narrative. That search was an act of faith.

And yet I was not willing to make a virtue of ordinariness. Something about Hannibal had to *matter*—not just to me, but to a reader. I think I've made it pretty clear by now that I am against pandering, but I am equally opposed to writing as self-help therapy; as a way of "getting in touch with your feelings." If you must think of writing as a gift, think of it as a gift from yourself to the culture you live in; or at least as an offering. You must have something to say.

As I probed into the contending forces within Hannibal's Sesquicentennial, I relied on the insights I'd developed as a journalist. Journalism is not inherently opposed to the writer's craft; it is the commercial mutations of journalism that the writer must understand and control.

It may strike some people as a lucky coincidence that my preoccupation with history and memory led me straight toward a narrative theme involving a test of history and memory. I can only repeat what I've said a couple of times now: when you're writing, everything is connected. This is just another way of saying how vitally important the *imaginative act* is, even when you are working in nonfiction. In this form, your imaginative challenge is not to *invent* symbols, nor to *impose* a formal symmetry, but to discover these qualities—*in vitro*, as my wife the biochemist would say. (I can assure you that I've found at least three other narrative themes in Hannibal that would probably support a book—but I'm not going to tell you what they are!)

To summarize a little further: my personal memories and images of Hannibal are worth little in themselves—except as *context* for the story of the town's struggles in time present. By the same token, the story of that struggle loses a lot of its power over a general reader when it is separated from the context of those personal memories. The memories have the function of allowing the reader to "inhabit" Hannibal as I knew it, and to feel a certain concern for its fate.

And finally, I am operating here out of respect for another sort of memory as well. Call it "cultural memory," the sense of a lineage of American writers who have reached their literary power not so much by sublime invention as by sublime clarity: a clarity that allows them to invite the reader to participate, in a sensory way, with the universe they've apprehended on the page.

By the way, my working title for the book is *White Town Drowsing*, which itself invokes yet another echelon of memory. Near the beginning of *Life on the Mississippi*, Mark Twain wrote these lines:

> After all these years I can picture that old time to myself now, just as it was then: the white town drowsing in the sunshine of a summer's morning; the streets empty or nearly so . . . a sow and a litter of pigs loafing along the sidewalk, doing a good business in watermelon rinds and seeds . . . two or three wood flats at the head of the wharf but nobody to listen to the peaceful lapping of the wavelets against them; the great Mississippi, the majestic, the magnificent Mississippi, rolling in its mile-wide tide along, shining in the sun.

They've already put up an artifical lake on top of the prairie near the house where Mark Twain was born (they call it "Mark Twain Lake"), and now the more visionary of the city fathers are talking of the day when someone will enfold the Mississippi in concrete, making it an efficient viaduct.

It seems like a good time and a good place to be writing a book of nonfiction that involves memory. There are other good places, and you can find them if you're willing to step outside the formulas and write, not as an exploiter of a cancerous culture, but as a friend on behalf of a community.

"Don't Think of It as Art": Nonfiction and the Inflected Voice

Writers in our time face a tension between the fading legitimacy of the printed word and the competing authority of images, in particular the mass-produced photographic and video images of this century. I think this tension holds clues as to why serious people sometimes question whether writers, especially nonfiction writers, are lately producing something less than literature, something less than Art.

We are approaching the end of a morally catastrophic decade, a decade marked not so much by a growth of wickedness and venality as by a withering of the consciousness of wickedness and venality. It is not sin but sinlessness that has made the 1980s so uniquely sordid; not the assault on the common good but the incapacity to imagine a common ground.

Not at all coincidentally, it has been a catastrophic decade for the common language, a decade in which both intellectuals and the mass of people seem anesthetized from any hope or interest in the regenerative power of words: "The normalization of crisis," as Christopher Lasch has put it. Propelled by mass media, the tendency to frame everyday issues in the rhetoric of life and death has inflated the commonplace and deflated the significant.

A saturation of cheap public rhetoric has numbed us both to the authentically spiritual and the authentically profane. Truth and falsehood have been mostly relieved of their opposing qualities, thanks to the linguistic behaviorists of corporate public relations. As for the dark redeeming purgative of obscenity,

1. Adapted from Bread Loaf Lecture, 1988. Reprinted from *The Kenyon Review,* *Summer* 1988, pp. 139–52.

consider the most fashionable new bumper sticker of the suburban middle class: "Shit happens."

But if this decade has been marked by linguistic and moral bankruptcy, it has been bathed in a compensating richness: an unprecedented *pictorial* brilliance. We are at the peak of the Visual Age. As our language declines, we see the rise of special effects, of postproduction, of computer-generated graphics, of fashion and packaging and design and the establishment of entire nonverbal communications systems, complete with their capacity to lie and distract. It is an age when people can, and do, judge a book by its cover.

In keeping with these wised-up trends, and the fascination with the power of image, the prevailing style of nonfiction today is intensely pictorial and morally benumbed. At first this sounds interesting, progressive, exactly right for the times.

Consider the furtive-snapshot aura that pervades the memoirs of Administration goons and torpedoed network television news bosses. Notice the hint of airbrushing that softens the self-images of former Secretaries of State and former whores—if I am not being redundant here. And let us add to that list the photorealistic biographies of the convenient freshly dead, the hidden-camera grave robbing of snuffed celebrities whose remains are pried from their crypts for one last posthumous photo opportunity.

We are well into the age of the nonfiction writer as open aperture, an age in which the piling on of pictorial detail, unencumbered by personal voice or moral argument, seems like a kind of manifest destiny. This age began with Christopher Isherwood, who wrote in 1930, "I am a camera." It continued into the era of Andy Warhol, who may actually have been one.

I want to be precise about what I mean by "nonfiction." It's a term that begs for precision. It includes everything from recipes and bumper stickers to property deeds and the works of Freud and Macaulay and Lenny Dykstra of New York Mets, who in his autobiography *Nails*, according to the *Harper's* Index, used 167 repetitions of the word *fuck*—a National League record. Nonfiction also embraces historians and critics and social philosophers and authors of scientific papers.

But each of these categories creates, in effect, its own specialized readership. I'm interested in discussing the great vital center of nonfiction writing in this century, and the legitimate source of its claim as literature, which has been precisely its connection with unspecialized, general readers: readers who seek in nonfiction an access to surrogate experience that matters; who seek reliable and textured information from frontiers beyond their daily reach, information of a kind that was abandoned first by the novel and more recently by the daily newspapers.

Something has happened to that center, and it has happened fairly recently, since about the middle years of the last decade: the center has lost its intensity, its sense of purpose. In a very specific and nonfigurative way, it has lost its voice.

This spring and summer I talked to some magazine and book editors about what they felt was typical of manuscripts they were seeing in nonfiction. I had doubts as to whether there was any way to answer such a question—just because nonfiction is a sprawling category. What can you say about it that is in any way typical?

But I was surprised. The answers were quite emphatic, and they clustered around a common complaint: that nonfiction writing lately has lacked an inflected and recognizable voice.

One editor defined the "inflected and recognizable voice" this way: "It is you, the writer," he said, "in the middle of the story, thinking out loud. Making it clear to the reader at all times, this is what *you're* doing. Transmitting the feeling that you're *there*, mud on your shoes, observing, writing what you see and what you can infer from what you see. Having the courage of your own conclusions and observations."

Now: *clearly* this kind of writing is "pictorial." It's pictorial by definition: its function is partly to trigger images in the reader's mind. That's partly the function of all writing.

So "write what you see," as this editor prescribes, by all means. But pay attention to the other component of this request: *Write what you can infer from what you see. Have the courage of your own conclusions and observations.*

This is a necessary ingredient of the "inflected and recognizable voice."

The editor I am quoting was expressing something central to the very origins of American writing—American as distinct from the European culture from which it departed. The great visionary of the American epoch, Emerson, insisted that the new country must declare its cultural as well as its political independence from Europe, or else it would simply replicate the European experience, with its fixed and finished ideas, in the new land. Intellectual freedom would be founded on the divinity within common experience, and would be advanced by the poet. Emerson called poets the Namers, the Language-Makers; he thought of poets as liberating gods: and by "poet" it is clear that Emerson was not just speaking of bardic rhyme-smiths. He meant any true writer, anyone writing out of representative experience for others, irrespective of literary specialization. And famously, in his essay "The Poet," he had this to say about the nature of the "poet's" work, which he was pleased to think of as God's wine:

> For it is not metres, but a metre-making argument, that makes a poem—a thought so passionate and alive, that, like the spirit of a plant or an animal, it has an architecture of its own, and adorns nature with a new thing. The thought and the form are equal in the order of time, but in the order of genesis the *thought* is prior to the *form*. The poet has a new thought: he has a whole new experience to unfold; he will tell us how it was with him, and all men will be the richer in his fortune.

The metre-making argument, the thought so passionate and alive—the writer writing what he sees and what he can infer from what he sees, with the courage of his own convictions: these are two halves of the same ideal whole, separated only by 160 years of validating experience.

And now, welcome to time present, a time in which the onslaught of mass-produced visual images, most of them now capable of instant mass transmission, has joined with certain other social forces to attack the historic primacy of the "metre-making argument," a time when the thought so passionate and alive, the inflected voice, has given way to a phenomenon that I think of as the Disinvolved Stare.

I'm going to consider a couple of selections from a big book of popular nonfiction that is in many ways typical of what has happened to the vital center of the craft, to its inflected voice, in our own visually sophisticated time: a best-selling biography of the late NBC newswoman Jessica Savitch.

Jessica Savitch died accidentally and quite horribly a few years ago after living of life of what seems to have been extraordinary pain and pathos. A true child of the media age, she left behind a convenient retinue of friends, lovers, maids, and other voyeurs willing to gossip about the clinical details of her misery. She even left an autobiography. I should add, with no disrespect to Jessica Savitch, that her public significance consisted mainly in this: she was one of the first and most successful women anchors of the 1970s, and she went on to anchor the NBC News Digest. She made the world safe for Connie Chung.

The author of the biography is one Gwenda Blair, a New York magazine writer, state-of-the-art. She is perhaps best known as the ethics columnist for *Mademoiselle*.

Here's passage from *Almost Golden: Jessica Savitch and the Selling of Television News* in which Gwenda Blair describes an incident early in Savitch's broadcast apprenticeship in Houston, Texas (Savitch's mentor here is a veteran cameraman named Bob Wolf). Pay close attention to the "metre-making argument," the "thought so passionate and alive":

> The first story Wolf and Savitch did together [writes Blair] was about a dead body, or "floater," that had been fished out of the ship channel between Houston and Galveston. Well known in local circles for having been [Dan] Rather's cameraman on the Hurricane Carla story, the pistol-packing Wolf had the local "fuzz factory"—police headquarters—as his beat and had photographed dozens of floaters. When he and Savitch arrived at the piers, he tried to keep her away from the rotting, maggot-filled corpse. But when Savitch insisted on viewing the body herself, Wolf recalled, "I got sadistic. I took her right down close and got her downwind. She turned pale and walked away. I probably thought to myself, Goody, goody, that's what you desire, you nosy little broad." (119)

And you thought television news was all work and no play.

Well, the meanness of this passage leaps out at you, of course—and believe me, this passage is in no sense untypical—but I am equally struck by the deadness of the writing, the monotone, the complete lack of any betrayal or moral response, or even moral shading. Who is the main character in this passage? Savitch? Bob Wolf? Gwenda Blair? The corpse? There's no way of knowing. It's just there, an image, pictorial.

Certainly it is a scene as vacant of human empathy as anything you're likely to read these days—at least until you get to page 282 of the same book and watch Jessica discover the body of her hanged husband, Dr. Donald Payne. Again, pay attention to the eerie, uninflected detachment of Gwenda Blair's telling (or, if you are squeamish, skip this passage):

> The next morning she flew back to Washington and took a taxi to Embassy Park. Inside her house she found Payne hanging from a pipe in the laundry room. Around his neck was the leash of her beloved dog, Chewy. She later told a friend that Payne's tongue was hanging out and bloated, his eyes were popping out of his face, his body had no color, and his hands were swollen.

Nice and pictorial, don't you think? The swollen hands—that's a nice little detail. A lot of people wouldn't have noticed the hands.

What are we supposed to make of this scene? Something has been left out; in fact, everything has been left out except the picture. The impression is that Jessica Savitch was casually describing some bit of life-sculpture instead of the body of her husband. What else did she tell that friend? What was her state of mind when she told it? And perhaps most important, what does Gwenda Blair wish us to feel, or understand, from this information?

Does she wish us to understand anything at all?

Consider this passage from Susan Sontag's *On Photography*:

> Strictly speaking, one never understands anything from a photograph. Through photographs, the world becomes a series of unrelated, freestanding particles; and history, past and present, a

set of anecdotes. . . . The camera makes reality atomic, manageable and opaque. It is a view of the world which denies interconnectedness, continuity, but which confers on each moment the character of a mystery. (23)

The Dissolved Stare.
But let's be candid. The example I've given you is from the lower depths of the genre, the mass-market inferno, the supermarket nightscape stalked by Rupert Murdoch. What about serious nonfiction? What about the mandarin level of American prose writing? Does the Disinvolved Stare surface in the work of such virtuosos as Peter Matthiessen, John McPhee, Frances Fitzgerald, Renata Adler, Tracy Kidder?

After all, these writers form an exalted school (let's call it William Shawn Polytech). Their books and essays are always impeccable in concerns, always meticulous in scholarship, always vast in scope of inquiry, always clear and unpretentious in narrative style. Their work is always profound.

And almost never any fun to read.

Now I know this is nonfiction blasphemy; it's like a novelist admitting that maybe Joyce Carol Oates goes on a bit. But the fact is that these mandarins have grown just a little bloodless, just a wee tad wonderfully serene. Their work seems ever so slightly insulated from common passion, slightly prophylactic—as though they have grown afraid of contracting a vernacular inflection.

Where is the individual voice, the mud-covered shoes, the exhilaration, doubt, loss of temper, hint of sleepless nights? Why do the best lack all conviction? Why do they all sound alike?

I'm going to present three brief excerpts, two of them by mandarins, the third by a writer relatively unknown. In each example the writer is setting a pictorial scene, introducing the reader to an environment that forms the context of the book. Notice that in each passage the writer has chosen the device of motion to heighten the dramatic intensity of the moment.

Here is John McPhee, from his book *Pieces of the Frame*, getting us into a scene involving a field zoologist named Carol and her friend Sam down in the river country of Georgia:

Although Sam was working for the state, he was driving his own Chevrolet. He was doing seventy. In a reverberation of rubber, he crossed Hunger and Hardship Creek and headed into the sun on the Swainsboro Road. I took a ration of gorp—soybeans, sunflower seeds, oats, pretzels, Wheat Chex, raisins and kelp—and poured another ration into Carol's hand. At just about that moment, a snapping turtle was hit on the road a couple of miles ahead of us, who knows by what sort of vehicle, a car, a pickup; run over like a manhole cover, probably with much the same sound, and not crushed, but gravely wounded. It remained still. It appeared to be dead on the road. (409)

Now here is the opening passage of Frances Fitzgerald's essay on the Castro District of San Francisco, from her book *Cities on a Hill*. Again we're in motion, and again the details are meticulously catalogued:

It was one of those days in San Francisco when the weather is so perfect there seems to be no weather. The sun shone out of a cerulean sky lighting the streets to a shadowless intensity. It was a Sunday morning, and the streets were almost empty, so our pickup truck sped uninterrupted up and down the hills, giving those of us in the back a Ferris wheel view of the city. In Pacific Heights the roses were blooming, the hollies were in berry, and enormous clumps of daisies billowed out from under palm trees. . . .

Rounding a corner, we came upon a line of stationary floats. The balloons were flying—the lavender, pink, and silver bouquets crowding the sky—and the bands were just warming up. People in costumes milled about a crowd of young men and women in blue jeans. The Gay Freedom Day Parade had just begun. (25)

In many important ways, these passages are terrific. They are clear and perceptive and specific, and they evoke the scene. And yet I can't help feeling that if Frances Fitzgerald had gone to Georgia and John McPhee had gone to San Francisco, these two passages would have emerged pretty much as you have just read them.

Now consider a scene-setting passage—again with motion and detail—near the beginning of a book called *Blue Desert*, by an uncelebrated Southwestern writer named Charles Bowden:

Imagine you are on a train highballing through the desert night and out the window conflicting scenes flash across your eyes—a glimpse of mountain in the moonlight, a murder barely observed through a motel window—and that these experiences jar against each other as the train thunders toward its destination. This is the way to blue desert. (1)

Okay, it's a little florid, maybe a little film *noir*—and a little contrived: that image of the murder observed is after all a made-up detail. But I have to admit I like it. I like it better than the ingredients in the gorp and I like it better than those enormous clumps of daisies billowing out from under the palm trees. I like the recklessness in it; I like that cheap stunt about the murder, even though the referee in me wants to say that Chuck stepped out of bounds on the 30-yard line. Nonfiction prose should not have to borrow novelistic fantasy for its power. But we know that a gifted writer can present fantasy as a kind of truth, a mythic truth, as Harry Crews does in the first sentence of his nonfiction memoir *A Childhood*, when he writes, "My first memory is of a time ten years before I was born, and the memory takes place where I have never been and involves my daddy whom I never knew" (1).

In each of these latter two cases—Bowden's and Crews's—a note has been struck that seems urgent and strange. We know instantly that we've been plunged inside a private vision, a vision like no one else's, and that vision, that voice, is going to be our vehicle into unknown territory. We sense the underlying honesty. We also sense a kind of raw and restless will at work. These writers are on fire. Bowden isn't standing on ceremony. Crews doesn't seem to care whether you think he's creating literature or not: they're onto an idea that needs rooting out, and they're willing to improvise any style, any strategy that seems to work. It is the idea, the metre-making argument, and not the sentences, that drives these writers forward. And in the residue of their restless foraging, some very radiant sentences remain.

This is what's too often missing: passion, harnessed to an idea. This is the lost quality in so much of the genre we have managed to separate from Mr. Emerson's notion of poetry and stamp with the industrial label of "nonfiction."

Again, why?

It's not for me to impute motives to individual writers. Nor is it fair to trivialize the rational, scrupulous assembling and

organizing of facts that enrich the elegant essays we associate
with William Shawn and his *New Yorker*. This sort of writing has
often seemed to be the only sanctuary of narrative integrity
during times when the publishing world has been swept by fads
and broadcast lingo and the subversion of the language itself by
political bureaucracies and marketing specialists.

Nor should we forget what subtle force and passion can be contained in this outwardly opaque style of writing. Anyone who has
read John Hersey's *Hiroshima* knows this. *Hiroshima* first appeared
as an essay in the *New Yorker* in 1946, and it became the defining
standard of nonfiction for that magazine. It begins this way:

> At exactly fifteen minutes past eight in the morning, on August 6,
> 1945, Japanese time, at the moment when the atomic bomb flashed
> above Hiroshima, Miss Toshiko Sasaki, a clerk in the personnel
> department of the East Asia Tin Works, had just sat down at her
> place in the plant office and was turning her head to speak to the
> girl at the next desk. (*Reading* 474)

Flat, uninflected, detached, pictorial—but in this case, the
style is absolutely correct. There is no other way to begin this
story. How do you set up the atomic bomb with rhetoric?

And I cannot leave John Hersey's work without considering
one further passage that illustrates the moral power of uninflected prose when it is in the hands of genius:

> Everything fell, and Miss Sasaki lost consciousness. The ceiling
> dropped suddenly and the wooden floor above collapsed in
> splinters and the people up there came down and the roof above
> them gave way; but principally and first of all, the bookcases right
> behind her swooped forward and the contents threw her down,
> with her left leg horribly twisted and breaking underneath her.
> There, in the tin factory, in the first moment of the atomic age, a
> human being was crushed by books. (*Hiroshima* 23)

So, you see, the uninflected voice has its place and its function.

Sometimes I think that John Hersey's legacy has perhaps cast too
much of a spell across serious writers of nonfiction. And some-

times I wonder whether it's simply that the scale of things has shriveled in our time—that there's nothing left to write about so awesome as to justify this sort of terrible calm.

But I'd like to return to the question of American prose writing and its relationship to the photographic image.

There was a time when camera eye seemed to be a liberating force, a force for a new kind of realism in nonfiction; and of course if you read John Dos Passos or Isherwood, for the novel as well. the advent of the Leica, the hand-held 35-millimeter still camera in the early 1930s, gave photographers mobility and quick access, and the Spanish Civil War gave some of them a chance to use it. Suddenly the people of the world were opening newspapers and magazines to find images of soldiers in combat, sometimes at the instant of death, and of suffering civilians, images made by Robert Capa and Andre Kertesz and Henri Cartier-Bresson: images unprecedented in history. These photographs had the immediate effect of rendering romantic war journalism obsolete. Now people could see for themselves what it was like on the inside.

(And a hell of a lot of good *that* did, right?)

At about the same time, the Farm Security Administration project in America was assembling a remarkably gifted coterie of photographers who were similarly fascinated by this new opportunity for social realism: Walker Evans, Dorothea Lange, Ben Shahn, Russell Lee. Besides their great technical skills—their deep involvement in such matters as composition and light and geometry—these photographers were united by an older concern, one that traced back to Whitman: a concern for transcendence. Their photographs affirmed noble ideals. For instance, they dealt seriously with poverty, the poverty of sharecroppers. They trained their lenses directly into the faces of hardship and tried to evoke, or at least confer, an unquenchable beauty in those faces: a plea for redemption.

Walker Evans was after an affirmation, but of a certain kind: impersonal, marked by a noble reticence, a lucid understatement. Susan Sontag writes that Evans wanted his photographs to be "literate, authoritative, transcendent." And she adds this very pertinent observation: "The moral universe of the 1930s being no longer ours, these adjectives are barely credible today. Nobody demands that photography be literate. Nobody can imagine how it could be authoritative. Nobody understands how anything, least of all a photograph, could be transcendent" (31).

The writer James Agee, Evans's collaborator, understood. A Tennessee mountain boy by way of Harvard, on assignment by Henry Luce's *Fortune* magazine to get some profiles of poor whites in the South, Agee was nearly as affected by his companion's photographs as by his own eyewitness impressions. They moved him in fact to this great cry from the heart near the beginning of *Let Us Now Praise Famous Men*:

> If I could do it, I'd do no writing at all here. It would be photographs; the rest would be fragments of cloth, bits of cotton, lumps of earth, records of speech, pieces of wood and iron, phials of odors, plates of food and excrement. Booksellers would consider it quite a novelty; critics would murmur, yes, but it is art; and I could trust a majority of you to use it as you would a parlor game.
>
> A piece of the body torn out by the roots might be more to the point.
>
> As it is, though, I'll do what little I can in writing. Only it will be very little. I'm not capable of it; and if I were, you would not go near it at all. For if you did, you would hardly bear to live. (13)

James Agee's text in *Let Us Now Praise Famous Men* turned out to be one of the great flawed masterpieces in the history of American letters. Reading it fifty years later can leave you breathless and infuriated and overwhelmed with a feeling of radiance. It can leave you, to use a very old-fashioned word, *inspired*. It is by turns outraged, obsessive, lyrical, extreme, overwrought, exquisite, minutely pictorial, self-mocking, glorious—and poetic in the Emersonian sense of that word.

It is above all a towering manifesto of the inflected voice, an act of consciousness so sustained and so pure that you wonder it didn't burn out his soul—which it might have. He was twenty-seven when he started writing it and he died at forty-five.

Agee worked on the manuscript for four years. It is said that he developed a writer's callus on his right middle finger the size of a marble. He resisted having the work published, insisting at one point that it be done on newsprint. When it was finally published in 1941, most of the critics murmured yes, but is it art—the *Times* review called it "arrogant, mannered, precious," and "gross." Now the Depression was over and the country was focused on the World War. *Let Us Now Praise Famous Men* sold 600 copies in hardcover. Agee considered his text a failure, calling it in one letter "sinful" and "corrupt." Walker Evans mislaid the original manuscript that Agee had given him as a Christmas present.

Nineteen years later, and five years after Agee's death, Houghton Mifflin republished the long-forgotten work, and it has since sold more than half a million copies. More important, it inflamed the consciousness of a new generation of writers: academics, journalists, students, who caught the scent of the coming social revolution.

> For in the immediate world [wrote Agee], everything is to be discerned . . . with the whole of consciousness, seeking to perceive it as it stands: so that the aspect of a street in sunlight can roar in the heart of itself as a symphony, perhaps as no symphony can: and all of consciousness is shifted from the imagined, the revisive, to the effort to perceive simply the cruel radiance of what is.
>
> That is why the camera seems to me, next to unassisted and weaponless consciousness, the central instrument of our time. (11)

The surging nonfiction writers of the 1960s and the early 1970s did indeed write through the metaphor of the camera eye. But they also wrote in that inflected voice legitimized by James Agee; and the best of them, the ones who got beyond the artifice of New Journalism, reinvented Emerson's metre-making argument, the thought "so passionate and alive": Gloria Emerson and Michael Herr and the early Tim O'Brien in Vietnam; Norman Mailer on the election of John F. Kennedy and on the political conventions of the '60s; Dan Wakefield on American life; Joan Didion on the hallucination called California; Truman Capote on the slaughter of a family in Kansas; Gay Talese on Frank Sinatra and on the Bonanno crime family of New York; and dozens of others.

It was a fabulous time in American nonfiction writing, exciting and noisy and vital and filled with compelling, passionate voices. Popular magazines were publishing long, searching essays of personal reportage; even newspapers, those ancient seedbeds of American literature, seemed alive with young reporter-poets — creatures of mothlike avidity, as Ben Hecht, an earlier member of the breed, described them in *A Child of the Century*, "feeling a childish immortality within the days they occupied . . . haunt(ing) streets, studios, whore houses, police stations, court-rooms, theater stages, jails, saloons, slums, mad houses, fires, murders, riots, banquet halls and book shops" (112–113).

I knew some of those avid moths. In Chicago one night I saw a reporter by the name of Fitzpatrick get up and leave the *Sun-Times* city room to go out and cover a counterculture demonstration in Lincoln Park. The demonstration turned into a rampage; Fitz ran with the rioters through the Gold Coast streets, came back to the office and wrote seventeen pages of copy in short takes without revision. It won him the Pulitzer Prize. A few days after that assignment he was assigned to Paris to cover the atmosphere surrounding the Peace Talks. He phoned the city editor collect from Kennedy Airport in New York to say he only had twenty dollars left in his pocket and he didn't want to go to Paris anyway. Fitz was just a Chicago newspaperman.

It still astonishes me how recent that era was, how abruptly it ended and why — and how few traces it has left on the publishing landscape of the 1980s.

Or to be honest with you, the "why" of it does not astonish me. It seems inevitable. A realist might even say we should be grateful for the reasons: the end of a terrible war, the withdrawal of a disgraced Administration, a national cooling-down after fifteen years of riots and burnings and assassinations. Peace. And good times.

But the peace that came to America has not been a lovely peace; nor has the rhetorical voice of this decade been a very admirable voice; nor has the camera eye been much of a transcending eye. Somewhere along the way, and quickly, we became a nation of candy-colored newspapers expressing news in terms of percentile numbers, magazines about food and celebrities and the surrogate Self, books by political snitches and famous madams and people who have carefully tracked down the number of times Jessica Savitch was beaten senseless by her lover.

The line between social criticism and public performance has vanished. Critics have become value-free collaborators with the industries of processed fun. Vestiges of James Agee's great inflected voice may be heard in the transitional banter of television news teams, which marketing directors have discovered adds a "humanizing" touch."

The passion to perceive simply the cruel radiance of what is has been replaced, with startling abruptness, by the Disinvolved Stare. Walker Evans has been replaced by Diane Arbus, who trained her camera eye on freaks, and by Andy Warhol, who said this about his protégée Edie Sedgwick to his "super-star" Ultra Violet: "Should Eddie OD, we must film it. Stay in close touch with her" (47). And Ultra Violet adds in her recently published memoirs, "Andy was not at her deathbed to film her. At that time, her death was not nearly as interesting to Andy as it would have been at the height of her career. The fascination of the moment was gone for Andy. A cruel statement, but true" (47).

"The fascination of the moment was gone." Please pay very close attention to that statement, because I think it contains the key to everything I'm trying to express. It is at once an epitaph for the corruption of words by images that has been building in our society for many years, well before television—*and* it is a signpost that points the way out. It is a cryptograph that contains the seeds of redemption for writers still committed to the metre-making arguments.

The real reason for the debasement of rhetoric in our time has had very little to do with cycles of social change. Those cycles do color rhetorical styles and subjects, but they alone could not have unleashed the contempt toward narrative itself that is now routine in America, particularly within the print world.

The reason was technical and financial. Mass visual communication, with its brutal economic logic, had overtaken the typographic culture in the mid-1970s; the new surge of private hedonism merely gave it an idiom. Many publishing concerns were annihilated by television; most of the rest surrendered. They redesigned their products in the image of the oppressor. Check it out. The Disinvolved Stare was Everywhere.

And that is more or less where we stand today.

Now I'm going to tell you some very implausible good news.

The Camera Age is in decline. It has lost its capacity to move people by the force of its iconographic images. It anesthetizes. The Disinvolved Stare is met with a Disinvolved Stare in return. And let me assure you that the lords and ladies of the allied visual communications industries are quite aware of that fact.

I'll give you some evidence of this; but first the theory, expressed with admirable common sense by Susan Sontag. She is writing here not about television but about photography in its curve of aspirations:

> The vast photographic catalogue of misery and injustice through-out the world [she writes] has given everyone a certain familiarity with atrocity, making the horrible seem . . . ordinary. . . . In these last decades, "concerned" photography has done at least as much to deaden conscience as to arouse it. (20–21)

And, referring to Walt Whitman's ideal of populist transcendence, she notes, "American photography has moved from affirmation to erosion to, finally, a parody of Whitman's program" (29).

If that is true in photography, it is geometrically true in television. The big news of the 1980s is that television is losing its visual force. Like the movies, it has pushed "picture" to a succession of extremes, some morbid, some merely kinetic, and has found repeatedly that yesterday's extreme is today's unsurprising norm.

Example: a commercial not long ago, aimed at teenagers, the most suicide-prone group in America. Two teenage boys are in their cars, poised at the edge of a cliff over an ocean. A girl gives the "start" signal and the boys flatten their accelerators. The first boy laughs. The second is nervous. He tries to open the car door. It sticks. The first boy dives out of his car. The second boy screams as his car plunges over the edge of the cliff and crashes onto the rocks below. The first boy and the girl look over the edge, expressions of horror on their faces. The scene shifts to the ocean. A denim jacket and a pair of jeans are floating on the surface. The caption appears: "Union Bay—Fashion That Lasts."

The marketing director of this commercial explained to a newspaper reporter that the company was not trying to encourage reckless driving. They said the ad was chosen in the simple hope that it would have what the marketing director chose to call, doubtlessly without irony, "impact." She added that test marketing showed that kids found the ad amusing.

I think the real message of that story is not about the callousness of children. It is about the inevitable bankruptcy, if not the corruption, of the visual culture. Susan Sontag, speaking of the work of Diane Arbus, writes:

> Our ability to stomach this rising grotesqueness in images, moving and still, *and in print*, has a stiff price. In the long run, it works out not as a liberation of but as a subtraction from the self: a pseudo-familiarity with the horrible reinforces alienation, making one less able to react in real life. (41)

A less elegant way of putting this would be that the visual culture has skidded off the cliff of postmodernism. It can't even self-reference anymore. It can't have a catharsis. Its visual content has gone invisible.

This is why you rarely see coherent scenes on your television screen these days. More and more you are glimpsing blurred fragments. The emerging strategy, which has the scent of desperation, is to abolish the picture in favor of the edit. Pure transition is now the focus of energy on the video screen. The average television image now lasts less than a second and a half; in commercials and in music videos the time-frame borders on the subliminal. Visual as well as verbal narrative is abolished. The point now is the quantum, the smallest maneuverable bit of information. This is where video is now making its stand.

Does all of this suggest any plausible hope for some rehabilitation of the personal, the inflicted, the scrupulously narrative voice in American nonfiction writing? It's hard to say. A lot of damage has been done. A lot more is in the doing stages. The profound rupture in the narrative tradition—which has been deepening exponentially for the better part of a generation—could be extremely resistant of repair, especially given the steady encroachment of the video idiom (however debased, however atrophied) into American public education.

Just this past February the enterprising firm Whittle Communications of Knoxville, Tennessee, revealed a brazen scheme for intruding network-style programming into the high school curriculum: "Channel 1," a 12-minute daily "package" of news and educational features. Its executive producer is Susan Winston, a woman who, as producer of "Good Morning America," on ABC, was a leading *auteur* of content-free, value-free, disinflected video.

"Channel 1"—which has been snapped up by several schools around the country—offers one additional element not normally associated with basic education: commercials. For the first time in history, spots for blue jeans and candy bars will be, *ipso facto*, a part of the core curriculum of 15- and 16-year-old students.

And yet things may not have regressed beneath hope. The human wish for story, for tales told by a teller, rich and personal and flowing like a river, is an ancient wish—as ancient as myth, as ancient as words. It seems a little too neatly Orwellian (no offense intended to Orwell!) to suppose that such a wish—defining as it is to our very humanness—could be programmed out of the species in just one generation.

Story does crop up in the damnedest places. Just now it is making a significant resurgence in a relatively unnoticed corner of video: in the works of "independent" artists—that is, videomakers working outside the corporate bounties (and restraints) of commercial contracts, options, and budgets.

Independent video had quite a romp in the fields of nonnarrative, nonverbal impressionism through the 1970s and early '80s. But lately there appears to be a strong resurgence of interest in coherent exposition; in the exploration of aesthetic and social themes, developed with passion, clarity, a sense of involvement and moral probing.

There are many examples—Fred Wiseman and his unnarrated but crystalline black-and-white video essays; the critic and videomaker Helen DeMichiel completing her new work, a study of a

150-year-old Minnesota farm encircled by shopping malls and suburbia; the intense social journalism of Christine Choy and Renee Tajima in their five-year video study of a racial murder in Detroit, *Who Killed Vincent Chin?*

The point in citing these artists is not to suggest that their work (or even the work of hundreds more like them) will form some necessary new paradigm that writers, waiting helplessly for a new stimulus, will follow. The point is that there seems to be a nascent *cultural* revulsion toward anesthetized, dumbed-down, morally indifferent imagery; and that this new sensibility is showing up on the fringes of video, the form most congenial to the Disinvolved Stare.

Perhaps the emerging avant-garde of independent videomakers will replicate the great sudden flowering of literary journalists, those sons and daughters of Agee, who infused American rhetoric so vividly a generation ago. And perhaps the same cues, the same passions and discontents that are generating this new efflorescence, will energize a new generation of writers, and the process of rehabilitation will begin, quite unimpended by the defeatism and the sad disinvolvement that hang about the popular publishing world, the public school systems.

If that is the case, we might soon look forward to hearing some contemporary echoes of James Agee's obstreperous and liberating rant to his readers near the beginning of *Let Us Now Praise Famous Men*:

"This is a *book* only by necessity. More seriously, it is an effort in human actuality, in which the reader is no less centrally involved than the authors and those of whom they tell.

"Above all else: in God's name don't think of it as Art" (15).

WORKS CITED

Agee, James, and Walker Evans. *Let Us Now Praise Famous Men*. Boston: Houghton, 1980.

Blair, Gwenda. *Almost Golden: Jessica Savitch and the Selling of Television News*. New York: Simon, 1988.

Bowden, Charles. *Blue Desert*. Tucson: University of Arizona Press, 1986.

Crews, Harry. *A Childhood: The Biography of a Place.* New York: Harper, 1978.

Fitzgerald, Frances. *Cities on a Hill: A Journey Through Contemporary American Cultures.* New York: Simon, 1986.

Hecht, Ben. *A Child of the Century.* New York: Primus, 1985.

Hersey, John. "A Noiseless Flash." *Hiroshima.* New York: Knopf, 1946.

McPhee, John. "Pieces of the Frame." *The John McPhee Reader.* New York: Farrar, 1976.

New York. 9 March 1987: 47.

Reading for Rhetoric. 2nd ed. New York: McMillan, 1967.

Sontag, Susan. *On Photography.* New York: Farrar, 1977.

Toward the Light: Finding Truth Amidst the Virtual Reality

Ten years ago, in the summer of 1981—a very, very long time ago in our country's cultural and intellectual history—a younger and I think even more naive version of myself gave his first Bread Loaf lecture.

I can tell you that I was terrified. I had started writing the damn thing the previous February. I was still writing it a half hour before I delivered it.

I'd never talked to a group of writers before. I barely knew what they looked like in a herd. And to make matters worse, the writers I had sat out there and listened to the previous two summers, when I'd begun coming to Bread Loaf, fished out of the waters of journalism like an interesting but perhaps inedible species of basking shark, sounded to me like prophets. Their words seemed to glitter in the sunlight that came through those doors.

Frost had rested his elbows on the podium before them, I supposed. And Auden, and Carson McCullers. And now here comes a guy who had once covered a twenty-four-hour stock-car race for the *St. Louis Post-Dispatch*. What in the world was I going to say that could catch the attention of these drowsy ghosts?

I decided to stick as close as possible to the shore of my own experience and understanding. Perhaps this was not the moment to wax casually ironic over Trollope's astonishment that Mrs. Eustace had stolen her own diamonds. It wouldn't have done much good anyway, because I didn't know who Mrs. Eustace was at that time, and the only trollop I'd encountered had been associated with the twenty-four-hour stock car race.

In any event, my assigned field at Bread Loaf, then as now, was nonfiction—surprising, in light of the fact that my second failed novel was due out that very summer.

It seemed appropriate, therefore, to speak about Truth.

As I say, 1981 was a very, very long time ago in our country's cultural and intellectual history. "Truth" was one of those things we occasionally still spoke about then, along with phrenology and the recent writings of Mary Baker Eddy.

My interest in Truth had derived from my experiences in journalism.

Let me see if I can enlarge on that statement so that it will make sense to you.

My experiences in journalism had led me to observe a number of behaviorist experiments with the terms of truth in the mass media, particularly broadcasting. I felt that the effects of these experiments were rapidly resonating into more purified areas of our cultural life, such as literature. I thought I'd better get up here on the mountain and warn everyone before somebody got hurt.

Little did I know then that Jacques Derrida had already stolen his own diamonds.

Well, as I say, I worked hard on that lecture. I pulled together a lot of evidence from the fields of public-opinion sampling, and right-brain/left-brain response studies, and the strategies of motivational research as commissioned by the commercial television networks.

I tried to explain what one of the country's leading video theorists meant when he unveiled the good news that electronic visual transmissions had made truth obsolete as a social value. The constantly scrolling pattern of dots on a cathode screen, never presenting a coherent picture at any given instant, tended to enlist the human mind as a collaborator in an ongoing dream sequence. This collaboration was the exact opposite of the mind's function when assimilating the fixed and static symbols on a page of type: analytical, disciplined, dialectical, even querulous.

In other words, while the act of reading can evoke a memory of one's experiences in the world, including one's moral experiences, watching television evokes nothing so much as a memory of television. As this theorist summed it up: "In communicating at electronic speed, we no longer direct information into an audience . . . but try to *evoke stored information out of them*, in a patterned way."

And then, noting that the theories and practices of broadcasting had by then become well entrenched in a cowed and receding print world, I offered what I called "the most corrosive, the most insidious effect of broadcasting's influence on the world of writers." It was this:

"In separating ideas from any test of their authenticity other than how well they go over with a sample fragment of the mass audience, broadcasters are perhaps unwittingly rearranging the terms of truth."

I continued: "This is not the same as saying they are lying. What I mean is that the broadcast idiom has separated the concept of truthfulness from a sense of why truthfulness matters."

And I concluded by suggesting that the writers' great social task was to get back what was their own. And to get it back on their own terms. "Writers need to conquer both their deference to the colonizers from the broadcast world," I said, "and their contempt for the mass culture that has been its victim.

"Writers need to get angry over the fact that they have temporarily surrendered their language to a ruling force that does not love language, nor trust it, nor betray any interest in it beyond its propensity to sell things."

That was ten years ago. I was beginning a personal transition then: from the semibarbaric life of newspaper and magazine journalism to whatever the hell it is I'm writing now; I think the label says something like, "Serious Nonfiction."

In the summers since then, I have tried to pull farther and farther away from that familiar topical shore in my lectures here. I have tried to speak less as a courier from a distant battlefield, and more from the inside of the writer's craft, as I began to understand it. How to Convert Your Catharses to Cash, Let's Aerobicize Those Flabby Metaphors, the Five W's of Literary Immortality. That sort of thing.

But here I am, ten years later—and to my utter astonishment, I find myself swimming madly back toward shore. I still can't think of a topic more central to my identity as a writer, yet more confusing to my identity as a person in society, than this bewildering issue of Truth.

The 1980s saw the ascendancy of "nonverbal lying" in Western culture—a technique that George Orwell scarcely imagined when he published his great essay, "Politics and the English Language," in 1949. You'll recall that in that essay, Orwell drew attention to a new technique in manipulating the sentiments of a mass culture. This technique, arising from state political bureaucracies and soon to be imitated by statist corporations, was aimed at camouflaging true intentions. It accomplished this aim not so much by overt lying as by relieving language of its specific meaning. This in turn was accomplished by draining language of its imagery—its capacity to call up mental pictures.

"In our time," Orwell wrote, "political speech and writing are largely the defense of the indefensible. . . . Thus political language has to consist largely of euphemism, question-begging and sheer cloudy vagueness. . . . Such phraseology is needed if one wants to name things without calling up mental pictures of them."

He offered some examples; they're well-known; I'll cite just one: "Defenseless villages are bombarded from the air, the inhabitants driven out into the countryside, the cattle machine-gunned . . . this is called *pacification*."

Well, sometimes it's called Operation Desert Storm, but you get the point.

Willie Horton was still only a gleam in Roger Ailes's beady little kindergarten eye when Orwell published that essay. But Ailes and Horton were destined to turn Orwell's great formulation inside out and render it effectively obsolete. The Horton political ad for George Bush in 1988 consummated the emerging art of nonverbal lying. Instead of offering language drained of mental image, it presented a pure image that had no referent in language. Like television commercials generally, the Horton ad was impossible to refute with textual argument because its central message lived outside its text. It spoke neither the truth nor the opposite of truth. It simply evoked stored information out of us, in a patterned way.

If you're an irony fan, by the way, you may have noticed that the 1980s did see a continuation of Orwell's linguistic lobotomizing. Now it had been adopted, half a century later, by conscientious people seeking to save society rather than exploit it, but the results sounded curiously similar: "differently abled," "chemical dependence," "temporarily robust."

Meanwhile, the desanctifying of truthfulness accelerated in other ways—ways that would inevitably affect the world of writers. It wasn't so much that people and institutions were telling more lies in the 1980s, although that might well have been the case. The point is that in countless ways, the ethical pillars that had elevated the concept of truth above more relative claims were tumbling like goal posts after the Super Bowl. The wrecking crews portrayed themselves as liberators, saviors of the nation. Truth was elitist; truth was authoritarian; truth was hierarchical. Now, finally, after all these millenia, truth was becoming one of the guys.

Dramatic recreations of actual events began to appear on the network news, not to mention inside the cavernous sound stage of President Reagan's brain. Rock groups gained international fame by lip-synching the vocals of people performing behind the scenes, as did witnesses testifying under oath at the Iran-Contra hearings.

In letters, the hottest "ism" since minimalism became plagiarism, with big breakthroughs in politics, academia, and the popular press. Nor did it follow that if you were caught practicing the popular genre your career was necessarily in ruins. One young writer, suspended from a national magazine for lifting quoted material from a published text, announced to a friend that he had signed a contract to write a book. "Oh?" came the detached reply. "Whose?"

By the early 1990s, even those who had become heroes of the culture by the very fact of their truth-telling had begun to treat the truth as just another entrepreneurial resource. Bob Woodward, whose Watergate reporting two decades ago exposed the lies and deceits of the Nixon Administration, published a book earlier this year called *The Commanders*, an inside account of the secret policy discussions leading up to the United States assault against the Iraqui armies in the Persian Gulf.

No one has questioned the accuracy of Woodward's portrayals. What has been questioned is Woodward's withholding of certain facts that might have made a difference in the Congressional debate about the war if they'd been published when Woodward learned them. What this means is that they might have prolonged several tens of thousands of human lives.

Woodward learned last December, for example, that General Colin Powell, the Chairman of the Joint Chiefs of Staff, opposed a military assault and favored containment. Powell's opposition was not made public until *The Commanders* was published two months after the war ended. In the Senate, the resolution authorizing force in the Gulf passed by a mere seven votes. *The Commanders* is currently eighth on the *New York Times* nonfiction best-seller list.

It was not so much lying as surrealism that was replacing truthfulness in America—a strange new apathy toward any test of the authentic; a lassitude toward the legitimate.

Entire communities, threatened by economic decline, turned themselves into fantastic dioramic theme-park cartoons. They've gone Bavarian in Frankenmuth, Michigan; they're wearing lederhosen and eating sauerkraut and slapping their thighs. In Chicopee, Massachusetts, they've turned the riverfront into a tropical jungle, complete with live monkeys. You don't even want to know about Dolly Parton's hometown in Tennessee.

In fact, it has gotten to the point that the cultural critic Joel Achenbach now argues that in postmodern America, *nothing* is real anymore. And in fact, says Achenbach, Americans now prefer it that way. "The technology of falsehood," he writes, "has greatly outdistanced the progress of our judgment." And he notes an eerie sort of cultural submission to it all. "From this mess," he concludes, "has arisen a strange sort of *comfort* with artifice and falsehood. There may be an actual preference for the unreal."

Or the virtually real. The recent dawning of the Age of Virtual Reality in computer technology was practically a Darwinian sure thing, given the nearly complete deconstruction of *real* reality in our lifetimes, coupled with our starvation for authentic experience and our steadfast faith against all evidence in redemption through technology.

Virtual reality, according to its many advocates, is an even greater rush than reading the works of John McPhee. Now it's possible for reality buffs in the United States, Europe, and Japan to gird themselves up in video goggles, DataGloves, and wraparound display screens, and clump joyfully into a new Arcadia of simulated three-dimensional landscapes in which one can summon up and manipulate the objects in the environment at will, much as department chairmen were able to do in more primitive times.

The ultimate goal of this electronic pilgrimage is what virtual reality players call "presence," or the feeling of, quote, "being here now." Some have described it as not unlike being in the presence of the Almighty. Since it now costs about twenty thousand dollars to experience "being here now" through a pair of DataGloves and some video goggles, as opposed to about twenty-two dollars for an average hardcover book of narrative nonfiction, one does begin to fear that recent trends in literary theory have left some consumers vaguely dissatisfied.

Well, I've tried to give you a very compressed summary of what's been going down, truth-wise, in the culture at large. Now let's take things a little closer to our immediate concerns as writer and as readers.

Earlier this year a man named Simon Schama published a book called *Dead Certainties*, and subtitled, *Unwarranted Speculations*. Fair warning. Simon Schama is 45 years old, a distinguished historian, and currently Mellon Professor in the Social Sciences at the Center for European Studies at Harvard. His reputation is that of an unusually gifted writer of powerful narrative prose, a storyteller in the richest sense. And indeed, earlier in his career he was described by his own mentor, J. H. Plumb, as "the outstanding historian of his generation." His standing in academic circles has been neither tainted nor enhanced by any evidence of ideological special pleading or political partisanship.

Professor Shama has previously published four well-received history books, the first of which, *Patriots and Liberators: Revolution in the Netherlands, 1780–1813*, began in his words as "a trim monograph," but eventually ended up as 745 pages. Telling the complicated story of the destruction of the Dutch Republic required the British-born Schama, among other things, to master the Dutch language and the Dutch archives.   .

What I'm trying to say is, he ain't Kitty Kelly.

And in the interest of Truth, I want to acknowledge here the critical essay about *Dead Certainties* by the historian Gordon Wood in the June 27 *New York Review of Books* as a source of my knowledge of the issues at stake.

Dead Certainties combines two separate historical narratives. One involves the death of General Wolfe at the Battle of Quebec in 1759. The other deals with the murder of the historian George Parkman by Professor John Webster of Harvard in 1849. Perhaps some interesting Freudian wishes being thrashed out there.

As his subtitle indicates, Professor Schama is experimenting here in historical narration. Let me quote from Gordon Wood:

"In his storytelling, Schama has avoided neat chronological sequences and has in fact 'deliberately dislocated the conventions by which histories establish coherence and persuasiveness.' Both stories 'begin with abrupt interventions . . . and end with accounts at odds with each other as to what has happened.'

"He has given us," Wood writes, "what literary scholars would call interior monologues, shifting voices, and multiple points of view; and if these were not enough, he has invented whole passages, including a fictional account by one of Wolfe's soldiers of the battle of Quebec and a made-up dialogue between two of the figures in the Webster trial.

"It is an extraordinary book," Professor Wood sums up, "with important questions for the discipline of history, especially because of who Schama is."

Now, this combining of fact and fiction, and the theories supporting it, is yesterday's news in English and humanities departments by now; in fact it embarrasses me to admit that it was yesterday's news ten years ago when I first came galloping up the mountain with the bulletin that *television* was unhinging the terms of truth.

But apparently there are people in this world even more insulated than I am, and those people include paramilitary survivalists and academic historians. The act of combining fact and fiction is still pretty spicy stuff over in the history department. Professor Wood himself primly acknowledges that "Historians are usually the last to acknowledge current fashions, but so powerful have the postmodern, deconstruction theories become that even historians can no longer remain ignorant of them."

I don't get to say this very often, but—Professor Wood, wake up and smell the bacon.

But let's listen a little more closely to the considered anxiety that Professor Gordon Wood is expressing here. He seems genuinely to believe that Simon Schama's book has all but guaranteed the end of his profession as he has understood it. He is concerned for what his fellow historian Peter Novick has called "the demise of the founding ideals of the discipline of history with little or no hope of their rebirth."

Gordon Wood is honest enough to concede that the claims of the "new historicists," and of deconstructionists in general, are persuasive. Why should we cling to an almost theological belief in a past objective reality, or indeed in the possibility of objective reality at all? In the case of a gifted prose writer such as Professor Schama, why should he remain confined to the pedantries of specialization; why should he not let his language soar rich and unconfined?

Professor Wood celebrates this soaring language. "Schama develops his exciting tale with great skill," he acknowledges. "He introduces us to the principal characters and develops them fully and imaginatively as a sensitive novelist would."

He even allows Schama to speak for himself, quoting at length from an eight-page "Afterword" in which the historian tries to explain why he did what he did. In this Afterword Schama writes that since historians can never truly recover a past world, they are "left forever chasing shadows, painfully aware of their inability ever to reconstruct a dead world in its completeness, however thorough or revealing their documentation."

Schama also cites the alternative accounts of the events that he uncovered in his research. These, he argues, "dissolve the certainties of events into the multiple possibilities of alternative narrations. . . . These are stories, then, of broken bodies, uncertain ends, indeterminate consequences . . . flickering glimpses of dead worlds."

And then Professor Wood begins his rebuttal.

He begins with some insider stuff: historians know quite a bit more about the events covered in the book than Schama implies. It is no good, he insists, "for the historian to wring his hands and simply lay out 'all the accidents and contingencies that go into the making of an historical narrative.' It is the historian's responsibility to analyze and evaluate all these different views and narrations and then arrive at as full and as objective an explanation and narration of the events as possible."

Now, I suspect that a lot of you are thinking about this last assertion and muttering, "Oh, yeah? Sez who?" It's a legitimate reaction; Wood seems dangerously close here to moralizing in an arbitrary and unsupported way.

But this summons, this invoking of *"responsibility,"* cuts to the heart of the entire debate, I think: not just in academic historical writing but in any writing, or any attempt at communicating, that presents any blend of fact and fiction to an audience without renouncing the claim of history. For we are all historians—we poets, novelists, biographers, nonfiction writers, journalists. We are all historians.

Let's see how Professor Wood supports his assertion—and then I'll add some tentative thoughts of my own, just to see how they play.

First, Woods asks an entirely reasonable question of his own: have Schama's novelistic techniques led him to tell a better and more convincing story *than a novelist could write?* And if not, then why the experiment? For Woods, and I suspect for many general readers, the answer is self-evident: his story is less convincing, for the simple fact that the reader is never sure at which moment she is reading fact, and at which moment she is reading fiction. Since Schama provides no footnotes, no references, no conventional proof, the purely invented parts of his book taint the credibility of the whole.

I'd like to add a footnote of practical, pragmatic, value-neutral advice to that point. In my experience the addition of make-up material to an essentially factual text seldom works on the page because the reader *can* tell it apart. The reason the reader can tell it apart is that the made-up stuff is generally badly written. It stands out from the rest like a guilty conscience. "Truth," writes the Custer biographer Evan Connell, "no matter how startling, customarily rings with a distinctive note, rather like the high hard ring of a silver coin dropped on a table, (while fabrication) clinks like a potmetal counterfeit."

It's interesting to note the context of Connell's observation. Like Simon Schama, he sifted through hundreds of conflicting accounts, views, and narrations for his great work, a study of George Armstrong Custer called *Son of the Morning Star*. Unlike Schama, Connell made it his business to determine as best he could which accountings had that high hard ring of truth, and he had the charming idea, plus the absence of pretension, to let the reader in on the game. Again and again he supplies us with alternative descriptions of an event—journals, diaries, letters—then gives us his reasons for believing in one over the other.

This openness of method, by the way, has an attractive side effect: it enlists the reader as a kind of dialectical partner with the writer; or a welcome companion on a journey—which is of course one of the most ancient and magical functions of narrative.

And while we're enjoying this "practical and pragmatic moment," let's return to that notion of "guilty conscience." If we're honest with ourselves, it's very often the operative impulse that prompts writers to blend fiction with nonfiction in the first place. We can talk a good game about epistemological skepticism and Nietzschean denials of the possibilities of objectivity, but what we're really concerned about is getting sued, divorced, or beaten up.

You won't find that theory in the *MLA Journal*; just remember that you heard it here first.

Now, please don't misunderstand; I'm not saying that essayists are better writers than novelists. I'm not saying that it's impossible or even unusual to switch back and forth successfully between the two forms, and even write a little poetry on the side. I am certainly not indicting the historical novel. I am saying that the two states of mind are so fundamentally in opposition to one another that unless you are a far better liar than I am, you had best not risk trying to do both at once.

I want to return to Gordon Wood's response to *Dead Certainties* one more time before we move on. His last major rebuttal to Schama's book addresses the matter of imagination head-on; and in my experience, the myth of "absence of imagination" is perhaps the most pervasive and wrong-headed indictment against the field of nonfiction.

Wood cites Schama's remark that although the two stories in his book, quote, "follow the documentary record with some closeness, they are works of imagination, not scholarship." And then he responds:

"These are not contraries. Historical scholarship should not be set in opposition to imagination. History writing is creative, and it surely requires imagination; only it is an imagination of a particular sort, sensitive to the differentness of the past and constrained and constricted by the documentary record."

James Agee, one of the founding voices of American nonfiction in this century, expressed the same idea more than fifty years ago. Near the beginning of *Let Us Now Praise Famous Men*, his factual and yet magically realistic study of three Alabama sharecropping families in the 1930s, Agee thrashed about for a few paragraphs, moaning and groaning about the impossibility of rendering on the printed page the authenticity of the lives that he and Walker Evans had encountered. At first his tone was sullen and defiant, almost contemptuous of the reader.

> If there are questions in my mind how to undertake this communication [he wrote], and there are many, I must let the least of them be, whether I am boring you, or whether I am taking too long getting started, and too clumsily. No doubt I *shall* worry myself that I am taking too long getting started, and shall seriously distress myself over my inability to create an organic, mutually sustaining and dependent, and as it were *musical* form: but I must remind myself that I started with the first word I wrote, and that the centers of my subject are shifty; and that I am no better an 'artist' than I am capable of being . . . and that this again will find its measurement in the facts as they are, and will contribute its own measure . . . to the pattern of the effort and truth as a whole.

And then Agee unleashed this glittering passage, of which Professor Wood's more recent protest is but a faint echo.

> For in the immediate world, everything is to be discerned, for him who can discern it, and centrally and simply, without either

dissection into science, or digestion into art, but with the whole of consciousness, seeking to perceive it as it stands: so that the aspect of a street in sunlight can roar in the heart of itself as a symphony can: and all of consciousness is shifted from the imagined, the revisive, to the effort to perceive simply the cruel radiance of what is.

"The cruel radiance of what is."

What Agee was *trying to say* . . . in his halting and reticent way . . . was not that truthful writing lacks imagination or art. Don't let him kid you about not being concerned with boring the reader; he was a meticulous wordsmith and spent four years revising this book, until a callous appeared on his right middle finger the size of a marble. And, yes, the finished work did indeed have musical form; the weight and structure of a great elegiac symphony; he played Beethoven at earsplitting decibels as he wrote.

What he was trying to say was that great art can be the *residue* of a sustained effort to perceive . . . simply . . . the cruel radiance of what is. It's interesting that Agee's commitment to truthfulness in this book was so obsessive that not once, in its 471 pages, does he render actual dialogue from the Ricketts or the Gudger or the Woods families. To do so, he believed, would only diminish and trivialize what he thought was the sacredness of their language.

He did change the families' names, out of respect for their privacy.

Agee's legacy of passionate witness lives on into our time. In fact it's fascinating how many good writers, in this time of Nietzschean denials and reader-response theory, continue to write out of a heightened concern for reader's *needs*. It's fascinating how some of the most radiant prose of our time, cruel and otherwise, takes its radiance from the bond of trust that the writer has established with the reader: having assembled evidence in a transparent and scrupulous way, and never denying the elusiveness of truth, the writer then releases his imagination into the text, with thrilling results.

I want to bring you a passage from Ian Frazier's stunning book *Great Plains*, published in 1989. Ian Frazier is well known as an urban satirist and ironist whose droll essays in the *New Yorker* have been assembled into collections with titles like *Dating Your Mom*. In 1982 Frazier burst loose from this life and did something completely outside his public persona. He moved to Montana. He lived in a cabin and tried to produce a novel about high school. What he finally did produce, seven years later, was an astonishing work of nonfiction, a book that reads almost like a burst of religious ecstasy, an evocation of American place that occupies 214 pages of text and 65 pages of source notes. Frazier hung out with Indians, ranchers, kids out drinking, Park Service guides, the singing Robinson sisters, and food chemists dressed up like frontier buckskinners. He haunted libraries and museums. He got it all down. His chapter on the life and death of the great Sioux warrior chief Crazy Horse is, for my money, one of the most original passages of American historical scholarship ever written.

You need to know that Crazy Horse was at the head of the attack that wiped out General Custer at the Little Big Horn. He was hounded by the U.S. Army for a year after that until he gave in to the inevitable and surrendered. He was taken eventually to an Army post at Fort Robinson, now part of Nebraska. There, through an unbelievable series of misunderstandings and treacheries, he was stabbed twice through the abdomen by a sentry. He was carried to an adjutant's office, where he was offered the comfort of an Army cot. He refused, and several hours later he died on the floor.

Ian Frazier has brilliantly restored this epochal event. No interior monologues, no shifting voices, no invented passages. He has proceeded from documentation; the source notes alone for this chapter cover 13 pages.

And here is his concluding section:

> I believe that when Crazy Horse was killed, something more than a man's life was snuffed out. Once, America's size in the imagination was limitless. After Europeans settled and changed it, working from the coasts inland, its size in the imagination shrank. Like the center of a dying fire, the Great Plains held that original vision longest. Just as people finally came to the Great Plains and changed them, so they came to where Crazy Horse lived and killed

him. Crazy Horse had the misfortune to live in a place which existed both in reality and in the dreams of people far away; he managed to leave both the real and the imaginary place unbetrayed. What I return to most often when I think of Crazy Horse is the fact that in the adjutant's office he refused to lie on the cot. Mortally wounded, frothing at the mouth, grinding his teeth in pain, he chose the floor instead. What a distance there is between that cot and that floor! On the cot, he would have been, in some sense, "ours": an object of pity, an accident victim, "the noble red man, the last of his race, etc., etc." But on the floor Crazy Horse was Crazy Horse still. On the floor, he began to hurt as the morphine wore off. On the floor, he remembered Agent Lee, summoned him, forgave him. On the floor, unable to rise, he said goodbye to his father and Touch the Clouds, the last of the thousands that once followed him. And on the floor, still as far from white men as the limitless continent they once dreamed of, he died. Touch the Clouds pulled the blanket over his face: "That is the lodge of Crazy Horse." Lying where he chose, Crazy Horse showed the rest of us where we are standing. With his body, he demonstrated that the floor of an Army office was part of the land, and that the land was still his.

I submit to you that that section has everything to do with the literary imagination. Lyric, insistent, incantatory, it is a metaphoric meditation on the nature of metaphor, certainly on American metaphor. Note that phrase, "Crazy Horse had the misfortune to live in a place which existed both in reality and in the dreams of people far away; he managed to leave both the real and the imaginary place unbetrayed."

I believe that Frazier is talking here about something infinitely complex and tragic in the American saga. He has chosen to approach this theme, which I'll name in a moment, within the disciplines of a writer accountable to historic truth—the cruel radiance, you might say, of what once was.

But his very accountability has now permitted him to release his imagination upon his foundation of the actual, and the residue of that release is a charged and elegant language.

I can't read that passage of Frazier's without thinking of Nick

Carraway, sitting on the beach below Jay Gatsby's huge incoherent failure of a house, watching America grow dark:

> And as the moon rose higher the inessential houses began to melt away until gradually I became aware of the old island here that flowered once for Dutch sailors' eyes—a fresh, green breast of the new world. Its vanished trees, the trees that had made way for Gatsby's house, had once pandered in whispers to the last and greatest of all human dreams; for a transitory enchanted moment man must have held his breath in the presence of the continent, compelled into an aesthetic contemplation he neither understood nor desired, face to face for the last time in history with something commensurate to his capacity for wonder.

Here's what I think that infinitely complex and tragic quality is that Frazier was pursuing, and Scott Fitzgerald and Emerson and a lot of others before him. It's a quality that reaches out from our history, whether we like it or not, to embrace us or smother us, however deeply we try to burrow into our tunnels of Nietzschean denial or the electronic labyrinths of virtual reality.

That quality is innocence.

American writers, like Americans in general, have a tortured but inescapable relationship with innocence. Innocence is something we currently despise in this country—or at least we've convinced ourselves that we despise—and the pursuit of truthfulness is viewed as a concomitant of innocence. In a world of relativism and ambiguity, we at least have an unimpeachable source of authority for *that* view. We have the French.

But of course it isn't that easy. Innocence is in our national bloodstream, along with the very viruses that always corrupt it. The Puritans escaped here to have another crack at innocence, and innocence has always remained at the foundations of our optimism, our terrifying belief in perfectability, and yes, even our cynicism. "When men are innocent," wrote Emerson, "life shall be longer, and shall pass into the immortal as gently as we awake from dreams."

But Americans never quite seem to awake gently. We never got the hang of it. It's those damn human voices that keep awaking us; the voices of progress; Emerson's own voice: reinvent, push outward. "Things are in the saddle, and ride mankind." And somehow before we know it, before we're fully conscious, we have ruined what it is we've awakened to worship; we've screwed up the frontier and stabbed Crazy Horse and cut down the trees for Gatsby's lawn.

No wonder we like to pretend there isn't any such thing as truth. Agee again: "I'll do what little I can in writing. Only it will be very little. I'm not capable of it; and if I were, you would not go near it at all. For if you did, you would hardly bear to live."

So: what am I saying here? What is this lecture all about?

Am I saying that Truth, with a capital T, is knowable? Of course not. "Whoever wants the total reality," as Jacques Barzun has said, "must first gain access to the mind of God." And even my old fellow townsman Mark Twain sends down a veiled warning from the nineteenth century: "Truth is the most valuable thing we have," he says dryly. "Let us economize it."

There is no objective Truth, just as there is no objective literature. I know this from reading Terry Eagleton, who's not even French. "Literature, in the sense of a set of works of assured and unalterable value, distinguished by certain shared inherent properties, does not exist."

I know this.

Value judgments about literature, and about Truth, have a close relation to social ideologies.

I know this.

The text is nothing more than a pure embodiment of the author's consciousness.

I know this.

The reader then appears on the scene to finish off whatever might be left of the author's pathetic intent by "reading," in effect, about himself.

I know this.

I *know* this, as Tim O'Brien wrote toward the finish of *The Nuclear Age*, but I believe otherwise.

I believe that writing in pursuit of Truth, however unattainable Truth may be, is a legitimate pursuit for writer. Perhaps it is even ennobling, made so by the very fact that the pursuit is doomed, to some extent, to fail.

In saying this, I don't mean to attack the integrity of fiction, or deny fiction's capacity to elevate the consciousness. I don't mean to attack the historical novel or the fiction that draws on the personas of living people in recognizable contexts. Unless one of those personas happens to be my own.

I can even accept the legitimacy of a literary experiment such as *Dead Certainties*. I think I can accept it. Providing that the terms of the experiment are made available to the reader.

What I'm pleading for—what I hope we can preserve in our literary tradition—is the endangered custom of empirical writing that I have come to think of as "passionate witness."

It is our most native prose. It is what we improvised and refined and gave to the world during the great century of flowering that Alfred Kazin called "The American Procession."

It is the journey outward. The journey across terrain, from the familiar into the unknown. The journey across physical territories and across the inner territories of the heart. Motion. Risk. A fugitive flight in which the writer, questing, becomes an outsider, an *isolato*, drawing upon a mixture of fright and ecstasy to see with heightened clarity the luminous evidence along the way.

But what quest, and what evidence? Doesn't matter; usually the journey itself tugs the writer toward the truth. Agee in Alabama, expecting to interview sharecroppers for *Fortune* Magazine, finding himself in a religious trance before a rotting bureau in the front bedroom of the Gudgers' shack:

> The mirror is so far corrupted that it is rashed with gray, irridescent in parts, and in all its reflections a deeply sad thin zinc-to-platinum, giving to its framings an almost incalculably ancient, sweet, frail, and piteous beauty, such as may be seen in tintypes of family groups among studio furnishings or heard in nearly exhausted jazz records made by very young, insane, devout men who were soon to destroy themselves, in New Orleans.

Ian Frazier, fled from New York to Montana to write his novel about high school and now drowning in the unexpected ecstasies of the Great Plains. He finds himself in the town of Nicodemus, population fifty, founded by black homesteaders in 1877. He's sitting in the township hall watching a fashion show of ladies' hats modeled by the Robinson sisters, Kathleen, Karen, Kaye, Kolleen, Krystal, and Karmen.

Suddenly I felt a joy so strong it almost knocked me down. It came up my spine and settled on my head like a warm cap and filled my eyes with tears, while I stood there packed in with everybody, watching Mrs. Robinson's lovely daughters dance.

And I though, *It could have worked!* This democracy, this land of freedom and equality and the pursuit of happiness—it could have worked! There was something to it after all! We didn't have to make a mess of it and the continent and ourselves! It could have worked! The Robinson sisters danced; Prince sang about doves crying; beauty and courage and curiosity and gentleness seemed not to be rare aberrations in the world. Nicodemus, a town with reasons enough to hold a grudge, a town with plenty of reasons not to exist at all, celebrated its Founders Day with a show of hats and a dance revue. For a moment I could imagine the past rewritten, wars unfought, the buffalo and the Indians undestroyed, the prairie unplundered. Maybe history did not absolutely have to turn out the way it did. Maybe the history of the West, for example, could have involved more admiration of hats, more unarmed get-togethers, more dancing, more tasting of spareribs.

Or Annie Dillard, in a town near Yakima, heading up to the top of a mountain to watch an eclipse of the sun and finding herself looking into eternity.

From all the hills came screams. A piece of sky beside the crescent sun was detaching. It was a loosened circle of evening sky, suddenly lighted from the back. . . . At once this disk of sky slid over the sun like a lid. The hatch in the brain slammed. Abruptly it was dark night, on the land and in the sky. The hole where the sun belongs is very small. A thin ring of light marked its place. There was no sound. There was no world. We were the world's dead people rotating and orbiting around and around, embedded in the planet's crust, while the earth rolled down. Only an extraordinary act of will could recall to us our former, living selves and our contexts in matter and time.

The second before the sun went out we saw a wall of dark shadow come speeding at us. We no sooner saw it than it was upon us, like thunder. It roared up the valley. It slammed our hill and knocked us out. It was the monstrous swift shadow of the moon.

This was the universe about which we had read so much and never before felt: the universe as a clockwork of loose spheres flung at stupefying, unauthorized speeds. How could anything moving so fast not crash?

We had all died in our boots on the hilltops of Yakima, and were alone in eternity.

Fright . . . ecstasy . . . the capacity to see with heightened clarity the luminous evidence along the way. The literary residue of the journey outward. The journey across physical territories and across the inner territories of the heart. The endangered custom of empirical writing that I call passionate witness.

What I respect so much about each of these three passages of nonfiction prose is that they accomplish exactly what Simon Schama was reaching for in his puree of fact and fantasy: a higher truth. A state of transcendence.

I have quoted each writer at a pitch of consciousness that is neither strictly true, in the factual sense, nor in the slightest way converted to fiction. We know, for example, that Annie Dillard was not among the world's dead people orbiting around and around at that moment of the solar eclipse—but we also know that she did not for a moment expect us to suspend our disbelief and assume that she was.

We allow Annie Dillard her metaphoric flight—just as we allow James Agee and Ian Frazier their flights of visionary speculation—because they have allowed us to journey with them through the terrain they covered to reach that pitch of consciousness. They allowed us to see and hear them gather evidence . . . listen to language . . . describe people and objects . . . examine and evaluate the written records of the past . . . to pursue elusive Truth with steadfast truthful*ness*. And now we can share with them, not as manipulated spectators but as knowledgeable companions in the quest, the imaginative discharge of the journey.

* * *

I think this is such a valuable part of our literary tradition, this quaint-seeming commitment to truthful writing. Valuable, and so endangered.

The moral philosopher Sissela Bok tells us that we are truth-telling creatures; it's part of our biological makeup. That's why lie detectors work. As a corollary, we are truth-seeking creatures. Bok is unambiguous on this matter. "Deceit and violence," she writes. "These are the two forms of deliberate assault on human beings." And a bit later she adds, "Trust in some degree of veracity functions as a *foundation* of relations among human beings; when this trust shatters or wears away, institutions collapse."

Look around you. Look out beyond the mountain. Remember where you came from. We are living in a society, and indeed in a Western world, that is as besotted with deception as the mind of man can make it possible to be, and the mind of man is growing more inventive with each passing fiscal quarter, each approaching primary season. Perhaps not coincidentally, we are besotted with violence as well.

I began this essay with some thoughts on the receding value of truthfulness in the popular culture. Television and television advertising, political bureaucracies, corporate empires.

Truth, we have been told by the legitimizers of television, is an artifact of the print culture. So be it. But if writers are willing to blur fact and fantasy on our pages, what right do we have to be outraged when Oliver North does it on the witness stand? Why can't we accept our Environmental President as one of our own, a fellow experimenter in shifting points of view, when he decides that 10 million acres previously called wetlands are not wetlands at all—just land—and therefore suitable for development? Give that man a fellowship in nonfiction!

Why should we be indignant when a scholar decides that there was no Holocaust? Why should we not be complacent when a White radio talk-show host for the ABC flagship station in New York, a man named Bob Grant, defines the Black underclass as "mutants" and hints that the solution lies in genocide? Mr. Grant is just offering a fresh perspective on our social text. Or when an influential Black chairman of the African-American Studies Department at City College in New York, whose name is Dr. Leonard Jeffries, Jr., charges that a Jewish conspiracy is responsible for the low image of blacks in the movies, "planned, plotted and programmed out of Hollywood."

I believe that we are at the edge, if not over the edge, of a kind of social chaos in this country: a kind of "virtual reality" without DataGloves, in which nothing is right, nothing is wrong, nothing is true, nothing is false, nothing is quite what it seems to be, and yet nothing is quite the opposite of what it seems. We are in the landscape of Lear; of madness and suffering brought on partly by our overweening pride, our belief that we are perfectible, through our technologies and the manipulation of public opinion.

What's missing in this equation is love. In a new essay examining the parallel myths of King Lear and Job, Robert Pack has focused on the qualities of love and acceptance and forgiveness as necessary to the restoration of sanity and peace. When maddened Lear, awakening to see Cordelia leaning over him in Act IV, admits that she has "some cause" to poison him, Cordelia responds, "No cause, no cause." This, writes Pack, "is the human equivalent of creation out of nothingness. . . . Cordelia offers her love to Lear beyond cause, not as reward or in the fulfillment of duty, but as a gift that generates its own goodness."

This is our opportunity as writers at the close of this dark century: to work at the business of creation out of nothingness by treating our maddened readers with love; to offer them our truthfulness if not the Truth; and to invite them with us on a journey, out of the darkness and toward the light.

Before We Disappear: Affirming Words in the Age of the Gun

There are days—and they are drawing ever closer together—when it seems impossible to wake up in America and not feel that one is trapped inside the dark prophecies of Don DeLillo: specifically as he charts the withdrawal of the written word as a moral or aesthetic force in our culture, and the compensating encroachment of the fired bullet, the exploding car bomb.

I find myself thinking again and again of the famous conversation that unfolds early in DeLillo's 1991 novel, *Mao II*, between the legendary recluse-novelist Bill Gray and the photographer Brita Nilsson, who has arrived in the night at his concealed bunker to make the first photographs of him in 30 years. (Looking through the Bread Loaf brochure, I find that a lot of us must think we're Bill Gray.)

I'll read that exchange to you in a minute.

I thought about this conversation on the day that Salman Rushdie went underground, of course, as did a lot of people. I thought about it again last February, when a bunch of terrorists blew a hole in the basement of the World Trade Center, and several hours later that group of young schoolchildren came trooping down through the smoke from the top story. The world later learned that their teacher had led them in singing songs down all those stairwells, to keep their spirits up. This time the illusion that we writers live for held: the words of the songs seemed mightier than the bomb.

I can't escape noting, by the way, that DeLillo cites the World Trade Center, with his typically eerie deadpan, just one page before the decisive passage in that famous conversation. "The size (of the towers) is deadly," Brita Nilsson remarks to Gray.

"But having two of them is like a comment, it's like a dialogue, only I don't know what they're saying."

And Bill Gray replies, "They're saying, 'Have a nice day.'"

And finally, I've thought of this exchange countless times in the past two years as I have sat with morning coffee and the Metropolitan section of the *New York Times*, safe for the time being within my own bunker that is Middlebury, Vermont, and read of some new unspeakable human defilement in the larger world.

Most recently, last July 12, it was the story of a woman in the housing projects in Bedford-Stuyvesant named Frances Davis, who on the previous day had suffered the third death among her three sons by gunfire in the neighborhood. The deaths were spaced over a period of six years. Mrs. Davis is forty-two years old. She was photographed sitting on her bed, a small woman wearing hoop earrings and a Detroit Pistons basketball T-shirt, mercifully dazed from medication. She had told the reporter, "After these things happen, I question God. I'm not religious anymore. Today, I don't believe."

Who would blame her? God knows, today is not a time to believe in much of anything. Part of our inheritance as writers, certainly as American writers in the lineage of Mr. Emerson, has been the hopeful belief that what we write matters. That it might even matter, in some magical way, to Frances Davis and to the people who killed her children. That our words, like Walker Percy's message in the bottle, might find their way across time and distance to enhance the consciousness of suffering strangers.

"Poets are the liberating gods," Emerson assured us. "The poet has a new thought: he has a whole new experience to unfold; he will tell us how it was with him, and all men will be the richer in his fortune."

Emerson wrote, of course, in the antiquity before mustard gas blew in the twentieth century on the battlefields of the Somme, and has lately been blowing it out from within the French academies.

I read about Frances Davis, and I wonder what possible connection there can be between her consciousness and mine; between what I do and what she knows; between my books and her grief; between my puny and episodic wish to bear passionate witness and the hard futility of the witness that she has borne.

And I feel the baleful truth of that crystalizing exchange between Brita Nilsson and Bill Gray in Don DeLillo's *Mao II*.

Brita has just inserted a new roll of film in her camera, and Gray, who is famously untalkative , asks her:

"Do you ask your writers how it feels to be painted dummies?"

And Brita replies, "What do you mean?"

"You've got me talking, Brita."

"Anything that's animated I love it."

"You don't care what I say."

"Speak Swahili."

And then Bill Gray says, "There's a curious knot that binds novelists and terrorists. In the West we become effigies as our books lose the power to shape and influence. . . . Years ago I used to think it was possible for a novelist to alter the inner life of the culture. Now bomb-makers and gunmen have taken that territory. They make raids on human consciousness. What writers used to do before we were all incorporated."

"Keep going," says Brita Nilsson. "I like your anger."

"But you know all this. This is why you travel a million miles photographing writers. Because we're giving way to terror, to news of terror, to tape recorders and cameras, to radios, to bombs stashed in radios. News of disaster is the only narrative people need. The darker the news, the darker the narrative. News is the last addiction before—what? I don't know. But you're smart to trap us in your camera before we disappear."

"Before we disappear." That, I believe, is the dread, mostly unspoken, that haunts serious writers as this century draws to a close. Nor is it just the terrorist and the gunman who threaten to annihilate us, metaphorically speaking. The pure products of America, to update William Carlos Williams, are driving us crazy. Vast new systems of language have arisen in our age. They have arisen from the electronic mass production of images and the engineering of mass-produced thought. They are rooted not in typography but in movies, television, architecture, weapons.

These new languages and semiotics are public, yet anticommunal; gargantuan, yet hostile to true variety. They tend to serve the needs not of the individual seeking truthfulness and participation in society, but of collective, often multinational entities seeking standardization and control: entertainment conglomerates, the advertising industry, political image making and corporate public relations. In their aggregate, these systems have added to the epidemic blurring of truthfulness and illusion; they have placed the narrative idea under tremendous assault, and have devalued the system of obligations and rewards that links narrative writers and readers.

It's perhaps inevitable, given the tendency of extremes to converge, that terror and violence have become the content of choice within these new languages . . . a convergence that does not escape Don DeLillo's baleful eye. In *Mao II*, Bill Gray's assistant, a young man named Scott, plunges into a Warhol exhibit during a foray into New York City.

> He walked past the electric-chair canvases, the repeated news images of car crashes and movie stars, and he got used to the anxious milling, it seemed entirely right, people eager to be undistracted, ray-gunned by fame and death. Scott had never seen work that was so indifferent to the effect it had on those who came to see it . . .
>
> He moved along and stood finally in a room filled with images of Chairman Mao. Photocopy Mao, silk-screen Mao, wallpaper Mao, synthetic-polymer Mao. A series of silk screens was installed over a broader surface of wallpaper serigraphs, the Chairman's face a pansy purple here, floating nearly free of its photographic source. Work that was unwitting of history appealed to Scott.

I think we all understand that American writing has been monumentally affected by these currents in the culture. Not all the effects have been harmful; sixty years ago the dawning visual age transfused our literature with new, vigorous pictorial images and metaphors, and also with a new political concern for human life as lived down at the gritty grass roots—in sharecroppers' cabins and out on the American road. "The camera seems to me," wrote James Agee in 1937, "next to unassisted and weaponless consciousness, the central instrument of our time."

Even today, the very violence and rootlessness that tear at our national life are producing their opposite effect on the printed

page: a defiant small renaissance, an exciting literature of reclamation: poets, novelists, and nonfiction writers dedicated to
work that insists on history and its moral consequences—
especially the history that coheres in specific place and community. These writers reaffirm the hard old task of reconciling the
passionate self with an indifferent world.

I think of Jane Smiley's astonishing novel, *A Thousand Acres*,
about the dark fealties of an Iowa farm family, which won the
Pulitzer Prize and the National Book Critics Circle Award a
couple of years ago. I think of Russell Banks's scrupulous tales of
trailer parks and working-class dreamers and a school bus driver
whom the town must find a way to forgive for the deaths of its
children.

I think of Rosellen Brown's *Before and After* and Richard
Rausch's *Violence*, novels that take us into the familiar pit of
American rage and mayhem, and then venture beyond that into
the truly outlandish concept, which is regeneration.

In nonfiction we find a growing cadre of new voices who have
synthesized two prose forms long thought to be in hopeless
opposition: the personal essay and the searching reportorial
document. These writers, many of whom are also accomplished
poets, typically choose to unite their intimate concerns with those
of a community in crisis, or to the threatened natural world.

I think of Terry Tempest Williams—Utah naturalist, curator,
Mormon, and writer. In her work *Refuge: An Unnatural History of
Family and Place*, Terry chronicles the slow death of her mother by
cancer, a legacy of nuclear-bomb testing in the 1950s. But her
steadfast personal witnessing resonates constantly into a larger
context: the degradation of Utah's many life systems by various
manmade malignant intrusions into the land.

This literature of reclamation, I believe, is absolutely vital to our
interests in preserving our culture. I admire Don DeLillo, but
these and other writers eloquently refute the nihilism of his alter
ego Bill Gray. The gunman's triumph is not yet absolute.

This society cries out through its rage for a true accounting; for
honest and useful history; for replenishing metaphor; for reasons
to live.

But from what sources in our loud public conversation is a true accounting available? Not from the false proletarians at CNN or Geraldo or Rush Limbaugh; not from the movie-making elite who give us summer sequels about winsome corpses; not from advertising; not from most political discourse or analysis; not from a dispirited and overwrought academic "theor-ocracy"— not from the fraudulent semiotics of the shopping mall.

Not even, I am afraid, from corporate book publishers, whose cynicism and moral cowardice have lately produced a catastrophic watershed in the pollution, and the repression, of ideas.

No—the true accounting must come from within the souls of individual poets and writers.

Never before has this country so desperately needed a good-faith connection with its poets and writers.

And never—here I drift partway back toward DeLillo's dark vision—never has the connection seemed in greater danger of dissolving. Not so much from the pressure of the forces I've just outlined—although each of those threats is as serious as a heart attack.

The threat to writers' legitimacy that concerns me the most is a threat from within: a ripe sort of indulgence, a symptom of this self-regarding age, that is enervating our craft and sealing it off as a force for moral and aesthetic renewal. I will speak here about nonfiction writing, because nonfiction is what I practice. Perhaps some of you will think of analogies in the form you are working in.

The threat I speak of is that of unbridled narcissism: the preemptive surge of the writerly Self. The Self claiming dominion over the world, and abolishing the very notion of a distinction between reality and invention. (When President Bush declared a few years ago that the wetlands were not really wetlands after all, I couldn't help thinking, "This guy's already gunning for tenure in the English department at Duke.") The Self viewing the world not as a beloved habitat to be investigated and replenished, but as a mirror, or as a blank slate upon which to project the Self's fantasies, grievances, fears and desires.

This narcissism has infected nonfiction writing in many forms and on just about every conceivable level, from college and workshop composition papers through the latest confessional, recovery or "personal growth" best-seller, and on upward through the reaches of biography, social criticism and academic historical work. I'll give you some examples of what I mean in a minute. But first I'd like to remind you of the richness of this form at its most irreducible, and within its particularly American traditions.

"Nonfiction" covers everything, I grant you, from bicycle repair manuals to the works of Nietzsche. (Some bicycle owners, and maybe Nietzsche himself, might disagree about this.) But I speak now about the great flow of inquisitive, sojurning, and fact-based narrative literature rendered in this century by Agee and John Hersey and Joan Didion, who drew in their turn upon sensibilities inherited from such former journalists as Theodore Dresier, and Walt Whitman, and Mark Twain.

This tradition is expansive, outward-seeking, voracious in its effort to discern the world—an effort that by its nature can never be consummated. Truth is infinitely elusive; the great nonfiction sojurners have always known that. Their fulfillment, and their great value to the culture, have always lain in their truthful accounting of the quest.

In that quest they have marshaled the same inventory of rhetorical techniques available to so-called "creative" writers: metaphor, and description, and vernacular language, and structure, and rhythm and voice. ("There, in the tin factory," wrote John Hersey, famously, in *Hiroshima*, "in the first moment of the atomic age, a human being was crushed by books.")

Our inheritance of American nonfiction literature is rich with such voices . . . rich with miracles of imagination, as when the scientist/essayist Loren Eiseley encounters a man on a beach at Costabel, skimming stranded starfish back into the sea, and finds in that act a reconciliation between "the dead skull" of modern determinism and "the great atavistic surge of feeling" inherent in sowing life—the secret thing that the Star Thrower knew.

Our inheritance is rich, in other words, with the presence of the writerly Self. Which, of course, is the foundation of its claim to literature.

But haven't I contradicted myself? Have I not just complained that it is "the preemptive surge of the writerly Self" that now debases our nonfiction writing?

I'm glad I asked that question.

The critical distinctions, it seems to me, are distinctions of proportion and distinctions in faith. (Not faith in God, necessarily, but faith in the communal, reciprocal process of writing and reading.) I submit to you that the Self's proportion has expanded exactly to the extent that faith in the process has collapsed.

Let me give you some examples of what I mean.

Two years ago the distinguished young historian Simon Schama sent a shock wave through his profession. He published a book that explicitly violated the most fundamental taboos of formal historical writing: he made things up. The book was *Dead Certainties*, a study of two events in American history. Professor Schama proclaimed, in an Afterword, that he had buttressed his historical evidence with interior monologues, shifting voices, and multiple points of view, and that several passages contained fictional imaginings and invented dialogue.

The reaction among many professional historians was a kind of numb bewilderment, laced with dread: dread that the deconstructionist torrents had finally burst the levees of literature and were now flooding the field of history. Here was what one observer called "the demise of the founding ideals of the discipline of history with little or no hope of their rebirth."

In a troubled review of Schama's book, a review not without respect and even sympathy, the critic Gordon Wood focused on a key remark from Schama's Afterword: that although the relevant sections in his book "follow the documentary record with some closeness, they are works of imagination, not scholarship." And then Mr. Wood offered what I believe is an absolutely crucial rebuttal.

"These are not contraries," Wood wrote. "Historical scholarship should not be set in opposition to imagination. History writing is creative, and it surely requires imagination; only it is an imagination of a particular sort, sensitive to the differentness of the past and constrained and constricted by the documentary record."

In other words, Mr. Wood was calling upon Mr. Schama to recognize his inheritance, and the imaginative possibilities within it. And clearly, Mr. Schama, for all his acknowledged brilliance and profundity, had ceased to believe that such an inheritance mattered.

*   *   *

If Professor Schama's decision was indeed a tragedy, it didn't take long for it to replay itself as farce . . . in the hands of Joe McGinniss, that Bart Simpson of American letters.

McGinniss's peculiar fate, it seems, is to go down in history as the one journalist who fails Janet Malcolm's standards of responsible behavior.

His biography of Teddy Kennedy published this summer, *The Last Brother*, is so besotted with the writerly Self that most reviewers simply gave up trying to analyze it and instead used it for target practice. The *New York Times* said it wasn't bad, it was awful; the *Washington Post* critic found it the worst book he'd ever read, without a single truthful page.

In fact, it seems that Joe McGinniss might have ended up performing a weird kind of public service. If this is what the Golden Age of Detextualization is going to look like, you might as well cheat a little and tell the truth.

Maybe it would be well to pause a little at this point and consider what the writerly Self has always implied in American prose writing. And what it is coming to imply.

The writerly Self in its classic nonfiction form is a kind of vivid host, an engaging and trustworthy, if inevitably fallible, guide across frontiers. Its tacit message to the reader is: "Come along with me. See what I have seen, hear what I have heard. Apply your judgment to the evidence I have gathered. Perhaps a little understanding, a little wisdom will emerge."

The writerly Self unbridled is an autocrat: proportionately less interested in crossing frontiers than in dwelling on received personal experience, usually with family or love interest. This Self is less interested in probing unknown territory for thematic riches than in forcing epiphanies from mundane events. It tends to assert religious and spiritual awakenings based on dreams, and expressed in a semiprivate sort of language. When this kind of writing reaches beyond the quotidian, it almost unerringly grasps at trauma: the writerly Self as prototypically abused, alienated, discriminated against, or otherwise aggrieved—and seeking, somehow, to achieve restoration or self-healing through the process of writing as a therapeutic release.

What is missing, in any case, is the stuff that has in this century given nonfiction its exalted connection with the culture: a narrative journey into place, into history, into political and social conditions external to the Self's narrow purview; yielding both scholarship and rich empirical detail of locale and human character. A vigorous inquiry into cause-and-effect and into moral consequences of action. And finally, a shared sense of revivifying discovery, achieved through some kind of identifiable risk or effort, and offered as a companionable gift to the reader.

I will give you an example of writing that flagrantly fails every one of these conditions, and is thus state-of-the-art in popular American nonfiction. It is a book currently making its way through trendy ecclesiastical circles, entitled, *The Feminine Face of God*. Published by Bantam—coauthored by Sherry Ruth Anderson and Patricia Hopkins.

No one could deny the timeliness or legitimacy of the theme. At a moment in history when feminists are making headway against the patriarchal bias in the organized church, a new tide of biblical scholarship, led by Elaine Pagels and others, is restoring a lost sense of Judeo-Christian women's prominence in ancient times.

So I'm not assailing this book because of its theme. I'm assailing it because of its prototypical failures to connect with the reader—failures grounded in the writerly Self unbridled.

The failures are apparent at the outset, when one of the coauthors describes the occasion of her transforming insight that the Almighty is a person of gender. Typically of the genre, it is not an experience or set of experiences in the world, but a dream.

"In the dream, I happily soar high above the clouds on a great golden dragon," she writes, "until I wonder, 'Is that all there is?'"

No problem. The dragon immediately descends to earth and alights at the side of a jewellike temple, a kind of celestial EPCOT Center. A tour guide immediately appears, an old man with regulation long robes and beard. He lets her know, "without actually speaking," that his name is Melchizedek. (Try letting someone know, some time, without actually speaking, that your name is Melchizedek.) He hands her a souvenir dagger made of turquoise and jade, and ushers her inside.

Long hallway, high ceiling, red tiles. At the end, a polished cabinet. "Built-in," in fact. Melchizedek opens the doors to reveal a jackpot unimaginable even on "Let's Make a Deal." It is the Torah.

But no ordinary Torah! "This is a very special Torah," Melchizedek tells the author. She notices that its pages are blank. "The Torah is empty," Melchizedek tells her, "because what you need to know now is not written in any book. You already contain that knowledge. It is to be unfolded from within you." Then he places the Torah inside her body—God's empty calorie of Love.

Then, spinning around, the author sees that it's showtime. The room is suddenly filled with long-bearded patriarchs wearing black coats and trousers. "They're holding hands, laughing, singing and dancing jubilantly around the room. They pull me into their celebration." As the author dances, she spots a few celebrities: Moses, King David and King Solomon, and Abraham, Isaac, and Jacob. Women Who Dance With the Prophets.

"Finally the dancing stops and I ask, 'What is this all about?' The news couldn't be better. Melchizedek answers, 'We are celebrating because you, a woman, have consented to accept full spiritual responsibility in your life. This is your initiation as one who will serve the planet.' When the author asks with attractive humility whether the patriarchs will help her, they reply in Animatronic unison: 'We have initiated you and we give you our wholehearted blessings. But we no longer know the way. Our ways do not work anymore. You women must find a new ways.'"

The dilletantish fatuousness, the self-congratulation, the idiom of upscale consumerism, scream out, of course, from every sentence. But if you're looking for a single key as to why this kind of writing fails, begin with that unintended metaphor of the blank Torah.

No history here. No physical or political present. No *process*; no surrogate involvement in any kind of authentic community or human character. Nothing risked, nothing earned. No content to the platitudes—"accept full spiritual responsibility," "serve the planet," "find a new way." Not even a particularized narrator. The Self in this piece has been apotheosized into a deity by the time we meet her: a seraphic version of that nauseating woman who keeps singing "If You Could See Me Now" on that cruise ship in the television commercials.

Why do I dwell on writing that is so easily lampooned? Because it is rampant and infectuous. Because it is linked to the nonlanguage of the afternoon talk show and the midnight infomercial, and thus is a powerful enemy of narrative, and cause-and-effect. To be blunt, because I have seen it to often in applications for this writer's conference.

"We have seen," writes Wendell Berry, "for perhaps a hundred and fifty years, a gradual increase of language that is either meaningless or destructive of meaning."

Concerned as he is with the epidemic illnesses of our time, the disintegration of communities and the disintegration of persons, Berry insists that there is a hidden relation between these disintegrations and the disintegration of language.

In a seminal collection of essays called *Standing By Words*, Berry pinpoints the reason for the failure of what he calls "internal language." It fails, he says, because it is incomprehensible. "If the connection between the inward and the outward is broken—if the experience of a single human does not resonate within the common experience of humanity—then language fails."

It's hard to improve on Wendell Berry. But I now want to read you a passage that I believe extends and illuminates Berry's plea for connection between the Self and the world. I apologize for the embarrassment that I am about to cause my friend Richard Hawley, but this is from a letter that Richard wrote me this summer as we continued a long-standing discussion on this issue.

Richard wrote, "The liberation from narcissism and solipsism is not important only for writers, although it is indeed important for them. It is," Richard continued, "an applied ethics—an approach to living honesty and well, not merely writing that way. Polity, community, school, family, self—all need to be informed by the credo that maturation, improvement, fulfillment and salvation itself are described by the progress of the self's apprehension of greater and greater contexts, more and more otherness. To live better in the given world (including behaving more considerately to the ozone layer, rain forests, etc.), is to meet it more respectfully, more carefully, more much more objectively. This is how you love others and otherness, at least at first."

* * *

Kathleen Norris has spent the last twenty years of her life learning to live better in the given world. She is a poet who lives with her husband, the poet David Dwyer, in her deceased grandmother's house near the tiny town of Lemmon, South Dakota, in the High Plains vastness of the central United States. So her contexts are at once large and small.

Like the authors of *The Feminine Face of God*, Kathleen Norris is preoccupied with questions of religious faith and the response of a woman to the institutional church. Unlike those authors, she has rooted her quest, not in dreams but in physical terrain. Not in workshops but in human community. Not in case histories, but in the full and textured history of inheritance and tradition and paradox. The language that has flowered from this rooting is at once miraculous and inevitable.

Norris moved from to Dakota from the fringes of the Warhol crowd in New York in 1974—just briefly enough, she thought, to claim the legal inheritance of her grandmother's house. She's still there—in a town so small, she writes, that the poets and ministers have to hang out together. She and her husband remained on that hard, isolated, forbidding land precisely because, as she writes, "Dakota is a painful reminder of human limits, just as cities and shopping malls are attempts to deny them."

Her quest for inheritance expanded and transmuted. It began to haunt her. Agnostic by habit, exasperated by a religion that "has so often used a male savior to keep women in their place," she was nonetheless drawn to the strong old women in the congregations of her ancestral ground. The old women are one with that ground, she perceives; and the insight provides her with what she calls "Access to the spirits of land and of place."

Dakota: A Spiritual Georgraphy is Norris's contribution to the literature of reclamation that I mentioned earlier. It was published this year by Ticknor & Fields, and it is in itself a glorious paradox: intensely personal and self-revealing, it shows us how the well-proportioned writerly Self can thrust us deeply into the objective world, and earn our empathy with another Self's concerns.

No swans, no turquoise daggers to prettify the quest. The

inheritance exacts a price. "Religion is in my blood, and in my ghosts," Norris writes.

> My grandmother Norris lived with the burden of a hard faith. She had married my grandfather—a divorced man whose wife had abandoned him and their two small children—after his conversion at a revival meeting. (She) found her mission in . . . raising seven children as the wife of a Plains pastor who served in seventeen churches in thirty-two years. Their first child . . . was born with rickets. While my grandmother was still nursing she conceived again; her doctor found her too exhausted and malnourished to sustain another pregnancy and performed an abortion. Early in their marriage her husband had rejected her affection in such a way that it was still fresh in her memory sixty years later. Long after he was dead she could calmly say, "You know, of course, he never loved me."

Yet for most of her life, Norris writes, her grandmother "would ask of anyone she met: 'Are you saved?'

"It's this hard religion, adding fuel to an all-American mix of incest, rape, madness and suicide, that nearly destroyed an entire generation of my family," she continues. "My aunts suffered terribly, and one was lost. She died the year I was born. She died of lots of things: sex and fundamentalist religion and schizophrenia and postpartum despair. She was a good girl who became pregnant out of wedlock and could make no room for the bad girl in herself. She jumped out of a window at a state mental hospital a few days after she had her baby.

"I believe I became a writer in order to tell her story and possibly redeem it."

This seems a somewhat grittier task than "finding a new way" to "serve the planet." And yet for all its reckoning with death, and isolation, and the unforgiving nature of her inheritance, Kathleen Norris has hardly written a despairing book. It is filled with earned hope. Speaking of those poets and those Christians thrown together in uneasy proximity, she acknowledges the mutual suspicion of the two groups. But "There is also trust," she writes. "We are people who believe in the power of words to effect change in the human heart."

So how do we do it? How do we writers achieve this proportionality between Self and World? How do we burst through the invisible cocoon that imprisons us in our narrow concerns and ambitions—and make our way, filled with terror but also ecstasy, into the Unknown? How do we intervene? How do we find out things? How do we ask questions of strangers? How do we *survive* strangers? What hope is there for us, realistically, in making sense of the unknown world as it is, in all its secrets, its mysteries, and its dangers?

I have long believed that these are the central questions that confront writers, especially emerging writers. Clearly they are not "literary" questions, but behavioral ones—and thus they are rarely addressed at writers' conferences. And yet I believe that literary growth is next to impossible if we do not address them. That catastrophic old adage, "Write what you know," has permitted too many of us to write about dreams of swans and turquoise daggers.

My colleague Richard Hawley has provided a strong theoretical answer. He suggests that the liberation from narcissism and solipsism is not just a writing technique but an applied ethics—an approach to living honestly and well. I think that you heard in Kathleen Norris's prose a splendid application of that theory: her book as the seamless extension of her voyage of discovery from New York to the unfamiliar land of her inheritance.

I want to end this talk by offering you a couple more examples of the literature of reclamation. These are from papers turned in by students in my notification writing class at Middlebury College. These have been glorious classes, and some of their brightest stars are here at Bread Loaf this summer.

My role in these classes has been minimal. I simply give the students an impossible task, and then step back out of the way while they achieve it.

The impossible task is to stop writing about themselves, and set forth to find stories in the world. The world they must enter is a small, peaceful New England village surrounded by dairy farms. A world in which so much happens below the surface and subtle barriers separate townsfolk and college students.

I might add that like all composition instructors, I give my students reading assignments, both from standard anthologies and from magazine essays. Last February we spent a couple of class periods discussing the narrative techniques in an *Atlantic Magazine* essay by Eric Larson. The essay was a journey inside the culture of handgun sellers, buyers, and users in America; its title was, "The Story of a Gun."

One day last winter, at about midterm, Alvin Ung dumped a twenty-six-page manuscript into my mailbox: about six times the suggested minimum. It was based on two weeks he had spent hanging out with a night watchman on campus named Jack Simpson. Alvin conferred his powerful and sympathetic attention on this character, a man whose work made him virtually invisible to most students, and found his mythic dimensions. Jack became Alvin's guide beneath the literal surface of an affluent New England college and into its mostly unimagined depths.

In this section Jack and Alvin are in the basement of Proctor, the student dining hall. It is midnight.

As we prepared to turn back to the first floor, we heard a muffled, raspy cough. And again.

Jack walked toward the sound and turned the corner.

"Look who's here—Connie!" Jack had reached the door and opened it. Light flooded the corridor.

"Almost forgotten about me, haven't ya, old Jack?" she rasped in that ghastly, tobacco-voice of hers. Just as I entered the room, Connie flung two sodden pieces of Kleenex toward me, and into the trashcan by my feet. How unbecoming.

I looked around me. Just a basement. It was pitch-black outside, so I saw nothing through the windows just below the ceiling of the room. Jack introduced us. And I began to observe the two of them.

Jack had just unbuttoned the top of his jacket; it hung loosely against the side of his Falstaffian paunch. Connie, on the other hand, wore a stained denim jacket, padded all through, over an old sweater of undistinguishable color. Beside her were three large plastic bags. The first was filled with empty soda and beer cans; the second, with two-liter plastic containers; and the third contained some bits of paper and cloth. Connie is a custodian and every Saturday night, around midnight, she would come to

Proctor and spend two hours cleaning up the basement kitchens. Like Jack, her routine never changes.

My attention drifted to some of Connie's conversation with Jack. I heard her rasp.

"We just can't help falling sick, you know. Look here, I've been to the doctor three times already." She aimed another Kleenex toward the trashcan. Once again, her aim was true. The Medic Alert chain around her wrist rattled as she did so. I carried on eating my sandwich.

"See, during the normal days, I take up all the student trash. I handle everything they don't want. With all the broken glass, and beer cans. And they clear their nose, they spit into the trash, or just throw in used condoms. So, I also have to mop off blood—can't see why they cut themselves so often—and I have to handle urine and all that too. So if the students are diseased, we also become diseased. Don't you see, I think this bronchitis here came from the flu epidemic with all those students, just two weeks ago." As if to emphasize her point, she sneezed a few times.

Jack kept quiet this whole time. But he did not appear uncomfortable. He had grabbed an unwaxed paper cup and boiled himself some coffee while Connie talked. The silence beyond Connie, and the darkness in the kitchens, actually evoked a calming other-worldly effect. As I peered down the darkened hallway from our lit table-area, I saw the moon shining through one of those windows just below the ceiling. Its rays bathed one of the sleek, steel tables used for dough-mixing and made it look like a placid moonlit lake.

Of course not all journeys from the Self into the World need be journeys across physical terrain. The journey can also be a journey of the heart, or a journey of ideas. Toward the end of the course another splendid student named Taylor Fravel asked permission to try such an essay. Since Taylor had already achieved Phi Beta Kappa, had been named a Rhodes Scholar and a Truman Fellow, I figured it was okay to let him have the keys to the car, as it were. And since his area of interest lay in Eastern studies and the Chinese language, I braced myself for some fairly heavy breathing.

What I got was a paper on Dr. Seuss. I treasure it, because it brilliantly affirms the moral essence of nonfiction writing; or all writing . . . all discourse, in this age of the terrorist and the gunman. It inspired and educated me. Taylor used it as his address to the Senior Class of 1993. I'm going to repeat part of it for you.

"In *Horton Hatches the Egg*," Taylor wrote, "Dr. Seuss tells a tale about Horton the Elephant and Mayzie the Lazy Bird. Mayzie is tired of sitting on her egg; it was hard work. So she asks Horton to watch it for her. And honest and sincere elephant, he obliges while Mayzie flies off to Palm Beach for a long vacation. He takes his task seriously, claiming that 'I'll stay and be faithful. I mean what I say.' "

And here Taylor educated me about the cover design of Wendell Berry's *Standing by Words*—that inexplicable rendering of a Chinese character.

"Horton's story," Taylor continues, "reminds me of the Chinese word for faith and trust. The Chinese language consists of thousands of characters, each a small picture that represents a common object or action. The character meaning 'faith' is the picture of a human being placed next to the symbol for speech. The image created by this juxtaposition is that of a man standing by words—defining as 'faith' or 'trust' the bond between us and our language.

"Our words," Taylor writes, "cannot be separated from our deeds. Horton's determination to protect Mayzie's egg reflects the essence of standing by words, the importance of accountability."

Like Horton, we have stood by and observed growing violence, confusion and frustration. Within this environment, what does it mean to "stand by words"? What makes Horton's story so special?

Just before the egg was about to hatch, Mayzie the Lazy Bird returned. Horton had done all the work, but she wanted her egg back. When the egg did hatch, however, it was not a bird, like Mayzie. Rather, a tiny elephant with wings appeared. Horton hatched an elephant from a bird's egg. As Seuss says, "because Horton was faithful! He sat and he sat/He meant what he said/And said what he meant."

We can understand Horton's message. But we must also act; we must use this knowledge. And so we must choose, choose between Horton and Mayzie, between being active participants or passive observers. We can either be like Horton, accountable and determined, or we can be like Mayzie, irresponsible and lazy.

From now on, we must have the courage and conviction to decide where to help; to choose our center; to pick an egg and protect it. We have learned too much to turn our backs and fly away. No matter what we decide to do with our lives, which path we follow, we can succeed. We will become doctors or lawyers, teachers or artists, thinkers, believers or doers. But while busy becoming, we should always remember Horton, elephant birds, and the necessity of standing by words.

Those of you who have taught in college classrooms will perhaps recognize in Taylor's essay the poignance of a keen and ardent young intelligence . . . unscarred, as yet, by painful reality. But these are times, as I said earlier, when it seems impossible to wake up in America and not feel that one is trapped inside the dark prophecies of Don DeLillo: specifically as he charts the withdrawal of the written word as a moral or aesthetic force in our culture . . . and the compensating encroachment of the fired bullet, the exploding car bomb.

Taylor learned fast.

Just a few weeks ago, while I was well along in the drafting of this talk, I received a handwritten letter from him in Washington. It had not been ordered into finished prose; it was an anguished burst of plainsong, and it read in part:

"I wish I could be writing to you under better circumstances, but given what I am about to tell you, I think you will understand. Last Thursday, my cousin was one of eight people shot and killed in a San Francisco law firm. He died—shot six times— while trying to protect his wife, also a lawyer, who happened to be in the office that afternoon (he jumped in front of her). He was 28; they were married last fall. Such a tragedy is too sudden—too tragic—to believe. One day an angry man ends eight lives, devastates many, many more.

"I wanted to tell you all this because the coincidences with our class and my speech are almost too similar. This is the violence I discussed in my paper. This *is* 'The Story of a Gun.' The gunman," Taylor wrote, "used two of the semiautomatics described in that article. This is all too real."

I read Taylor's letter, and I wondered again: what possible connection there can be between his consciousness and mine; between what I do and what he knows; between my books and his grief; between my puny and episodic wish to bear passionate witness and the hard futility of the witness that he has borne. To say nothing of his cousin's widow.

Is Bill Gray right? Have we writers become effigies as our books lose the power to shape and influence? Is it no longer possible for a writer to alter the inner life of the culture? Have bomb makers and gunmen have taken that territory, along with the pure products of America? Is news of disaster the only narrative people need? Are we about to disappear?

I don't know. But I do know this: to the extent that the answer to each of those questions is "yes," we writers must write and live all the more fervently as if the answer were "no."

We must accept paradox: writing as if language matters while conscious of the theories that tell us it does not. Honoring our inheritance as truth seekers is an age that has disproven the possibility of truth. Investigating unknown territory beyond the Self on behalf of that provisionally interested reader whom market research tells us no longer exists.

And why must we accept these paradoxical standards for ourselves? Only in order that we may then begin the most impossible task of all; the only task that matters; the task that perhaps only writers can now honestly contemplate:

And that is the task of reclaiming our broken world, and rebuilding it with words.

Part Two

EXCERPTS FROM BOOKS

Face Value (1979) has all the earmarks of a journalist's first novel. I wrote it with great glee and energy and innocence of craft in the spring and summer of 1978, pouring into it my journalist's love of bold character, decisive action, and mise-en-scene, all in the service of a form I'd yearned to explore since adolescence: social satire, developed as narrative.

In the mid-1970s, while I was working as a TV commentator at station WMAQ in Chicago, I grew absorbed in the seismic shift of American temperament that had begun to reveal itself. Fifteen years of intense political and social preoccupations had either decelerated or abruptly ended: the civil-rights and early "women's liberation" movements, demonstrations against the Vietnam War, assassinations of political leaders, urban race riots and student takeovers of college administration buildings, the beginning of a move to impeach a President.

Replacing these epic concerns in the national consciousness was a sudden, almost hysterical compulsion for immersion in private pleasures, accompanied by an efflorescence of celebrity worship. The emblematic event that year was the death of Elvis Presley, from an overdose of pills, in a Las Vegas hotel.

Face Value was a mock-heroic, satirical speculation on the overflow of American celebrityhood from its own precincts into other areas, such as news and information and, inescapably, to the political arena. (The book was optioned for a movie, but its chances were scuttled with the election in 1980 of Ronald Regan as President. Clearly the moviegoing public was in no mood to treat such fantasies lightly.)

The (mock-) hero, Mark Teller, is, through the merest of coincidences, a commentator at a TV station, the eponymous WRAP in New York. His whimsical impulse to spotlight a spectral, eerily funny young standup comedian named Robert Schein has the unintended effect of catapulting Schein into a fast-accelerating trajectory of popularity.

In this final chapter, Schein—who remains nearly devoid of personality out of the spotlight—is on the verge of capturing the nomination for U.S. Senator; he's the front for a wicked political cabal. The horrified and repentant Teller is hard on his heels. Jennifer Blade, a star TV reporter and Teller's fickle girlfriend, has cast her lot with Schein. Lon Stagg, who appears briefly here, is the station's hunky and vacuous anchorman. (After the book was published, I was struck with the wish that I had included a chapter in which all the principal characters gather over drinks to discuss the oddly allegorical nature of their names.)

Toot-Toot-Tootsie, Good-Bye (1981) was a gentler novel, more focused on character and fate. It had as its design the portrayal of a man growing old in America—a craftsman, whose craft was being rendered obsolete by rapidly advancing technology. It could have been any artisan's craft. I chose the one that had fascinated me since childhood, and went to Spring Training in Florida to observe its practitioners in action.

L. C. Fanning is a beloved baseball announcer, a radio play-by-play man who has outlived his time but doesn't know it. In October 1951 he called Bobby Thomson's famous home run to win the playoff series against the Dodgers ("Toot-Toot-Tootsie, Good-Bye!" was his patented home-run call), but his career, like his host society, has been in slow decline ever since.

In this, his final season, Fanning has been turned into a buffoon, a living piece of ironic performance art, by the new general manager of his radio station, a hip and cynical young whiz named Jeffrey Spector. Spector has paired Fanning in the broadcast booth with an ambitious former Miss America, Robyn Quarrles. He promotes their constant miscommunications as campy comedy; and though Fanning is slow to catch on to the joke, his beloved long-time color man, a former catcher named "Turtle" Teweles, sizes the situation up astutely and bolts the broadcast booth, heading back home to Arkansas.

In this chapter, Fanning, belatedly realizing that his imagined grandeur has been reduced to mockery, has also fled his on-air duties. He leaves Robyn in sole charge of the microphone in St. Louis as he launches a desperate foray into Arkansas to persuade Turtle to come back and make things the way they were. His need to confront the hopelessness of his quest to preserve the past—a precondition of his final liberating gesture—grows dimly apparent through a series of encounters in diminishing stages of light.

Super Tube: The Rise of Television Sports (1984) marked a return to nonfiction, a form that I have since pursued. The chapter entitled "The Iceman Clowneth," an account of a weekend of televised boxing by NBC at Atlantic City, is among my favorite pieces of reportage from direct observation; I am happy to see it given a new life here.

White Town Drowsing: Journeys to Hannibal (1986) is the book closest to my heart. A combination of reportage and personal memory, it is an account of my visits back to my home town in the summer of 1985, the 150th anniversary of the birth of Samuel L. Clemens. The town fathers, stirred to action by the blandishments of a "commemorations consultant" from New York, have planned a gigantic Mark Twain Sesquicentennial celebration that they hope will generate millions of dollars in tourist revenues and boost the struggling old Mississippi river town into a new era of prosperity. My narrative chronicles the inevitable calamities that resulted. Since its publication I have returned several times, in books, articles, and lectures, to the larger questions that *White Town Drowsing* raised: What is the fate of American small towns? What are the civic and spiritual costs of America's new penchant for "attractions," "historic redevelopment," vast and glittering theme parks, and other devices for superimposing a synthetic community on an authentic one?

from *Face Value*
(A Novel)

The chairman of the Schein for Senator Committee—a Wall Street investment banker (and a member of the Phaëthon Society)—announced a rally for Robert Schein on the night before Election Day. The rally would be held at a location of particular sentimental importance to the candidate, the campaign chairman announced—in front of Stitch's, where Robert Schein originally came to the attention of New Yorkers. The master of ceremonies for the evening would be Al Gnagy, proprietor of Stitch's and "longtime friend" of Schein.

It would be the candidate's first appearance in front of a public gathering. Accompanying him would be his fiancée, Mary Ellen Olds, and her father, former President V. W. Olds.

Jennifer Blade strode into Lon Stagg's office without knocking. The anchorman looked up from his desk in surprise. He flushed and hastily attempted to sweep away a sheaf of papers that he had been reading when Jennifer burst through the door.

She thought for an instant that she had caught Stagg in the act of reading porn. But she glimpsed a page before it disappeared into his middle desk drawer and realized that Stagg had been absorbed in the week's ratings totals. Lon Stagg read ratings pamphlets with the same furtive enjoyment that other men experienced from flipping through *Penthouse*. On the walls of his office were pinups of ratings sheets from weeks in which he had done especially well.

"*Jenny!*" He stuck out a hand, but did not rise—probably trying to cover an erection, Jennifer thought. "Hey, I thought you were in the Golden State, big-time lady!"

She mentally crossed her eyes. "I came into town to cover

Schein's rally. We're going live on the network with it and I'll get some extra footage for *Face to Face.*"

"What brings you over *WRAP-Around* way?" His face cracked open with his best lopsided little-boy grin.

That man should not be permitted to open his mouth without a TelePrompTer, Jennifer decided silently. Instead of replying right away, she fixed him with a long gaze and a mysterious smile.

Then she turned around and walked back to the door, letting her hips undulate in a parody of sensuality that Stagg undoubtedly perceived as a woman's rightful style.

She pushed the door to his office closed and slid the bolt into place. She turned around to face him and slid her hand deep into her shoulder bag. The motion was somehow carnal.

When she withdrew it—from Stagg's expression, he might have been expecting a garter—she was holding the cassette.

"I have two surprises for you," she said softly. "One of them is this."

Stagg squinted at the object.

"What's the other one?" he asked. He thought he might know—but he didn't dare believe it. Stagg had had the "hots"—as he liked to call them—for Jennifer ever since she had first showed up at the station. But something about her decisive, authoritarian manner inhibited him from approaching her with the line that he found sure-fire among stewardesses and cocktail waitresses: "How's your sex life?"

Was she about to come on to him? Jesus, think of the time he'd wasted . . .

"This," she said. She was wearing a suede skirt that came to mid-calf. Under the skirt she was wearing boots. She seemed to be undoing the buttons that held the skirt together down the side.

Stagg couldn't believe it! It was just incredible what being with an anchorman did to women in the eighteen-to-thirty-four age group. They couldn't leave him alone! But now came a moment of decision. The beautiful woman stripping in his office was between him and the clothes hanger. On the one hand, he wanted to tear off his clothes and ravish her right away, before she somehow came to her senses . . . changed her mind . . . on the other hand, he was wearing a brand-new Adolfo three-piece

charcoal chalk stripe . . . elegant set of threads . . . really ought
to get those pants on a hanger . . .

Unbuttoning his vest (the jacket was already hung, thank God)
he began moving away from his desk, circling Jennifer, holding
her gaze over his left shoulder. His best side. He got the vest
off—she was down to bra, panties, and boots, *incredible body*—
and reached for his belt buckle.

His boots! He was wearing the damned Botticelli pull-ons, they
came practically up to his knees, he'd have to get them off first or
the pants would get snagged; he liked his pants tight, especially
in the ass, women liked a guy's ass, he'd read that in *Viva* . . .

Still holding Jennifer's gaze, Stagg reached down carefully,
bringing the heel of his right boot up across his left leg, and
tugged.

The boot slid off.

Now the other one.

Jennifer was moving slowly toward him, her hands at the
clasp of her brassiere. *God, she was going to keep her boots on!* What
a turn-on! He felt his excitement surge; it made his knees weak,
made it hard to stand on one leg . . .

He had to get to the clothes hanger behind her. Not to make it
obvious! Tugging now at his left boot he began to hop, carefully,
one hop at a time, trying to circle her, trying not to spoil the mood
of her sudden desire . . .

"Hey, baby, I'm a great big bunny rabbit. Come get me."
Maybe if he made it a game. She was smiling now—almost
laughing, it seemed. Funny how women react when they get their
juices up . . . some of 'em are screamers . . . he hoped Jennifer
wasn't a screamer . . . still, it wouldn't be bad for his rep if the
word got around the office that he was banging Jennifer Blade.

She was stalking him now, and in his haste he lost his balance.
Still gripping his right boot, he went hop-hopping backwards,
toward his desk, like some demented Scotsman doing the High-
land fling. She was on him as the small of his back hit the desk,
and together they went plummeting back across the surface, and
her expert hands were at his trousers, and he was free, and they
slid back further still, down the other side, in a tangled heap of
tanned skin and Adolfo fabric and hot mouths sucking . . . his
hand grasped at the top of a file cabinet as he went down, her on

top of him, honey-blond hair cascading, and a stack of ratings sheets fluttered down around them, covering them with the sweet sticky musk of *demographics*, and all the statistically concupiscent ladies of the eighteen-to-thirty-four age group coated him like a Xerox harem as he came and came . . .

Afterwards, after she had finished undressing him and lay with her legs entwined with his, her hand gently massaging his satiated member, Jennifer Blade pressed her lips to the base of Lon Stagg's ear and whispered to him:

"I've been dying to do that for months . . . I wouldn't let myself while I worked here . . . I make it a rule never to get involved at the office . . . but after I left I couldn't stop thinking of you . . . your hair . . . that fabulous smile of yours . . . those sexy looks you give . . . those *clothes* . . ."

"Hey," he whispered back. "I can dig it. But don't let yourself get involved, Jenny, I'm not into deep commitments . . ."

She snickered into his ear—she didn't believe him, he guessed. None of them did. What the hell . . . but she put a finger over his lips to silence him.

"Lon . . . I have something else for you . . . remember the first thing I showed you, that cassette tape . . . Lon, it's got dynamite on it . . ."

After she had dressed and gone, Lon Stagg sat at his desk in his snakeskin-pattern Jockey undershorts (the same pattern Lydell Mitchell of the Baltimore Colts wore in that full-color ad) and tried to figure out all that had happened in the last thirty minutes of his life.

One: He had Done the Trick with one of the foxiest women in the United States.

Two: He had been presented (by this same chick) with a piece of news material that could give him the instant national renown he longed for.

Three: He had ripped the bottom of the best pair of suit pants he had ever owned.

Three did not matter for the moment. Stagg turned the cassette over in his hands and frowned at it. Jennifer had said she wanted to see him as a network anchorman. (So did he.) And not on a low-rent network like CBN, either. (He'd had the same thought.)

But one of the Big Three, one of the blue-chip networks, a quality organization that a man of his stature and reputation deserved. (Exactly.)

Don't waste this bombshell on WRAP or even CBN, she'd urged him. Play it. Listen to it. See if he agreed with her that it was major-scoop, dynamite stuff. Then call her at the Hilton . . . she'd explain who the guy was that did all the talking on the tape . . . and from there, they'd figure out how to get it, and him, on a network news show. He'd be an instant star, she said . . . it was a revelation on a par with Woodward and Bernstein . . .

Why waste another minute? He pulled a cassette recorder out of his desk drawer and played the tape.

It was dynamite, all right. Even Lon Stagg, with his limited understanding of politics, grasped that. Robert Schein a stooge for a secret businessmen's cabal! Everything arranged behind closed doors, like in that television movie a couple of years ago.

In a way, Lon Stagg felt almost personally betrayed. He'd been a big Robert Schein fan. Used a lot of his jokes at parties, in fact. Thought he was terrific. But if all this was true . . . bugger Bob Schein, it was Lon Stagg's ticket up!

He wondered who the man was. Obviously the guy who pulled Schein's strings. The voice sounded awfully familiar, but Stagg couldn't quite place it.

His course of action was clear: Call Jennifer at the Hilton and get the ball rolling. The sooner the better.

No. One thing to do first.

Call his agent. His new manager. The new guy he'd hired just before this incredible windfall, to help him out with what he felt was a stagnating image. No pun intended.

The guy who'd been recommended to him by the Big Boss himself, the Colonel, Eddie Donovan.

California guy. But he was in town, too, Stagg recalled. Be good to run over this thing with him first. The guy had made it clear—he expected to know every last detail about Stagg's life. Professional and personal.

So be it.

He dialed the Hilton and asked for the suite of Mal Book-master.

* * *

Stitch's was ablaze in the cold November night air.

Spotlights and television lights seared into the seedy little establishment, turning its dark facade into a glowing ember of garish red.

The police had reluctantly agreed to cordon off this block of Second Avenue, sending traffic into confusion throughout the Upper East Side. But even this cleared space was not enough for the throng of fifteen thousand people that surged and pushed into the area to see Robert Schein return to the point of his first fame.

The street was already clogged with police cars, mobile vans from New York television stations, and a brass band that played from the platform of a truck. Scaffolding had been erected in the street directly in front of Stitch's; it was upon this surface, piled with bunting and backed with a giant, billowing photograph, that Candidate Schein and his fiancée would greet his supporters.

The rally had been scheduled for eight P.M., but the crowd had started gathering as early as six. Now the streets around Stitch's were a nighttime wheatfield of straining humanity. Bookmaster, nearly invisible near the base of the scaffolding, noticed expensive leather coats, angora turtlenecks, fashionable scarves. This crowd was not rabble. These were the cognoscenti, the people who waited in lines around a city block in freezing rain for the latest Woody Allen. Hip. Serious fans. A killer crowd. He had selected these people out of their separate lives as surely as if he had lifted them up by tweezers, and set them here. There was a bright moon, and the crowd's faces were bright and cold with a skittish intensity. They pressed in on the scaffolding, their collective voice high with manic chatter. Bookmaster permitted himself to feel very proud.

Because of the national interest in Robert Schein's phenomenal climb to the threshold of political power—the latest poll showed him the slight favorite, with a scant plurality of voter support— the four networks had decided to preempt prime time programming and telecast Schein's rally live. The networks and the New York stations agreed to share four "pool" cameras, due to the shortage of space. Three of the cameras would be at fixed points. The fourth would be a roving minicam.

Among the reporters present would be Jennifer Blade. Bookmaster kept glancing toward the shiny, roped-off area where the silhouetted cameras stood mounted like machine guns; where correspondents and crewmen flitted in and out of the harsh light like sentries in an armed camp.

There was a matter he had to settle with Jennifer tonight. Here, in the midst of the crowd. It would only take a minute.

At seven thirty, the band on the truck bed swung into a series of Sousa marches. The guests of honor began to pick their way up the metal stairs to the top of the speaker's platform: a few independent candidates for lesser offices. A sprinkling of New York entertainers and celebrities who claimed longstanding friendship with Schein. Bodyguards.

As each new arrival emerged at the top step and crossed into the field of arc lights toward the folding chairs, the moiling crowd set up a howl of recognition. They were deep-throated howls, animal roars, and they carried a suggestion of something deeper, darker, more urgent than mere campaign fervor.

The personalities on the platform felt it, and shivered. Stepping into the arc light's glow was, for many of them, like stepping into a field of fire. The crowd's intensity rolled up onto the platform in hot waves, dispersing the pleasant chill of the November urban night. Under the moon, their white glistening faces waited, slack and grinning.

A cheer greeted the arrival of Colonel Eddie Donovan, president of the Continental Broadcasting Network.

The loudest roar came as former President V. W. Olds reached the top step, stumbled briefly, and swung his arms in a jaunty winner's wave toward the wheatfield of people. The crowd—most of whose members had ridiculed Olds in their private lives—unleashed a great cascading roar that swept down Second Avenue like a tidal wave, crashing into Midtown.

Olds ushered his wife, a terrified woman in a pink coat, into the cross-hairs and across the stage. The band played, "The Bear Went Over the Mountain."

Teller could hear the *wheep* of the public-address system from as far west as Lexington Avenue. As he ran toward Second down 68th he could feel the crowd begin to thicken and slow, like stream water rushing into a deep pool. He was breathing hard, concentrating on his pace, on the running, breath coming in regular gasps. He didn't want to think what was going to happen once he reached the rally. He didn't know. He didn't really have a plan. Avoid Bookmaster and his goons . . . keep from getting killed if he could . . . *get to Schein*! Dismantle him. It would have to be that way, he saw. Somebody would literally have to take Schein apart in front of a crowd. He could not be destroyed by the media. He ate the media. Every one of Teller's attempts to ruin Schein on the air had failed—worse, had been turned into fuel to further propel Schein's phantom image. Schein was impregnable in the studios, invincible on the airwaves. After tonight, Teller knew, after the election, Schein would vanish from corporeal presence forever. He would ascend on the airwaves, he would rule on the airwaves. It would be the beginning of a new order: medium and messenger forever intertwined, indistinguishable.

So the confrontation, if it was ever to take place, would have to be in the flesh. A primal reckoning under the November moon, on a temporal street, under the witnessing eyes of human beings.

Teller's pace was slowed by jostling bodies. He had not expected the crowd to be on this scale. Could he worm his body through it? He sensed the hysteria in the collective temperament around him. He should have arrived hours earlier. But that would have left him open to Bookmaster . . . he could hear the echoing voice of the Schein for Senator chairman as the man began to make introductions. The platform and the red facade of Stitch's were small bubbles of light across an acre of human flesh.

He came to Third Avenue and sprinted uptown for four blocks, across the current to 72nd. At that intersection he encountered an immobile mass of humanity, a blackening pond.

Like a swimmer about to plunge into dark and icy waters, Teller hesitated, took a breath, and knifed into the crowd.

"WHAT WE ARE HERE TO CELEBRATE TONIGHT IS NOTHING LESS THAN A REVOLUTION IN THIS COUNTRY'S ELECTORAL PROCESS . . ."

Jennifer Blade drew the lapels of her coat close around her. Despite the heat of the crowd and the warmth here in the TV pit, she felt a deep-winter chill. The crowd frightened her. She had seen madness in the faces. The crowd had come here not just to cheer, not just to worship, but to devour something. There was the kind of ecstasy that she had seen in sweat-soaked faces at Tennessee churches when she reported the Bobby Lee Cooper phenomenon a year ago. But this ecstasy was tempered with something else—a kind of crackling current of raw power, undirected, capable at any moment of whipping out of control.

" — WE ARE ON THE EVE OF A NEW ERA IN THE SYMBIOTIC DIA-LOGUE BETWEEN A PUBLIC OFFICIAL AND HIS PUBLIC — "

They were all mad. She was, certainly. She had come here to devour something, too. Schein. But she had come unarmed. The tape—what had happened to Stagg? Gutless bastard. Like Teller. Covering his own ass, probably. The men she had turned to were ineffectual. She would have to carry it out herself.

But how? If she'd had the tape, she might rush onstage and stick a recorder in front of a microphone, let it play until they dragged her away. But she didn't have the goddamn tape.

"A NEW WEDDING OF COMMUNICATIONS TECHNOLOGY AND THE HUMAN COMPASSION NECESSARY TO PRESERVE OUR TRADITIONAL VALUES — "

Perhaps she would rush the stage anyway, seize a microphone, blurt the connection that linked Bookmaster and Schein and Colonel Donovan's foolish group . . .

It wouldn't work. The papers would play it the way they'd played Teller's outburst on the air. A lover scorned. A sideshow.

And Bookmaster would kill her.

In the first heat of his betrayal of her, in that first wrenching knowledge of Schein and Mary Ellen Olds, and for weeks afterward, she had felt that death would be an insignificant price for revenge on Schein and Bookmaster. She wasn't sure she felt that way now. Death was heavy around her in this crowd, unconscious perhaps to the crowd itself, but palpable to her. It made her sick with horror. She wanted to live.

"AND NOW, BEFORE WE MEET THE CANDIDATE HIMSELF, IT IS MY VERY GREAT PLEASURE TO — "

But what of this crowd? How to explain its stench of death? She recalled old conversations with Teller—he would talk earnestly about the things one gives up in one's adulation of the famous. It's impossible, he would say, to identify so heavily with someone else, and not lose a corresponding measure of your own identity.

Was this crowd an ultimate expression of that truth?

No time for such thoughts. She turned her gaze to the base of the speaker's platform. There in the shadows stood Bookmaster like a coiled snake on a rock. The sight of him filled her with dread and loathing. But he had said to look for him there—he had something for her.

Something, perhaps, that she could use, a scrap of information she could twist around in some way to hurl at him and his hideous puppet.

She glanced at her watch. Ten minutes until eight.

"Back in a minute," she called to her producer.

She headed for the shadows.

Al Gnagy was at the microphone now.

Dressed in a robin's-egg-blue tuxedo, his eyes as wild and distended as the crowd's eyes, Gnagy clutched the microphone close to his mouth, popping his *p*'s like gunshots as he rambled on about his early association with "this man of genius, this populist visionary." Gnagy's spittle glittered in the arc lights; there were rivers of sweat on his skull face despite the cold air.

The crowd gaped at him with a large loon smile. He was the warm-up act before the main rock'n'roll show.

Teller was deep in the crowd by now, wedging and squeezing his way forward. It was a nightmare journey. People turned around to see who was pushing them from behind. Some of them recognized him as the man who had tried to destroy their idol on television, and these people were not kind. A red welt had opened under Teller's left eye from an elbow thrown there. A hand had come across his mouth, bruising his lips. He had been shoved, tripped, cursed, ridiculed. The crowd hated him. Teller sensed that it was capable of killing him at any moment. He fought claustrophobia, fought the terror of sinking deeper into a mass of human quicksand, and pushed on.

"MANY'S THE TIME AFTER HIS ACT, BOBBY SCHEIN AND I WOULD SIT LONG HOURS HERE IN THIS ESTABLISHMENT YOU SEE RIGHT BEHIND ME . . . 'AL,' HE'D SAY, 'THE PEOPLE OF AMERICA NEED A

NEW VISION, THEY NEED SOMEONE TO HELP THEM REDISCOVER THEIR
ESSENTIAL HONESTY AND DECENCY AND COMPASSION . . ."

"Hello, Mal." She had virtually to scream to make herself heard
above the din from the crowd and from the speakers over their
heads.

Bookmaster gave a jump. He turned flashing serpent's eyes on
her.

His mouth formed the word, "Jenny."

She put her mouth to his ear. "You said you had something for
me."

The crowd had somehow broken past the rope barrier around
the scaffolding; bodies pressed in on them.

She saw Bookmaster smile; saw him nod his balding head in
vigorous affirmation.

He reached a hand inside his overcoat.

He withdrew it, clutching a small, thin rectangular object.

He brandished it in front of her eyes.

It was a tape cassette. She recognized it: the cassette she had
given Stagg.

In that instant Jennifer Blade knew that she was about to die.

The fixed smile was still on Bookmaster's face. His eyes
glittered. His free hand was sliding back into the pocket of his
black outer coat.

She knew he had a pistol inside.

In a flash, Jennifer understood that Mal Bookmaster had
picked the perfect setting in which to kill her. No one would hear
the pistol go off. In this crush of humanity, she would not even
fall. No attention would be drawn to her. Her body would not be
discovered for hours—another random, senseless incident of
gunplay in New York. It could even happen to a television
personality!

With his usual thoroughness, Bookmaster had thought of
everything.

He had even created the crowd—Schein's crowd—to absorb
her murder.

The crowd!

Jennifer thrust her mouth into the moonstruck face of the fan
nearest her and screamed at the top of her lungs:

"THIS MAN'S GOT A GUN HE'S GOING TO SHOOT ROBERT SCHEIN!"

Faces turned.

"—LIKE MY OWN SON—" Gnagy droned on the platform.

"Hunh?"

"What the fuck!"

"Grab him!"

Hands reached out for Bookmaster. Something glinted at his waist and then was lost in the shadows. In the instant before the crowd closed on Bookmaster, his wild eyes met Jennifer's.

"*Who's got the power?*" she mouthed to him.

Then, in the loudest shriek she could muster:

"THERE! HE'S THE ONE! STOP HIM HIT HIM KILL HIM KILL HIM KILL HIM KILL HIM!"

She could feel all the animal lust in the crowd coalescing into the small group of people who had now encircled Bookmaster and flung him to the pavement. The energy surged into them at the speed of light. Men, women, middle-class; there were perhaps a dozen of them. She glimpsed expensive leather overcoats, tweed jackets, a woman's handbag rising and falling. But some mania now gripped these people. Their teeth bared, their voices cursing, laughing, snarling, they seemed to have absorbed the collective electric frenzy of the animal crowd. She could almost see the currents flashing from body to body, in a gigantic but ever-receding V, until they grounded in the twelve or so men and women who were now beating Mal Bookmaster into a bloody sponge.

Even through the din of the loudspeakers and the general crowd noise, Jennifer could hear the rhythmic, oddly monotonous sough and thog of fists and boots slamming into Bookmaster's flesh. There were splotches of blood on some of the leather coats now. Jennifer realized that if she did not get herself out of the way she could be drawn into the melee and crushed along with Bookmaster.

Her back pressed against the scaffolding. She felt along it with her palms, gripped the cold metal tubings that formed a network below the platform. Spinning around, she reached as high as she could and pulled her body up. Her arms trembled. She could feel the entire speaker's platform sway with her weight.

Her feet found purchase on a crossbeam. Turning carefully, she gripped the beams behind her and looked down at the murder taking place beneath her.

Bookmaster's face was a scarlet, pulpy sausage. The crowd had formed a perfect circle around him now, kicking and smashing him with an almost ritualistic precision. She wondered whether he could still see, could make out her form on the scaffolding above him.

"Who's got the power?" she screamed down at him. "*Who's got the power, Mal?*"

A heavy face turned from its work to stare up at her, like a sheepdog with blood on its chops. What if he thought she was Bookmaster's accomplice? He'd pulled her down and kill her.

On impulse, she waved merrily at the suspicious face. "Jennifer Blade," she called into a cupped palm. "CBN News!"

The murderous face split into a grin. "Hi, Jenny!" The man flipped her a jaunty salute and turned back to his labors.

"—GIVES ME GREAT PLEASURE TO INTRODUCE THE NEXT UNITED STATES SENATOR FROM NEW YORK—"

The metallic voice above her brought her out of what had been a hypnotic daze. A cold wind whipped down from dark Uptown, above the crowd, and stung at her eyes.

The horror of what had passed beneath her knifed in on the wind. She turned her face and retched into the scaffolding—once, twice, three times. Her body convulsed, and she was seized with the fear that she would faint and tumble back into the feral crowd.

She tightened her grip, and held. She was sobbing.

Above her, they were introducing Schein. Spotlights swept over her head. The crowd let loose a roar that made her ears ring, a roar that she could feel in the palms of her hands as it coursed along the metal girders. She saw the silhouetted TV cameras swivel and pan, and she remembered that she had deserted her station. The Continental Broadcasting Network was covering Robert Schein's ascension without her.

She became aware that there had been a small noise at her side for the last several minutes—a persistent *pip-pip-pipping.*

Her beeper. They were paging her on her beeper.

Directly above, she knew, Robert Schein was advancing toward the microphone. People were screaming, sobbing, embracing one another, waving their arms like sinners about to be redeemed.

She forced her gaze again to the foot of the scaffolding.

She saw that the horror was not yet over.

A curious thing was happening. She gazed in stupefied fascination. The hideous red wreckage that had been Mal Bookmaster's body had begun a macabre journey back into the bowels of the crowd.

It had been an isolated killing.

Most people in the vicinity had scarcely torn their eyes from the speaker's platform long enough to comprehend more than a scuffle.

It was as though the crowd itself had unconsciously detached a portion of itself, a set of jaws, to do the necessary work.

But now, even as Robert Schein's hand caressed the microphone above her, Jennifer could see the pattern of rippling awareness, the turning of heads, wheatstalks touched by a gust of night wind.

It was a chain reaction—an outward impinging of information, a combustion of turned heads, *like the airwaves*, Jennifer imagined. And behind the widening ripples floated the corpse of Mal Bookmaster—passed back along the crowd from hand to hand, quietly, without panic, until the body disappeared into the maw, and Jennifer could follow its passage only as a receding oval in the darkling field of humanity, a gray blip on the screen of heads . . .

The crowd was *digesting* Mal Bookmaster.

She clung to the metal scaffolding, her consciousness fading into the collective deafening whisper of the crowd.

From another direction, another small oval of movement was pushing its laborious way toward the platform.

"—FULFILL A PROMISE TO YOU THAT . . . I MADE MORE THAN A YEAR AGO AT THE DEATHBED OF ONE OF THIS NATION'S IMMORTALS . . ."

"He looks a little distracted," observed the pool director, a CBS man. "Stand by, Two."

"You'd be too, in his position," muttered the technical director.

"He keeps looking back onto the platform."

"—NEVER BEFORE HAS THIS COUNTRY STOOD, stood . . . STOOD AT THE THRESHOLD OF SUCH GRAVE DANGER OF SATURATION BY SOVIET PROPAGANDA . . . uh . . . DELIVERED NOT THROUGH ENEMY CHANNELS BUT ON OUR OWN MISGUIDED, uh . . ."

"Why's the bastard keep looking around? *Take* Two."

Teller's ribs and shoulders ached from a constant pounding of elbows, hands, bodies. He was drenched in sweat. The closer he pushed toward the platform, the more resistant the crowd became. Now he was nearly at a standstill. The figure in front of him, a beefy stud with a Fu Manchu mustache, was refusing to budge.

"I don't give a fuck who you are, fuck off, you fuck."

Now there was a pressing in from their left. People jostled against him. He fought for breath in the sudden crush. Something heavy was passing back through the crowd alongside him. People were turning and stepping backward, onto his feet, against his shins, to clear the way.

The man ahead of him turned a half-step—and gave Teller six inches of open space. Teller plunged into the opening.

It was like stepping out of heavy underbrush into a creek bed. The line of people in the wake of the heavy object seemed somehow more pliant, more willing to step aside, clear room. He was within thirty yards of the platform now. He could see Schein's face illuminated in the spotlights and the TV lights, could pick up the glint of his ice-blue eyes. Even in his preoccupation with the crowd, Teller could sense that something was not right with Schein. The voice was hesitant. He kept pausing to sweep the speakers' chairs behind him with searching glances.

Bookmaster would have him off the stage in no time. Teller lowered a shoulder into the pliant crowd and bulled his way ahead.

"—AN AIR ATTACK NOT FROM ENEMY . . . from enemy . . . MISSILES BUT AN AIR ATTACK ON AMERICA'S OWN AIRWAVES . . ."

The chairman of the Schein for Senator Committee had been scowling intently at Schein, arms folded, from his seat behind the candidate. Now he leaned toward Colonel Donovan and asked in a rasping whisper:

"What the hell's the matter with him? Is he drunk?"
Donovan shook his head. "I don't see his manager anywhere.
I think the boy is at a loss without him."
"Well, I'm going to stop this thing before he pisses away the
election."
Donovan nodded.
The chairman cursed under his breath and sprang up from his
seat, arranging his face in a jaunty television smile as he did so.
He strode up the aisle until he was directly behind Schein. He
clapped a hand on the candidate's shoulder.
"LADIES AND GENTLEMEN—" the campaign chairman began.
He felt Schein's shoulder tighten like a steel coil. Schein spun
around as though he had been attacked from behind in a dark
alley. The campaign chairman found himself looking into the
panic-stricken eyes of a stranger.
He tried to salvage the instant. "HA-HA, SCARED 'IM! BOOOOY, IS
MY FACE RED!"
Scattered boos from the crowd.
"LADIES AND GENTLEMEN, THIS MAN HAS HAD A HARD AND
EXHAUSTIVE MONTH OF CAMPAIGNING! I THINK IT WAS A MARVEL-
OUS TRIBUTE TO YOUR SUPPORT THAT BOB SCHEIN IS HERE WITH YOU
TONIGHT! I KNOW HE'D LIKE TO BE HOME RESTING UP FOR THE BIG
DAY TOMORROW! I THINK WE SHOULD ALL GIVE HIM A BIG HAND, A
BIG SHOW OF OUR SUPPORT—"
Cries of "No!" "No!" "Let him speak!"
Teller crashed through the last remaining rows of people and
burst upon the small clearing at the base of the scaffold.
He threw his bruised head back and stared upward. His
quarry was directly above him. Robert Schein looked like a
waxen dummy on a high shelf, a doll that Teller could not quite
reach. The platform was more than twice his height. The steps
leading to it, on the side to his right, were ringed with policemen.
The facade directly in front of him was a hopeless arrangement of
vertical steel tubing. He saw that he could pull himself partway
up by standing on crossbeams that were four or five feet above
the pavement. But his stretching hands would still fall a couple of
feet short of the platform base.
He had the strangling sensation that he was living in a
nightmare. He had clawed and battered his way this far, absorb-

ing the blows of the crowd, only to stand helplessly at the feet of the monster, his monster, while the last seconds of hope ticked away.

"WE WANT TO THANK EACH AND EVERY ONE OF YOU WHO HAVE BEEN A PART OF THIS MAN'S PHENOMENAL SUCCESS STORY — AND WHO WILL DEMONSTRATE AT THE POLLS TOMORROW THAT THE PEOPLE OF AMERICA CAN BREAK THROUGH THE ESTABLISHED POLITICAL MACHINERY AND SPEAK WITH THEIR OWN VOICE—"

The frustration, the futility of his quest washed through his body and left him limp. The ringing idiot voice in the loud-speaker pounded and mocked at his skull, a funhouse shriek lulling the gullible to their pre-assigned complicity in their doom. There was nothing more he could do. He wanted to seize the steel girders with his hands and shake the platform down. Instead he grabbed at them as though they were prison bars, hung his head, and gazed stupidly at the rotting newspapers and food wrappers in the Second Avenue gutter

"Mark!"

The voice came at him from above, to his left, apart from the general murmur of the crowd. It seemed to float in under the platform, through the scaffolding—a familiar woman's voice calling his name.

He raised his head and looked to his left.

The silhouette of a woman clung to the girders on the far end of the scaffolding. Her feet rested on the crossbeams.

The voice was Jennifer Blade's.

He scrambled to the left side of the structure and rounded the corner. Jennifer looked down on him from above.

"You want up there?"

"Yes, goddammit!"

She held down her hand.

He took it, grabbed a beam with his other hand, and pulled himself even with her.

"Lock your fingers!"

He placed a foot inside the sling she had made with her hands and, as she lifted, pulled himself upward on the vertical beam with all his strength. His hands felt the smooth edge of the speaker's platform. Jennifer's hands were above her now, and he felt her arms tremble under his foot. He placed his palms flat on the platform, elbows high, and pushed with all his might. The center of his gravity shifted, and he rolled onto the stage floor. He found himself looking up at the pink coat of the former First Lady of the United States, who screamed.

He smiled up at her husband, who was frantically fumbling to free his foot from its entanglement in his metal folding chair so that he could spring into action . . . escape . . . somehow cope with the welt-faced intruder who had rolled in out of nowhere.

"Mark Teller, *WRAP-Around News*," he said, as conversationally as possible.

"Yes," said the former President, breaking into a broad smile of relief. "How are you? Uh, no comment at this time." He reached an arm around his wife, who was in hysterics.

"—AND SO WE WILL SAY GOOD NIGHT TO YOU ALL, AND WE'LL GREET YOU FROM OUR WINNING HEADQUARTERS IN JUST ABOUT TWENTY-FOUR HOURS, TO USHER IN A NEW ERA—"

Teller got his feet under him. There was a clear path between him and Candidate Robert Schein. Down a long row of chairs filled with dignitaries, the path was free. He was on his feet now. The dignitaries had turned their horrified faces to him, their expressions frozen into masks of bewilderment and fear. Beside the former President and his wife, there was Mary Ellen Olds, open-mouthed and uncomprehending. There was Colonel Eddie Donovan, his old boss—caught in a rigid stare of scowling indignation. For all his immobility, he might have been one of the Six Captains festooned on a stake. There was Al Gnagy, the Master of Ceremonies, serene in his blind moment of stardom. Several other people whose faces Teller had seen on TV and on billboards—candidates. Two melon-faced giants who could only have been bodyguards. Behind them on the platform, a receding sea of pink, prosperous faces.

And, of course, Robert Schein.

Teller absorbed the whole scene in an instant—in that elongated beat of time that expanded under the TV lights. Bathed in that harsh white glow, the dignitaries in the folding chairs seemed permanently frozen in the pop of some giant flashbulb.

Teller's throbbing eyes swept the platform for the one man who could unfreeze the tableau and send all these statues into a frenzy of action that would engulf him, smother him, kill him perhaps, certainly keep him from reaching his final goal. Book-master was nowhere to be seen. Surely he was there. Teller had to act in the second or two of grace before the superagent spotted him and willed his destruction.

He sprinted down the platform, crashed into the chairman of the Schein for Senator Committee, and sent the beefy man staggering. Teller snatched the microphone from the man's hand as he shoved.

In their respective studios, the four network correspondents had already begun their analysis of the Schein rally.

MacGregor Walterson of CBN put his hand to his earpiece and glanced at his monitor screen.

"Something's happening up on stage," he told his viewers. "Let's go back live."

The other three networks followed suit.

"Camera One, get on this!" yelled the pool director. "We're still in business! Where the hell's that minicam crew? *Take* One!"

Mark Teller was alone on the platform with Robert Schein.

He gazed into ice-blue eyes that seemed to fill the universe. His own eyes throbbed. He fought against the sudden fascination, the rush of hatred and exhilaration, that threatened to hypnotize him.

He drew a breath and shouted into the microphone with all the volume his heaving lungs could master:

"MARK TELLER, *WRAP-Around News!*"

It was a lie, of course—but it didn't matter. The amplified echoes of his voice boomed off the buildings around, and sent shock waves through the crowd.

The reaction was instantaneous. The shock waves came rolling back in a thunderous wash of boos. This was the man who had tried to bring down their hero!

Teller's eyes darted around the platform again. Still no Book-master! Without him, the people onstage—even the bodyguards—seemed confused, paralyzed. Time was ticking by in milliseconds, freeze-frames. Schein's face, inches from his own, was a heaving landscape, a convulsion of skin, the blue eyes distended, the features a flickering, snapping screen of long-dormant emotions flickering to tormented life.

"I HAVE A QUESTION FOR THE CANDIDATE!"

Again the thunderous echoes boomed out over the crowd. The boos continued, but the volume abated. The shiny faces turned upward in renewed fascination. The man confronting their hero might have been a hated enemy—but he was a *celebrity.*

The crowd waited to see what would happen next.

Teller turned once again to stare into the universe of blue eyes. There was fear in the eyes now—an emotion he never expected to discover in Robert Schein. Fear clouded the eyes like static. Milliseconds.

Teller drew in his breath again.

"WHO ARE YOU?"

Schein flinched. His mouth flapped open, unhinged, hung there, in the shocked expression of a man who has just received an unspeakably withering insult.

(*"Tighten that shot, One! Tight! Tight!"*)

"WHO ARE YOU?"

The words boomed out of the loudspeakers again, over a crowd that had now fallen silent. Teller thought he heard a stirring on the platform. But he did not allow himself to take his eyes off Robert Schein.

Could it be his maddened imagination . . . was he already hallucinating . . . or had Schein begun, in some strange and subtle way, to disintegrate before his eyes? Teller's own senses expanded. He felt the collective fascination of America watching through the camera lens, watching something that was very much like a murder.

He knew that he had only seconds left before somebody on the stage snapped out of it and sent the goons to yank him into oblivion as though he were a piece of gristle that had landed there . . . and even now he head the heavy footsteps behind him; he planted his feet, waiting for the blow to come down . . .

"*Get away from him!*" . . . the hiss belonged to the Colonel . . . "Can't you see *we're on television!*"

The footsteps stopped. Teller spun around, smiled through his bruises into the melon faces of the bodyguards. He looked at the Colonel. The old man's entire life had come down to one

split-second decision—and he had opted for decorum. He would
not, in the end, violate the imperatives of the airwaves. The
moment had to be played out. Now his whitened face was turned
imploringly to Schein.

Teller was about to show the old man what a hideous thing
decorum could be.

He turned back to Robert Schein and placed the microphone to
his lips. In the background he was aware of men with earphones
moving quickly toward him—the minicam crew.

Jennifer Blade hurried along with them.

The air was white and cold with the essenced of arena. The
crowd was absolutely still. All the ruinous questions that candidate Schein had not been called upon to answer—could now be
laid down upon him like bludgeon blows.

The minicam's snout hovered over Teller's shoulder, leering
into Schein's quivering face. A fresh pool of light spilled upon the
golden hair, the ice-blue eyes. The very pores of Robert Schein's
skin filled the screens of shocked America.

Teller opened his mouth to deliver the first question—and
handed the microphone to Jennifer Blade.

Something persuaded him that it was her moment.

Their eyes met. She nodded almost imperceptibly. And then
Mark Teller withdrew, out of the arena, out of the light—back
into the far shadows of the stage.

"ROBERT SCHEIN, THERE ARE A NUMBER OF ISSUES WHICH YOUR
OPPONENTS CLAIM THAT YOU HAVE AVOIDED ADDRESSING YOURSELF
TO . . ."

Teller let his attention drift away from the scene, down to the
people below the scaffolding. He scanned the individual upturned faces—confused, frowning, not quite making sense of it
all. Fathers with small children perched on their shoulders.
People smoking, eating things, focusing Instamatics. The collective feral personality seemed to have flowed out of the crowd;
seemed to have broken up, to have rediffused itself into all the
fragmented impulses, the inner preoccupations, the transient
passion, of strangers gathered on a common ground to view
something—a juggler, a woman with a boa constrictor in her
purse, a body that might be drunk and might be dead, a
candidate, a beautiful child. A crowd. An audience. The same

audience that had waited down the generations, down the centuries, for television to take its mind off the pain of being human for a while.

"—CAN YOU, FOR INSTANCE, TELL THE VOTERS OF NEW YORK HOW YOU WOULD RESPOND TO THE QUESTION OF A PROPOSED FIVE PER-CENT ACROSS-THE-BOARD CUT IN FOREIGN ASSISTANCE—"

The crowd was not following the strange dialogue onstage. Its evening, begun in such high spirit and pageantry, was trickling away in anticlimax. Some confusion up there, reporters asking questions. The band wasn't playing. The night air was cold. It was time to go home.

The crowd began to dissolve, hands in its pockets.

Teller turned back to the stage. Most of the assembled dignitaries had fled the platform like thieves in the night. The little lighted pool of people left in the center—Schein, Jennifer Blade, the minicam crew—seemed somehow private, inconsequential. It was hard to believe their conversation was being watched by most of the households in America. Perhaps it wasn't. Perhaps the cameras were no longer even transmitting.

And then as Teller watched, a horrible and spellbinding thing happened. As Jennifer Blade held the microphone to Schein, Schein's entire body began to tremble. His yellow hair shimmered in the harsh light—for a moment, a trick of backlighting made it appear to Teller that a shower of sparks had erupted around his head.

The convulsion lasted only a moment. And then Schein became unnaturally still. He froze like an appliance whose cord had been snatched from the socket. Even from where he stood in the shadows, Teller thought that he could see the brightness in Robert Schein's ice-blue eyes recede into twin pinpoints of light, then disappear, leaving his face a blank screen.

He watched as Jennifer nodded to her crew and began to gather in the microphone cord. The light man switched off the beam that had bathed Robert Schein's face. Down below, in the television pit, the big cameras and lights had already shut down.

He listened to the clear footsteps as Jennifer and the crew made their way down the stairs at the far end of the platform. The interview, he imagined, had assured Jennifer of her network anchor job. Somewhere. Biggest political pulldown since Watergate. If Robert Schein still lived, he lived in Jennifer Blade.

Teller walked past the husk standing immobile in the darkness and descended the stairs of the platform. The moon was high and there was a cold energy in the air. No wonder, he realized, glancing at his wristwatch.

It was Prime Time.

from *Toot-Toot-Tootsie, Good-Bye*
(A Novel)

Yellow sunlight flooded into the little rent-a-car office, and the morning felt like Sunday. Fanning drummed his fingers on the counter top and whistled a fragment from an old tune. His nails were newly manicured; smooth and round as pennies. The morning was too fast for a Sunday; Sunday mornings were lone high saxophone notes, austere preludes to the variations of the double-header afternoons. The traffic that thrust and pounded behind his back, along the service road near Lambert-St. Louis International Airport, was fast workaday traffic. But Fanning stood outside all that. For him it was a Sunday. The fragment he was whistling was from "Toot, Toot, Tootsie! Good-bye."

"May I see your driver's license and a major credit card." The gum-chewing girl behind the counter might well have been speaking to the computerized typewriter at her red fingertips. She wore a yellow uniform dress and a matching yellow scarf, but the scarf had a penny-sized brown coffee stain down near the tip, and to Fanning that was wrong. He grimaced. The brown coffee stain spoiled something that might have been perfect, for the colors of the rent-a-car office were white and yellow, and the ashtrays were clean, and the morning light bathed the yellow and rendered everything in a clear light that left no shadows, no possibility of doubt. Everything stood certain: the ashtrays gleamed empty and waiting. The counter top ended at a point just so, and there was the window and that was the floor, and Fanning's decision was illuminated by a universe of summer-colored truth. Except for the little penny-size coffee stain on the reservationist's scarf.

Fanning studied the girl's thin chewing face as he brought his wallet out of his hip pocket. He remembered her from other times, when he and Turtle had come in here to pick up a car for a day of helling around before a night game. But she didn't give any sign of recognizing him. This, too, annoyed Fanning. As he slid out his license and credit card—the one with the intersecting orange-and-yellow circles, his name in proud relief like the tooling on an emperor's seal—he pressed his thumb against one of his gold-embossed business cards, as if by accident, an dropped it on the counter so the lettering faced her. It said:

L. C. FANNING

VOICE OF THE NATS

She glanced at it, chewing her gum, then raised her brown eyes to his smiling face.

"I won't be needing any additional identification," she said.

The car awaited him at the side of the entrance, a small mustard-colored compact, still dripping water from the automatic wash. Fanning got his suitcase squared away in the trunk. Then he took off the ash-gray cashmere cardigan he had brought along for the trip. Even in August heat Fanning never felt completely dressed in just shirt-sleeves. He arranged the sweater on a wooden hanger. This he fitted over the hook above the rear window. He had brought his Ambassador, with its peaked crown and two-and-three-quarter-inch brim. Now he removed it from his head and placed it on the front seat. He smoothed a hand back over his high forehead to set the hair in place.

He took two state road maps out of his attaché case and arranged them, folded to his route, on the seat beside the hat. He rummaged in the attaché case again until his fist was full of Life Saver packages. These he placed gently on the seat so that they wouldn't slip down the crack. On second thought, he picked up one of the Life Saver packages, a butterscotch, and got it started, pulling the small tab ribbon away until the waxed paper unfolded, exposing the first crescent of candy. He looked around until he spotted a trash barrel for the scrap. Fanning did not normally allow himself the luxury of Life Saver candy, on doctor's orders. Today was an exception.

Finally, he withdrew from the attaché case a fresh package of White Owls. He wedged these over the sun visor on the driver's side. He closed the attaché case and flipped it over the seat into the back of the car. Then he rubbed his nose several times, took a width of his limecolored checked trouserlegs between each thumb and forefinger, and pulled until they rode high and free on his shins. He settled himself behind the wheel. The pants were loose around his waist and hips now. They'd fit snug when he'd bought them just a few weeks ago. Time gets away. But the shoes on his feet felt just right. They were a new pair of tassled white loafers, the kind he and Turtle liked to wear, their hard rubber soles as fierce and inviolate as the walls of unconquered cities.

The attendant had left the engine running and the radio on. The radio was tuned to some Negro rock 'n' roll station up at the end of the dial. *Got*-cha, *got*-cha. As Fanning eased the car out into the traffic, his nostrils full of the warm molded-metal aroma of the dashboard, the syrupy vinyl of the seatcover, he twisted the dial back down toward the fat part of the spectrum. Toward the big old standard middle-of-the-road stations that he'd known about for years, the ones that covered the ball games. He tuned into a lively morning call-in show on the issues of the day. He thought he recognized the announcer's voice. He couldn't think of the name right off hand, but the voice was one of the good ones, one of the old standard voices, deep and rich as liquid gold. The voice of the eternal announcer. And he lit up his first White Owl and settled back behind the wheel to drive and listen. He wished he could think of the name.

He headed the little car south on Interstate 270, the expressway that formed an outer belt around the St. Louis metropolitan area on the western rim. As he drove, the orange morning sunlight shimmering on his windshield, it occurred to him how little of any given metropolitan area a radio announcer got to see over the course of a season. You slipped into groves. You didn't take advantage. You stay at the same hotel, you eat at the same restaurants, you play golf at the same links. All the while, the metropolitan area around you is constantly changing, expanding and you're not even aware of it; you might as well be a thousand miles away, or on the moon. A caller's voice came on the radio to wonder why it was that there were so few movies nowadays you could take your whole family to see. Fanning made himself keep a lookout for all the new developments along Interstate 270: the lowslung chrome-and-glass company headquarters that flashed by at extravagant intervals of open space, terraced and landscaped with sculpted fir trees and artificial lakes, mute architectural rebukes to the jagged upthrusting coziness of the central cities he knew. Well, you adapt with the times. He passed a valley on his left that contained a corporate headquarters set in a sumptuous verdancy of shrubbery and lawn. He glimpsed the corporate logo, a giant scarlet letter of the alphabet that seemed to rise like an iris from the land itself, and he realized that he was looking at the company that invented artificial turf for baseball diamonds.

Just south of the city of Kirkwood, he left 270 and got on Interstate 44, which knifed south and west through Missouri. Immediately the vestiges of metropolis dropped away behind him, and Fanning knew that he was in the country. On the rim of the horizon was a tree line: oak and maple and ash. The pavement under him was old now; great jagged chunks of ancient cement held together by ridges of tar. He whisked past a couple of truckers' cafés, the pennants of an amusement park, and a vast automobile manufacturing plant—white glass windshields in infinite rows—and then L. C. Fanning was in the bosom of the Ozarks.

It shocked him, at first, how the great boiling hills of the Ozarks rolled up to the very rim of St. Louis and then stopped, as if held at bay by the flimsy band of landscaped office buildings he had been observing; the "metropolitan area" now, in retrospect, an unconvincing shred. In all his trips into St. Louis over the years, Fanning had never realized the immediacy of the surrounding wilderness.

But as he rolled deeper into Missouri—skirting little towns named Eureka and Pacific and St. Clair, towns that sprang up like berries on a bush and then vanished—Fanning gave up his resistance to the boiling hills. The warm yellow light of morning had burned off into a whitish blue haze now. The world and all its possibilities opened to him. He put a match to another White Owl. He relaxed his grip on the wheel and settled his weight back into the seat. He leaned over and switched the radio dial away from the big station's call-in show; that was now a part of the world he'd left behind. He twisted through bursts of static until he located the flat voice of a middle-aged man reading the midday market reports. The man's accent was like an old tune played on a stringed instrument. It pleased Fanning. It was like a memory. It reminded him of Turtle Teweles. Fanning felt a brotherhood with the nameless announcer. He pictured the man in his cramped little studio somewhere, a fatbellied local boy with pink skin and a string tie, perched on a stool and surrounded by crumpled cigarette packages and thick sheafs of work schedules thumbtacked to the bulletin board and banks of ancient gray audio dials and a stopwatch somewhere in the mess of his desk and a girlie calendar taped up on the glass to the engineer's booth. He tried to picture how it would be if the man had any inkling he was being listened to by a famous broadcaster from the East—by L. C. Fanning himself. And he had to laugh out loud, a laugh that had been building in his belly since he left St. Louis. It was crazy, but he almost wished he had time to find the town the man was announcing from—it couldn't be far— and just pop into the station unexpected, and introduce himself and see the expression on everybody's face. The idea being that they were all fellow journeymen, all humble equals in the great brotherhood of the airwaves. Like the great Arthur Godfrey turning up in a small station somewhere, sending all the secretaries into a tizzy. Of course the local man would want to get him on the air for a few minutes, pump him about the Nats, about the tight Eastern Division race, get him on the record about his pennant picks—a real scoop for the local fans. And Fanning would have to oblige, of course. You never got so big that you couldn't take the time to give a boost to the little man in your profession, and if you ever thought you had gotten that big, God help you. Then it was time to get out.

And so he drove his mustard-colored rent-a-car with both hands firmly on the wheel (the way they used to make catches in the outfield, even the great ones; everybody had to do it the one-handed showboat way nowadays; you had television to thank for that trend); a fifty-five-mile-an-hour fleck in the rushing stream of eight-wheel rigs and flatbed pickup trucks with hard sunburned faces at the wheel, and the wild flickering motorcycle riders that were his new companions on this strange and lonely interstate slashing south and west through Missouri. Sometime after one o'clock in the afternoon the market-report announcer faded into static. Fanning's hand went to the dial automatically; he'd forgotten about the man before the needle reached the next clear station, which was playing a country and western ballad.

Near Rolla the landscape changed. The boiling hills deepened into abrupt peaks cut through with gullies and ravines. The Ozark forest crowded in on the highway's edge now. Birds with great black motionless wings circled in the blue-white sky, and once, coming out of a wide sweeping curve, Fanning caught sight of a roadside diner on the crest of a hill, beetle-shaped and silver-plated, in the style of the old cafeterias you used to find in the 1940s. He had a sudden inner vision of round gas pumps and a rainbow-colored jukebox inside. He couldn't tell for sure in the second or two that he had to glimpse it, but the place looked deserted, its curved art-deco lines oddly irrelevant to the eternal forest that pressed upon it, like a home run baseball lying abandoned in the outfield bleacher seats. Toot-toot-tootsie, good-bye.

Strangely, the image didn't depress him. (Nothing could dampen his spirits on this sunlit day.) on the contrary: the old diner reinforced a notion that had taken root in him: that on this expedition he had blundered upon the essential America that he had always believed existed, in spite of the evidence offered by the cities. (Perhaps the diner wasn't closed after all; it may just have been the time of day, getting on toward two in the afternoon, well after country people were used to taking their dinner.) These were the Ozarks: where people still worked the land and read the Bible and ate fried chicken on Sunday and listened to the radio. The cities give you a false impression of things. He smoked his cigar, tamping the ash into the tray, with an imperious flick of his finger, like a general riding through captured territory. At Rolla he turned off Interstate 44 and headed due south on a two-land highway, Route 63. For a while there was a national forest on his right. He could see blue and white tents that people had pitched. Families. He passed through towns named Yancy Mills and Edgar Springs; feed mills and stores with signs that said Bait; and running the radio dial along the band, he heard a man's voice say, "All righty, it's ninety-two degrees under Great God Almighty's fair skies."

He would say to Turtle: Why you old owlhoot.

And Turtle would say: You old hound dog.

And he would say: Why I was in the neighborhood, I thought I'd come around and see how the other half lived.

And Turtle would say: You crazy ole porkypine. You sumbitch.

And he would say: Where can a man find himself a cold bottle of Heine Meine beer in these parts?

And Turtle would say: Boys I want you all to shake hands with the greatest god damn sports announcer ever lived, L. C. Fanning, the Voice of the New York Nats. L.C. and me used to work together.

And the boys would say: *L. C. Fanning.*

And: *Toot-toot-toosie, good-bye.* Ain't that right, L.C.?

And: *Mister* L. C. Fanning. Why I lissened to you do the 'fifty-one World Series. That's the one where Thomson hit the home run in the playoff to get 'em in.

And: Off of Ralph Branca. He th'owed the pitch. Old Number Thirteen.

And: Why it's a pleasure, L.C. Heine Meine beer! Hot damn!

And he would say to Turtle: Now I have a bidniss proposition for you, if you don't think you've lost your touch. I know of a certain radio team where there might be a vacancy. Certain team looking to sign on an old pro, help carry 'em into the stretch drive.

And Turtle would say: I don't know. [Playing hard to get.] I done packed it in, L.C. Got my Bowl-A-Wile to look out for. Got my pals here. [That would hurt.] I don't need that aggervation anymore.

And Fanning (Turtle's biggest pal of all, after all) would say: Turtle, not to change the subject, but did I ever tell you the story about the time I got stuck up at the point of a gun outside Tommy Eagle's?

And Turtle would say: Boys, Tommy Eagle's is a famous honky-tonk right in the middle of New York City. It's where all the big-name ballplayers hang out, and all the writers and the sports announcers. Me and Fanning we used to drink there all the time. Ain't it the truth, L.C.?

He was coasting along the main street now of a small town whose name he had not noticed. There were sunburned squinting people lined up at a frozen-custard stand. A small movie mar-quee, jutting out over the sidewalk like a rowboat's prow, advertised: *Saratogo Trunk.* Fanning was so bemused with *Sa-ratoga Trunk* that he barely had time to hit the brakes before his car clattered over a thuddle of railroad tracks that split the middle of town. *Saratoga Trunk!* He'd seen it he didn't know how many years ago. With Eleanor. He passed gas stations, blue pennants shimmering in the hot sunlight, and then the main street ran through a brief neighborhood of white frame houses, their roofs nestled in shade trees, before the road opened up into the country again.

Front porches! In spite of the air conditioning there was perspi-ration on Fanning's forehead. He wiped it off with his handker-chief and helped himself to a Life Saver. The ashtray was growing thick with cigar butts; he would have to empty it soon. He fiddled with the radio dial until he found what sounded like another country station, a chorus of untrained women's voices singing "The Good Reuben James." He was going to need a beer or a Coca-Cola before long. But he felt good. In the clarity of the afternoon sunlight—blazing down just now on a barn roof, making the Mail Pouch lettering dance—Fanning could see the truth as clearly as he had seen Thomson's home run ball rise in flight: The great bedrock republic of his imaginings was still intact. It hadn't evaporated. It hadn't been paved over, spoiled, transistorized, turned into shopping centers, whatever the modern commentators were saying about it. Hadn't been taken over by the smart boys, the advertising hotshots, the modernistic kind of crowd that Robyn Quarrles came from. The blazes with them. The land that lay beneath the airwaves, the decent hardworking family people he broadcast to—they had never gone away after all. His eyes were wet, and a sudden memory from childhood sprang into his mind: He had drifted asleep one summer night, in his bedroom, with the radio on, the orange dial still glowing, the faraway voices still murmuring in his ear, and beyond them, the voices of his parents talking quietly downstairs. And he had awakened again, he did not know how much later, but the radio was hissing static, and in his confusion he thought he might have slept for hours—and then a dreamy panic had seized him: how much time *had* washed by in the darkness? Had he been asleep for years? The radio seemed dead; was he the only one left in time? Trembling with fear, he had thrown the sheet off and felt his way across his darken bedroom to the door. But when he opened it, he saw the light from the downstairs lamp still glowing on the stairwell; and when he listened, he heard the soft voices of his parents, talking still. The relief he had felt then had almost made him sob. Time hadn't washed by. It was as though he had been rescued from eternity. Lord, it must have been over fifty years ago that had happened. He'd forgotten it—but still, he'd never wanted to be around a stadium at night when they finally turned the arc lights out. And the old memory flooded back on him, fresh as yesterday, as he headed south.

Turtle would say: What about that new snatch sidekick of your'n?

And he would say: You mean that gash neophyte they sent us.

And Turtle would say: I mean that highheeled lipstick blond-haired little piece of Hollywood tail that come in there an' taken my job away.

And he would say: You mean Miss Yankeedoodle Poontang.

And Turtle would say: I mean Miss All-America Makes-My-Ass-Crave-Cold-Buttermilk. It's me or her. There ain't any other way I'm gonna do it. Them's my terms, L.C., and you can take it or leave it.

And he would say: Don't you worry about her, Turtle. You let me take care of Miss Robyn Quarrles.

Because he had a plan. Every contingency, every corner of L. C. Fanning's master scheme was as bright and clear as this sunlit summer day.

Yes sir. This was the Ozarks. This was the eternal heartland. The kind of country where most of the great ones came from. The Dean brothers, Paul and Dizzy, cotton-pickers from Mississippi. (Doctor to Dizzy, after examining the toe hit by that line drive in

1938, in the All-Star Game in Chicago, that ruined Diz's career: "This toe's fractured, Diz." Dean: "Fractured, hell. It's *broken*.") Ha-ha. He still had to laugh, thinking of that one. Pepper Martin, the Wild Horse of the Osage, who ran out the dugout and kissed the soil at home plate before a World Series. Vinegar Bend Mizell. Turtle Teweles. Decent, clean-cut, salt-of-the-earth boys, who represented the values of their families and their fans, of that great grandstand full of people called the United States of America. God rest her soul.

And putting it out for free for a buck nigger outfielder probably wasn't Mr. And Mrs. Average Taxpayer's idea of wholesome.

Ha-ha.

Fanning hated to use that kind of pressure. He was after all a respecter of the fair sex. But Robyn had made her own bed, so to speak. And while Fanning wasn't perhaps on the best terms lately with the press corps (thanks mostly to Miss Robyn Quarrles), he still had one or two key contacts who'd be only too happy to play around with that little tidbit of information.

Christ, he'd go to Fensterwald himself if he had to.

Getting on toward four o'clock in the afternoon, not twenty miles from the Arkansas state line, Fanning realized that his neck was sore and his pants were sticking to the seat from perspiration. This despite the air conditioning. Plus the fact that he had to see a man about a horse. He'd been holding it in for several hours now. The last radio station he'd tuned to had long since gone to static. He had been gripping the wheel with both hands since before noon, and he hadn't had anything to eat if you didn't count the Life Savers. The gas dial was wobbling near Empty. In his determination to get to Arkansas, Fanning had not taken stock of how the time had slipped away.

There was a combination diner and Texaco filling station off to the right. It sat on a harsh little island of white asphalt. Behind it was a scraggly cornfield dropping off into an indeterminate forest of scrub oak. The owner's name was painted onto a board above the filling-station door, and the diner section had been joined to the original cement structure like a tool shed. A torn screen door yawned open like a tired dog's jaw; it had the remnants of an

Orange Crush sign on it. Behind the station somebody's gray sheets hung limp on a clothesline.

In the lengthening shadows of late afternoon, the place had a pinched, forbidding air about it. But Fanning had to see a man about a horse.

A lone automobile commanded the lot by the diner: a long, pearl-gray Bonneville 500. One of the last of the full-size luxury cars. It was a few years old, but Fanning could see that the chrome gleamed to a high polish in the sun, despite the dust-choked roads the car must have traveled to get here. On the shining rear bumper was pasted a decal: an American flag.

Fanning guided his own compact to the Unleaded pump, feeling, as the car rolled to a stop, the exaggerated sense of stillness that envelops one who has been traveling at highway speeds for several hours. His muscles ached. A teen-age boy with long, caked hair and a goatee came ambling out of the station, sucking the dregs of a grape Popsicle.

The heat of the afternoon hit Fanning like a physical blow when he got out of the car. For a moment the world went purple. Then he was conscious of long shadows. He felt the hot asphalt under his shoes. He put a hand on the door to steady himself and the metal burned his hand. Damn the afternoon games to hell anyway. The kid was staring at him, the gas pump motionless in one fist. "Where's Turtle?" Fanning demanded of the parking-lot attendant. "Where's who?" said the kid. "Did he bring the net?" Fanning asked, and he could hear that his voice was loud. His throat hurt. "The *which*?" bleated the kid. The purple cleared from Fanning's eyes. He blinked. The kid retreated a step. Fanning remembered that he was in southern Missouri, not far from the Arkansas state line. "Fill 'er up," he said to the kid, who was now regarding him with chin tucked into skinny neck, as though gauging which way Fanning might jump. "I got to see a man about a horse," Fanning explained to the kid. "Which way?" The kid looked at him for a long time before he said, "Straight on th'ough 'at door."

Trudging across the hot asphalt toward the filling station men's room, Fanning noticed that the Bonneville 500 had a New York license plate. Fans of his, probably. He'd have to pay them a little surprise visit before he hit the road again.

He finished up in the men's room, which didn't have a light. On his way back to the pump he sneaked a glance inside the diner. Through the screen door he could make out two hazy figures seated at the counter. A man and a woman. Plump through their middles; middle-aged. The kind of people he had seen by the tens of thousands passing through the turnstiles at Flushing Stadium, the Polo Grounds. Solid-looking. Fanning's kind of people.

Yes. He really ought to stop in and say hello to these people before he got back on the road. The thought of it made him almost want to laugh, with a feeling like love.

He paid the boy in bills from his money clip. He got back inside the rented car and eased it away from the pump, over to the other side of the Bonneville. He transferred the White Owls from the sun visor to his shirt pocket. Stepping back into the glare of the sun, he thought about donning the ash-gray cardigan. He didn't want to. It was hot. But he hated to go sleeveless. When you're in the public eye, you have a certain image to maintain. He pulled on the cardigan. Then he picked the Ambassador off the seat, placed it atop his head, and strode into the diner.

The man and woman sat on counter stools, sipping cola through straws. On the other side of the counter a fat waitress fanned herself with a cardboard fan that had Jesus' picture and the name of a funeral home on it.

The man wore a western-style shirt and squared-toed cowboy boots. His silver hair was combed back in waves.

The woman had on a white blouse with embroidered figuring around the shoulders. At her throat was a ribboned bow tie with the ends dangling down.

The two looked up at Fanning when he entered, but no one spoke. From somewhere out of sight came the sound of religious music on a radio.

The only counter stools left vacant were in a pool of slanting sunlight, so Fanning took a seat on one. From this vantage point the place and the people in it looked dim, indistinct.

"I guess I'll have a large Coke with plenty of ice," Fanning announced to the woman behind the counter, although she hadn't asked him. He tried to roll his eyes to the left, to see whether the couple showed signs of recognizing his voice, but looking out of the glare into the dim light, he couldn't tell.

The woman behind the counter slowly got to her feet.

Fanning felt the sweat running down his back and sides. The feeling of lovelike urgency grew inside him. These people were of his generation: his audience. They would know him. It was almost as though, finding them here in the wilderness near the Arkansas state line, he had received a sign: a sign as clear as Thomson's home run ball, rising in flight.

He decided to test them right away.

"I see you folks are from New York." He put all the vibrancy he could muster into his famous voice. In the small room it seemed almost strident. People often recognized him just by his voice.

It seemed to be working. As one, the man and woman turned to him, smiling and nodding their heads.

Encouraged, Fanning extended his hand.

"Fanning's the name. L. C. Fanning."

He watched.

"Howdy *do*," said the man in a booming voice that made Fanning jump. "Hearty's the name. My real name's Donald R., but my friends call me Hale. Hale Hearty."

"Hale *Hearty*," the woman repeated pointedly, with a smile for Fanning.

Fanning turned to her. "And you must be Mrs. Hearty. My name's Fanning," he said. He paused. "L. C. Fanning."

"Oh yes," the woman cried. "Oh, yes. I'm the Little Missus. I'm Hale's Better Half. I'm *Mrs.* Hearty."

"Co'-Cola." The waitress pushed a plastic cup full of amber slush in front of him.

"Thank you," said Fanning. He cleared his throat. To the man, he said, "Well, now, how about those New York Nats anyway?"

The man said, "I'm sorry?"

The waitress said, "Fitty-fi' cen's."

Fanning reached into his pants pocket and slapped three quarters down on the counter. He glared at the waitress until she shuffled away.

He turned back to the silver-haired man with a smile on his face.

"The New York Nats," he repeated. There was no reaction in the man's face. Fanning was conscious of long shadows. How long had he been away? How much time had passed? His hand on the Coca-Cola glass was trembling.

"You mean the ball team." The man named Hearty grinned as though he had just solved a riddle, a brainteaser that Fanning had thrown at him. "We don't know about any of that," he said. "We're Angelenos, see. Why, we've just recently relocated to New York. But we put in most of our time in Los Angeles." He pronounced the *g* hard.

Fanning felt as though he had somehow been tricked. He was sweating hard now. "Well, you must have gone out to see the Nats when they come out to play the Dodgers."

"Of course *I* was born and raised in Kokomo, Indiana," put in Mrs. Hearty. "But Hale's an Angeleno all the way back."

"But I guess you must have heard a Nat game or two since you came to New York," said Fanning.

Mr. Hearty looked thoughtfully into his own Coke glass. "Well, I tell you, sir," he said after a moment. "The Missus and I are *doers*. That is, we don't believe in sitting around on our duffs. What we like to do is just pile in the car and go, see."

"It's a blessing to get away and see how people really live, without all the conveniences we're used to," said Mrs. Hearty. "Ours is such a vibrant country, and I wouldn't want to live anywhere else in the world." She turned to her husband with a radiant face.

"Myself, I'm a play-by-play man for the New York Nats." Fanning tried to make it sound like an afterthought. "I'm on the radio. Cover the baseball team, oh yes." He pulled a White Owl out of his shirt pocket. Mr. Hearty nodded and smiled.

"I don't know if you heard me," said Fanning. "I said that I am a major-league baseball announcer from New York City."

Hale Hearty winked and gave a sharp nod of his head.

"I like New York City," observed Mrs. Hearty, "but I miss the climate of Los Angeles. But I wouldn't live anywhere else in the world except the good old U.S.A., and we've been all over."

"Well, I'll tell you where all the top action is," said Hale Hearty. "Fiber optics. That's my game. Now you're a fellow in the communications trade. This is the stuff that's gonna transform the whole cable television setup. Boom! I've seen the stock triple in the last two years. Why, it is floating not one but two equity offerings." He reached over and put a hand on Fanning's shoulder; Fanning flinched. "Now you talk about an exciting bidniss to be in. Come on over to fiber optics." He winked.

Fanning clenched his fist on the counter and fought to keep himself from leaping at Hearty's throat.

"I don't suppose," he said through his teeth, "that either of you has ever heard the name Turtle Teweles."

Hearty sucked his teeth. "It doesn't ring a bell. Unless it's that new industrial supplies plant they're putting up over in Jersey."

It took a moment for Fanning to realize that he was on his feet; that the smiles on the faces of the two people were distorted with a kind of nervous fear.

He was looming over them, his breath coming in rasps.

He checked himself. Brought his wristwatch up to his face and made himself concentrate on the time.

In a few short hours it would be twilight. In a few hours Robyn Quarrles would be taking the microphone by herself at Busch Memorial Stadium in St. Louis.

Fanning took the unlighted White Owl from his mouth and placed it on the counter, as gently as a man placing a bouquet on a fresh grave.

He looked at the two friendly faces, still dim above the pool of sunlight. He said, as distinctly as he could manage:

"I'm sorry. There has been some mistake. I don't know you people after all."

Mrs. Hearty grinned and nodded. "Of course on this trip we're just about living out of a can of beans," her dim mouth said. "We can't seem to get in with the young people and have them tell us where the good restaurants are."

Fanning crossed the Arkansas state line on a country road in the late afternoon.

The day had passed by quickly. He must have been in the diner for longer than he thought. It was late. Time had slipped away from him.

His only hope now was to reach Turtle Teweles. Without Turtle, nothing else hung together anymore. Nothing made sense.

But Turtle would come back with him and be on hand for Fanning's Day. He was sure of that.

If he could only find Turtle. If only Turtle were at the place Fanning knew he must be—at the Bowl-A-Wile in the little town that Fanning had circled on the map.

If only Turtle were there.

This was the first time that Fanning had considered the possibility that Turtle might not be present at the end of his search. The thought made his hands go clammy on the wheel. In all his imaginings of what might go wrong on this journey— delays, wrong turns, car trouble, an accident, a stickup—Turtle had emerged at the end, inevitably, as visible and corporeal and eternal as a catcher squatting behind home plate when the pitcher turns to throw.

But now with the late-afternoon sunlight playing tricks on his eyes, he wasn't sure of anything. Black shadows laced the country road, cast by trees and barns. The alternating patches of light and shadow made the windshield, bug-stained now, seem to flicker, and he strained to concentrate on holding to the pavement. The blacktop road soared and dipped and curved. He wasn't used to this kind of driving. The woods and the pastureland that had seemed so open to him in the white afternoon, so emblematic of the lost America he craved, now glared at him in an angry luminous green under a red sky. White-frame churches, Baptist and Nazarene and Pentecostal, shone like burning sheet metal. He kept his eye on the speedometer; he was doing the limit. He passed boarded-up grocery stores and discount liquor stores and dust-caked ballfields and mobile homes. But he saw few people. The countryside had the empty sullenness of a vast stadium when the team was out of town. A black pickup truck shot up out of nowhere and hung on his bumper for a while, nosing across the center line and back again. Fanning scanned the rearview mirror. He expected for a wild moment to see Turtle's grinning face. But the face that looked back at him was the face of a cold-eyed girl. Fanning swerved to let her pass, his two right tires kicking up a funnel of dust as they dropped off the pavement. She was around him and gone in a flash, without looking back. Blond hair. He beat his fist on the wheel and screamed a curse, but no sound came from his throat. In an hour Robyn would be on the air.

She had known something was terribly out of kilter as soon as she arrived at the ballpark and discovered that Fanning was not there. That had been an hour and a half ago. Fanning was never less than two hours early for a game. She had delayed any action at first, praying that there was a reason for this exception; that he would somehow show.

When there was no sign of him forty-five minutes before game time, she alerted Danny Breen.

"No problem," said Breen. "You know the drill by now. I'll whip up some extra background material for you. Fasano pitched last night; Pachelbel won't be using him tonight. I'll see if Tommy'll send him up to the booth to do the color. You'll do fine. No problem."

"The problem," said Robyn, "is that L. C. Fanning is missing."

"Really?" said Danny Breen. "How can you tell?"

She steeled herself and walked into the pressbox area and asked each writer whether he had seen Fanning that day or heard whether he was ill. The writers grunted their noes without looking at her. Then she polled the press crowd still in the lounge. Then she called the hotel. And then she telephoned the police department to file the missing persons report.

She hurried down to the playing field to tape a pregame interview. She encountered Bogart Humphries in the dugout.

"Fanning didn't show up tonight. I'm worried about him. He may have had a heart attack or something in his room and nobody would know it."

Humphries, his arms folded, cap low over his eyes, made a hissing noise.

"That man didn't have no heart attack. I wouldn't be surprised if he didn't just go on and fly the coop, the way his buddy done."

"What makes you think that? that's crazy."

Humphries studied his highly polished baseball shoes. Then he turned his head to spit a line of tobacco juice—a trait that Robyn loathed—before he replied.

"Maybe Fanning can't take the competition."

"*What* competition?" Humphries had lapsed back into his

country-boy cadences, to her further annoyance. She had come to him for advice, reassurance—not smirks and riddles.

Arms still folded, he rolled his eyes to her under the bill of his cap.

"Shee-it. Man loves your ass. Way I hear it, he can't handle the fact that Bogart Humphries been beatin' out his time."

"*What?*"

Two or three players at the far end of the dugout turned, grinned.

"Hey, keep your voice down." Humphries glanced about, frowning.

"I want to know what you mean about 'Bogart Humphries beating out his time'! That's a disgusting thing to say, and furthermore I'd like to know how Fanning is supposed to know about us!"

"Hey. You know. Word gets around. I gotta run my sprints." In a sudden motion Humphries adjusted his cap, clattered up the dugout steps, and trotted down toward right field, a rippling chorus of shouts following him along the box seats.

But he didn't run fast enough to escape Robyn Quarrles's shocked, piercing cry:

"You pompous phony puffed-up . . . *bastard!*"

Now, just minutes before game time, Robyn stood at a pay telephone on the causeway that led to the WERA broadcast booth. If she chose, she could see a slice of the green outfield bathed in the stadium light, and above the wall, fans moving in their ceaseless scurry. But her head was bowed and her face was toward the wall.

The public-address system boomed with the starting lineups, so she held a finger to her free ear. On the other end of the line, tracked down at last by a WERA operator, was Jeffery Spector.

"Well, I mean I thought you'd want to *know*. Your number one announcer is *missing* and . . . sure, I can. Of course I can. That's not the point. The point is that L. C. Fanning has simply dropped out of . . . well, thanks, Mr. Spector. Thanks a lot for your concern."

By that time she was talking to a dead line. She turned away from the telephone and walked with short deliberate steps toward her broadcast booth, her head still lowered as if in thought.

When she saw the Nats pitcher, Fasano, seated in her old place at the second mike, she did not hesitate.

"Out."

"Huh? Hey, Danny Breen sent me up here to—"

"*Get out. Get out of this booth right now.*"

She didn't want to deal with Fasano. She didn't want to think about L. C. Fanning, or Bogart Humphries, or Jeffery Spector, or any other man. Their fears, their vanities, their idiocies repulsed her.

Only one thing mattered to Robyn Quarrles at this moment: The game.

Darkness had come by the time Fanning approached the Arkansas town where Turtle lived. Only a narrow ribbon of orange hung on the horizon, receding under the rich cobalt of country night, like a memory.

Fanning's neck and shoulders ached. Cold sweat matted his shirt to his ribs. His throat was giving him trouble. It throbbed with a new kind of ache, dry and pulsing at intervals—a weakening radio signal, now, on these night airwaves.

He had the window down and his elbow thrust into the cooling dark air, and when he slowed to make the turn onto the "Business Route" that would take him into the town, he became aware of crickets in the sudden silence. He stared upward at the yellow blinking intersection light with fascination, as though looking at a legendary character in the flesh. Turtle had told him about this light, illuminating the pavement and the desolate sumac beyond, and now Fanning beheld it; it was real. Turning toward Turtle's town, he felt a shudder coming over him, at least partly delicious, and he passed his hand back over his damp hair, as if to set it in place.

What lay before him was a desultory collection of shapes in the darkness: small buildings, houses with the lights out, parked cars, a darkened grocery—the town had gone to bed. Something on three legs flashed in his headlights; a glimpse of illuminated eyes, and it vanished. The town seemed entirely to have festooned itself along the two sides of the narrow macadam road.

There were two dull street-lights, one of them bringing up the colors of a Coca-Cola ad in the window of the grocery—an out-of-season Santa Claus, cheeks red and beard white, taking a swig.

Fanning slowed the car to a crawl and ducked his head, alert for clues to the whereabouts of the Bowl-A-Wile. Now the scent of the town came into his nostrils. It was a mixture of rust and gasoline and a sweet mulch, as of a creek backed up or old leaves rotting. The scent inexplicably brought tears to Fanning's eyes. Like the ribbon of orange at the bottom of the advancing night, it had the essence of memory.

He must have cruised the length of the town—about four blocks—a half-dozen times before he spotted the Bowl-A-Wile.

Actually, he heard the place before he saw it. He became aware of a muffled thud of music. At first, he thought it might be coming from somebody's radio. But then, wheeling the car around on the asphalt lot in front of the hulking grain elevator that dominated the town, he caught a flash of violet neon among trees, perhaps a hundred yards back off the road, on a rise of land littered with jagged shapes—rusting farm equipment.

Hitting the accelerator harder than he'd intended—the tires screeched on the asphalt—he swung the car about so that the headlights pointed toward the wisp of neon. The headlights were too far away to do any good, but peering through his bug-spattered windshield, Fanning was able to satisfy himself, after several minutes, that the swaying tree branches in front of the light concealed a half-extinguished script of neon tubing that had once spelled:

BOWL-A-WILE

He gunned the small car onto the macadam road, then slammed on the brakes, looking for the turnoff up the hill. Fortunately the road was otherwise deserted. It took him another fifteen minutes of retracing his route up and down the road, in ever lengthening laps, before he finally discovered the turnoff—fully a mile outside the town, and around the bend of the sloping hill on which the establishment lay.

He spotted several rows of cars and pickup trucks in a

makeshift lot illuminated by what looked like strings of Christmas tree lights. He pulled off the macadam road and stopped the car at the foot of the dirt lane leading up to the lot. He reached a nervous hand inside his pocket for a White Owl, but he had smoked them all. The inside of the windshield was filmy with tobacco smoke.

Now he could see the shape of the Quonset hut, glowing in the night—the sky was filled with stars. Turtle Teweles was inside there. He knew it. He waited until the trembling in his sides was under control. He rehearsed the things that he wanted to say. Then he reached down for the ignition, switched it on and at once heard the angry *buuuuuuurrrrrrrp!* of an engine that was already running.

He eased the car up the dirt lane, his heart going as fast as it had on October 3, 1951.

The country music thudded out from a jukebox inside. The ear-splitting throb of the bass seemed to make the very building vibrate like a tuning fork. Fanning pushed his bulk slowly from the car, the Ambassador on his head. He stood for a moment in the loud night air. He glanced upward at the skyful of stars. He tried to remember the last time he had stood out in a country night. The sudden awareness of years shocked him.

He shuddered against the memory and looked upon Turtle Teweles's Bowl-A-Wile, a spectral entity now in its ineffable closeness. In the black night—given relief by a single window at the front, from which yellow light poured—Fanning could see that the roof of the hut was crescent-shaped, an elongated rind of aluminum not more than thirty yards deep and scarcely twice the height of a man. This must be the bowling-alley part. Lashed, welded, and hammered to the front of the crescent was a smaller cabana made of corrugated scrap metal. Several beer cans littered the loose gravel near the entrance, a screen door yawning open like the lower jaw of a drunk. Fanning paused a moment before plunging through this entrance. It appeared as though the town's entire male population were stuffed into the little sardine can of a tavern.

He opened the screen door and stepped through, to a raucous enclave thick with jukebox music, ripsaw laughter, cigarette smoke, and men with dangerous eyes. He smelled stale beer and sweat and something else he could not distinguish, an aroma both acrid and sweet.

He spotted Turtle at the pinball machine.

There he was—the familiar balding crown, the elongated chin, the hard intelligent eyes. Turtle's long arms, more sinous than Fanning remembered, gripped the sides of the machine as he shook it with a violence that made a mockery of "Tilt." The rattle of Turtle's pinball machine competed with the country-music din for primacy in the general uproar.

Fanning gave a yelp and squeezed his way between two tables, each occupied by a gaggle of beery men in cloth hats like baseball caps. He forced his way toward the throbbing pinball machine, his hands outstretched. It was only when he was within four feet of the figure, on the verge of calling out Turtle's name, that he realized the man was a stranger. He turned his head, by degrees, to survey the crowded tin can of a room—to determine whether anyone had noticed his near embarrassment. Now a fresh confusion: It seemed to him that every man in the tavern had Turtle Teweles's face. Could they all be his relatives? A sweet and acrid sickness took hold of his throat, then coursed into his belly, and the room seemed to break apart, then run like liquid into colors of orange and yellow, and he saw the silver face of Hale Hearty grinning at him, uncomprehending, unlistening, and he knew then that he had found his way inside a kind of giant radio, and that all these faces were the inhabitants, the voices that lived there as he had known they did in his boyhood . . . *Ladies and Gentlemen of the Radio Audience!* . . . but the volume was too low; you could barely hear the thing from down the road, and no wonder Hale Hearty couldn't hear him, his *tubes* were giving out. . . .

He had lurched and felt his way up to a small corner of the bar, and wedged himself upright between the wall and one of the four occupied stools, and had ordered himself a beer, before it hit him with the weight of desire itself that the bartender was Turtle Teweles.

They had locked eyes at least once before, when Fanning ordered his beer. But Turtle hadn't even recognized him. . . .

Now Fanning gaped at Turtle, ogled him, wooed him with his eyes.

He hadn't changed, and yet he had. Gone were the flashy clothes that Turtle had affected as an announcer. He had on a short-sleeved shirt of some faded plaid design and a pair of stained khakis, over which he had tied an apron. He was moving up and down the short bar with a rolling gait, setting out bottles of beer and raking in change in short, professional movements. He seemed neither aloof from his clientele (as a baseball celebrity might be expected to seem) nor particularly involved with them. His face had lost its seamed, anxious expression. He looked like a man at peace.

When Turtle drew near, absently chucking quarters in his palm, L. C. Fanning, blissful between tears and laughter, reached a paw far over the bar top and grabbed Turtle by the elbow.

"Why, you old owlhoot!"

Turtle turned absently, a man distracted from private thoughts. He gave Fanning a cordial nod.

"Turtle! God dammit, it's me! It's L. C.!"

When Teweles looked back at him again, the eyes were penetrating but noncommital. Fanning waited for the flash of recognition, the sudden lunge, the old Turtle Teweles ribald grin, the uproarious cry.

What he got instead were three blinks. Turtle's eyes were as opaque as a reptile's.

The country song on the jukebox had a contemporary beat: *"Got-cha, got-cha, got-cha, got-cha."*

Turtle said, "Well, hello, L. C."

With something like a sob, Fanning blurted: "Why I was just in the neighborhood, and I thought I'd come around and see how the other half lived."

Turtle lowered his eyes to the beer in front of Fanning's heaving chest. It happened to be a Heine Meine.

"You all taken care of, now, are you."

"Turtle, for God's sake, it's me! It's L. C.! Can you hear me, Turtle?" In the din of the place he could barely hear his own voice, and he wondered wildly whether anything was coming out. But the warm bulk he'd been leaning against suddenly shifted. The man on the stool next to him slid out of the way with a curse and muttered, "Don't go gittin' you balls in an uproar, Grand-daddy!"

Fanning crashed onto the vacant stool without being aware of the motion. Turtle was staring at him fixedly now, like a man coming out of hypnosis.

"Do you recognize me, Turtle? Turtle, god dammit, do you hear me?" He groped crazily in his mind for the speech he'd rehearsed—all about his plan to get rid of Robyn, ruin her name so she would no longer be around to torment them. About how essential it was for the two of them to be together in the booth again. About the rhythms, the undefined but nonetheless sacred rightness of things that must be restored, to make it all come put pure and redeemed on the last day of the season, on Fanning's Day.

But all he could think to say now in the uproar of the tin tavern, this garbled inside of the giant radio set on the side of the nighttime Arkansas hill, was: "Turtle, can you hear me? Do you understand me, Turtle? Do you hear me?"

from *Super Tube: The Rise of Television Sports*

The Iceman Clowneth

On Saturday, Atlantic City is plastered by fog. But nobody has come here for the weather. Atlantic City was never what you'd call a weather type of town. Atlantic City's idea of weather is a thermostat. Inside the Atlantic Room, on the mezzanine level of the Tropicana Hotel, the weather remains the same as it always is: under control.

But even the visibility inside the Atlantic Room is limited today. Its Kiwanis-luncheon dimensions are choked with men and women who have come to see what the television lights are all about. Shouldering their way around the center of the room are half a dozen NBC Sports production people dressed in their official network windbreakers, one famous network sportscaster, a few cosmeticky women whose stiletto heels suggest a kind of festivity but whose faces seem stunned, and finally, the men: some of them young and lean and mustachioed, most of them middle-aged and short and thick. All the men are clad in nylon warmup suits with personal monograms ("Lou") stitched on the front. All the men are as expressionless as the fog. These people are the media chroniclers, the wives and girlfriends, the managers and trainers of professional boxers, and a few actual boxers—the inner circle of the fight crowd.

But this is not a Fight Crowd as Norman Mailer or Budd Schulberg would understand fight crowds. These people lack the suppressed eroticism that has always elevated fight people into folk myth. This, it strikes me, is the *made-for-television* fight crowd.

* * *

NBC Sports has come to telecast boxing matches from the Tropicana. On Friday, three white Freuhauf semitrailer trucks with the NBC Peacock painted on the sides rolled down to Atlantic Avenue from Rockefeller Center in New York. The three Freuhauf trucks (Mobile Unit N-2, as they were collectively known) have brought with them three RCA TK-760 "hard" color cameras; one RCA TK-76 minicam; three videotape machines; two hand-held "shotgun" microphones; several small lavalier mikes; a Chryon character-generator for creating names, statistics and other captioned information on-screen; a "video control area" complete with power supplies to feed voltage through Triaz cables and then to the cameras inside the hotel; a transmission area where technicians will monitor the visual signal as it leaves the truck and flashes first to New York and then over the NBC network; a maintenance bench area; and a miniaturized but self-contained control room, complete with some twenty television monitor screens on the forward wall, seats and desk space for five production staffers, a brace of headset phones for communicating with NBC people inside the hotel, as well as in New York, five wall telephones, innumerable clipboards, and, most important, the control room's nerve center, a sprawling panel of levers and square plastic buttons that glow in color-keyed hues of yellow, red, and green. This instrument, known as a Grass Valley Switcher and operated by the crew's technical director, will translate the verbal commands of the director, as he selects from possible camera shots displayed on the various monitor screens, into the "line" picture seen by NBC viewers across the country.

In addition to the equipment, the NBC Sports contingent also includes a manpower force of twenty-one staff technicians, five production assistants, a unit manager, a floor director, a "compliance and practice" supervisor, a public relations man, and a pro forma representative from NBC's executive management—in this case, the manager of technical sports operations.

Marv Albert, the most prominent of the three announcing Albert brothers, has come down from New York to handle the blow-by-blow duties for the telecast. Flying in to join Albert, from his residence in Tampa, Florida, is Dr. Ferdie Pacheco, the celebrated "Fight Doctor," who will provide color commentaries and feature interviews.

The fight people step back when Pacheco struts into the room. He is one of them; he is the surrogate TV star for all the hard, aging hipsters in the gyms and in the casinos who know the fight game and like the lights. Pacheco is a practicing medical doctor, but he talks in the fast impersonal patter of a good lounge comic, and he wears his collars open, the points as long as Sammy Davis's. Pacheco was once Muhammad Ali's personal physician, a fact he is not exactly shy about mentioning. His curious compulsion for one-line gags, and a certain shrewdness about the fight world, attracted the network peoples' attention, and Pacheco found himself, suddenly, in fleshy middle age, a TV celebrity. Now Pacheco has consolidated an impressive amount of power inside NBC Sports: besides his on-air commentator role, Pacheco is the man who approves—and sometimes informally arranges— every bout telecast on NBC.

What this means is that Dr. Ferdie Pacheco controls the destiny of every fight person in the Atlantic Room. In the 1980s, each television network has assembled what amounts to a repertory cast of fighters. Each network has its own version of Pacheco, a sort of impresario on the lookout for fresh talent. But this is television. Boxing talent isn't enough. A certain panache is also necessary; a knack for projecting warmth and sincerity—a way of relating to people. To have a chance at landing a spot in a network repertory, a professional American fighter—typically a young man, black or ethnic, trying to pummel his way out of poverty—is expected to be at the same time charming and articulate and clever: if not another Ali, then at least a Donny Osmond with eight-ounce gloves.

In the crowded Atlantic Room now, a small young man has taken a seat on one of the two wooden chairs positioned in front of some red velvet drapes that reflect the glare of the television lights. The young man has a peaceful Hispanic face. He is wearing a brown velour warmup suit. Except for the faint beginnings of scar-tissue crescents on his forehead and cheekbones, he might be mistaken for one of the Tropicana's bellhops, or a car-park attendant.

This is the featherweight boxer José Nieto. Nieto is one of fourteen children in a family so poor that its idea of upward mobility was to flee the Bronx for Honduras. That happened when José was four. He learned the trade of fighting as a child in Honduran slums. An aunt brought him back to New York when he was ten. He spent his teenage years in and out of detention homes. But José Nieto had his eye on the American middle class. He harnessed his brutality; made it respectable: he learned to box. He won the New York Golden Gloves, fought in the Marines. He got married, enrolled in a community college. Now, at age twenty-seven, José Nieto is one day away from boxing on television. His appearance on NBC will bring him about seventy-five hundred dollars.

Nieto will earn every cent: his opponent will be a former United States Boxing Association featherweight champion named Rocky Lockridge, whose 24–2 pro record included nineteen knockouts. Rocky Lockridge is the number-two ranked feather-weight in the world. As an amateur he fought 218 matches, winning 210.

But before he can climb into the ring with Lockridge, José Nieto must endure a trial for which his childhood of back-street violence hardly prepared him: he must record a television interview that will be put on the NBC airwaves just before his fight. The interview will establish to the American public what a charming, articulate, and clever guy José Nieto is; what a *cuddly* sort of guy. If Nieto performs well in the interview, his value as a promotable personality will soar. Of course, it will help if he wins the fight. But in TV boxing, winning is not necessarily everything. "I want to put on the air the kind of folks I'd like to see when I'm sitting at home," Pacheco told me earlier. "I want to see *real people* fighting."

But even before Ferdie Pacheco can commence the interview with Nieto, there is one additional layer of preparation.

Towering over Nieto now is a figure who might have stepped from the bosom of a highly affluent, rather suburban rock band. This figure is lean and flat-bellied like a lead guitarist, and his razored mane of red hair and beard sparkle when he glides into the field of TV lights. But his clothes are about power. In a roomful of people for whom "casual" is a sort of sacred ordeal, his own casualness seems almost catatonic: pale brown hopsack jacket over an open-collar dress shirt of rich blue with white pinstripes. The gray suede slippers are by Gucci.

This is Mike Weisman, one of network television's hottest young sports producers. Weisman, who is thirty-two years old, earns five hundred thousand dollars a year for producing NBC Sports programs. His authority in the room is tacit but unquestioned: "What we're gonna do is, we'll do what we call 'word association,'" Weisman is explaining in a slightly overmodulated voice to Nieto's upturned face. Some of the aimless shifting around in the Atlantic room stops. People begin to peer toward the TV lights. A cameraman is adjusting the focus of the minicam aimed at Nieto.

"Which means," continues Weisman, "that if we give you a word, you say the first thing that comes into your mind." Weisman pauses. He gazes down at José Nieto. José Nieto stares upward at Weisman. "Sometimes funny things come out of it," Weisman informs Nieto. Another pause. "Sometimes serious things come out." Yet another silence.

Weisman brings his hands together in a clap of finality that sounds just a shade forced. "Whatever comes to your mind," he repeats. "It's just as if we opened your mind, and whatever came out." Nieto listens. "We've done it with several fighters," Weisman assures him. "Trust us," he tells Nieto. "Believe me," he says. He hesitates for a moment, his hands still clasped. "Don't think about it," he suggests.

Ferdie Pacheco is now moving briskly through the onlookers and into the pool of television lights. He carries a clipboard in one hand. Nieto's body gives up some of its tension as Pacheco replaces Weisman under the lights and sits down on a chair opposite the fighter. Here, at last, is a known quantity.

Mike Weisman plunges from the pool of TV lights into the larger dimness of the Atlantic Room; it is as though someone suddenly switched his hair and beard off. He seems thankful that his conversation with Nieto is over.

I ask Weisman to explain the reason behind the word-association game with Nieto.

"My feeling is, I'm bored with just talking heads," Weisman whispers as Pacheco waits for his cue to begin. "Plus, the important thing is, we're learning something important about these kids. You get some really revealing responses on this game. We threw the word 'KO' at Alex Ramos a few weeks ago. You know what his comeback was? *'I hope to get up and finish strong.'* Revealing. He went on and lost the fight."

A few days later, in New York, I would ask another young NBC Sports programmer why he thought this sort of interview was in vogue. His answer was more blunt. "American television is always trying to advance the myth of a classless society," he said. "There isn't supposed to be any underclass in TV's view of the world. Americans associate boxing with a seamy, sort of barbaric segment of society. So naturally the impulse would be to make these guys cuddly and lovable. They're coming into our living rooms."

In the Atlantic Room, Mike Weisman checks his wristwatch and decides to get the Nieto interview going. He nods to the director. The director calls for quiet in the room. The minicam goes hot, the videotape rolls, and Dr. Ferdie Pacheco begins throwing words at José Nieto.

"Goal," is the first word on Pacheco's clipboard.

Nieto's face creases in thought. The dark brows draw together. He is silent for so long that one begins to suspect he may not have heard the question.

"Uh—*to win*," he murmurs, finally.

Pacheco is ready with another one. "Hero."

Again, Nieto sinks into some private abyss. Moments pass. Throats are cleared. Will someone offer a clue from the sidelines?

"*Uh—I'm one.*" Nieto steals a glance at Pacheco. The doctor's face is noncommittal; the answer apparently stands.

"Family."

Another pause, but not quite so vast this time; Nieto is getting the hang of it. "*Reunion.*"

"Fear."

"*None.*" At last, an easy question.

"Pain."

"*Defeat.*" Nieto is looser now, faster; he is perhaps beginning to sense that he can go the distance.

"Dream." *"Crown."*

*"*KO*." "Finish quick."*

"The greatest. *"Duran."*

"Hate." *"In the ring."*

"Food stamps."

Nieto does a take. The whole *room* does a take. *Food stamps?* What the hell kind of—? José Nieto is suddenly in trouble; that one came out of nowhere. *Food stamps.* You can almost see him trying to mentally cover up, wait for the bell . . .

Then Ferdie Pacheco bangs his clipboard on the top of Nieto's head and lets out a horselaugh. "Food stamps" was his little way of ending the session. A *joke.* The entire room chuckles. Once. José Nieto looks relieved. He has endured his "audition." Or so he thinks.

"Let's do it again," calls out Weisman.

Boxing once again found its way back to mainstream respectability on television. Just as Muhammad Ali single-handedly revived the sport in the sixties following the trauma of racketeering investigations and the demise of James Norris, another savior emerged to erase the taint of corruption that settled over ABC's 1977 "United States Boxing Championships." Sugar Ray Leonard.

Like Ali, Leonard restored to boxing a needed cachet of glamour, sexuality, and human charm. Unlike Ali, who became an antihero in a political age, Leonard was a hero in a new, apolitical disco age. When he fought Thomas (Hit Man) Hearns for the welterweight championship on September 16, 1981, the various closed-circuit telecasts of the bout reached 250 million human beings—one-sixteenth of the earth's population. Boxing was indeed back in style.

But in 1982, boxing was in style for another reason that had to do with network television's own interests. Already convinced that the threatened NFL players' strike would become a reality in the fall, the three networks were moving quickly to orchestrate large-scale viewer interests in "backup" sports that they could move into Sunday afternoons in the absence of football games. Boxing was the most logical backup sport. There were those in network TV, in fact, who believed that boxing, and not football, was the real TV game. The affinity between the sport and the medium was primal: boxing was drama compressed to an intensity perfectly expressed within the charged energy of the small flat screen. It was drama shorn of all complexities and qualifications—force against force, played out violently upon a bright, stark, claustrophobic landscape. It was the ultimate content of television—simplistic, random, morally neutral, pure sensation without past or future.

The matches in Atlantic City were a part of the first phases of this buildup. They took place several months before the new revival in boxing culminated in yet another dark, grotesque series of episodes: the fatal beating, televised on CBS, of the Korean Duk Koo Kim by the fists of Ray (Boom Boom) Mancini in November 1982; the shocking and prolonged pounding administered to Randy (Tex) Cobb by heavyweight champion Larry Holmes on ABC a couple of weeks later—a fight that inspired Howard Cosell to swear angrily that he would never again call a professional boxing match on TV.

In the Atlantic Room, Mike Weisman is back inside the pool of TV lights. Now he is going over some interview ground rules with another fighter: a middleweight named Bobby Coolidge, a twenty-nine-year-old left-handed boxer from Foley, Minnesota. Coolidge, whose professional record stands at 20–2–1, is nicknamed "The Iceman." Tomorrow, the Iceman will make his television debut; as with Nieto, the price will be high. Coolidge is scheduled to meet an Eastern seaboard legend on the rise: the baby-faced twenty-year-old Bobby Czyz, an unlikely mixture of brutality and intellect. Czyz graduated sixth in his high-school class of 330 and secured an appointment to West Point military academy. He decided to box instead. He has knocked out twelve of his first seventeen professional opponents, and no one has beaten him.

For the Iceman interview, Weisman has hit on a different premise. Now the crew is dragging its lights, cameras, cables, and microphones to the other end of the Atlantic Room and is reassembling this equipment directly in front of a large potted palm.

At first glance, Iceman appears to be the sort of personality who might make José Nieto look, by contrast, like Richard Pryor.

Tall and rangy, his blonde hair cropped close to his skull, Iceman peers at Weisman through flat blue eyes, over a nose whose cartilage has already been reshaped to a simulation of Dick Tracy's. He does not particularly strike one as a natural choice for cockamamie TV boxing hijinks. Nevertheless, Weisman is giving it a try.

". . . When he says *that*," Weisman is telling Iceman, "we're gonna turn on the *fan*." As he did with Nieto, Weisman pauses expectantly. There is not a great deal of visible reaction from Iceman.

"It's gonna be funny," continues Weisman. "It really is. You're gonna think he's gonna be *yelling* at you—and he *is* gonna be yelling at you. Then *you* say, 'Would you excuse me, Dr. Pacheco?' And you walk off the set, and . . . we're gonna do this a few times. Trust us. Don't worry."

Iceman studies Weisman for a long moment. He strokes his chin. It seems as though everyone in the Atlantic Room is hypnotically fixed on Iceman's moving fingers.

Then Iceman grins.

The effect on Weisman is electric. He all but springs into the air.

"*He likes it!*" screams Weisman. "*We got it!*"

Ferdie Pacheco materializes beside Iceman. At the same instant, an NBC technician begins to hurry toward them through the crowd. The technician is delicately cradling a Galaxy twelve-inch oscillating fan with bright blue blades. The technician abruptly flops down to the floor, on his back. He plugs the fan into a socket, flips the switch to "on," and aims the fan upward, so that its breeze hits Iceman and Pacheco.

Back out of camera range, Mike Weisman is whispering again. "Here's the bit," he says. "What we try to do at NBC is entertain as well as inform. Here, we're playing off Iceman's nickname. The bit's gonna be that Ferdie starts off telling the viewer that 'we're awaiting the arrival of Iceman Coolidge.' He's playing it very straight. Then he said, 'I think I hear Iceman now,' and the fans starts blowing Ferdie's hair. You won't actually *hear* any wind; they'll dub it in New York. But Ferdie's gonna raise his voice. He conducts a normal interview with Iceman, but all the time this terrific wind is blowing. Halfway through it, Iceman leaves the set for a minute. The wind stops blowing. When he comes back again, the wind starts up. So we can see it's the Iceman's wind. You got it?"

In the interviewing area, another NBC technician has now dropped crosslegged to the floor. He is gripping the potted palm by its base. He begins to shake it, so that the branches move as if in a gale. Someone notices that the Galaxy twelve-inch oscillating fan is not having much of an effect on Pacheco's thinning hair. Weisman orders a search for a larger fan. Pacheco calls across the room to Marv Albert, "Hey, Marv, loan me your hair a minute, will you?" After several minutes, a second fan—a square window model—is produced and trained on the two men.

Iceman is now getting deeply absorbed in the mood of the moment. "Can you hear me all right?" he calls professionally to the sound men in a high, reedy voice.

Weisman orders a couple of takes. Iceman performs his role with a certain rakish abandon, but something is missing from the heart of the scene.

"Is there any *intrinsic motivation* for Iceman to leave the set?" wonders an assistant producer.

"I got it," says Weisman. "It'll be: 'Iceman—*telephone!*'"

There is still not enough wind to unsettle Pacheco's hair. Mike Weisman begins to prowl the Atlantic Room. He snatches up a large cardboard rectangle—it is a billboard announcing a Tropicana nightclub act—and thrusts it at a stagehand. "Wave this," Weisman commands.

The crew tries another take.

"Cut," yells Weisman. "Shiver, Doc, shiver! You're dyin', Doc! Shiver."

Another take.

"I understand you do roadwork with a goat," Pacheco shouts at Iceman. "I understand you live in an earth shelter."

"No, no, no, no," calls Weisman. "He starts to walk off when you say 'southpaw.'"

Another take. Perhaps forty minutes have gone by now.

"I don't know how much longer I can do this," says the stagehand who has been waving the cardboard. "My thumbs are killing me."

"Get him out after 'southpaw,'" calls Weisman.

"I thought all I had to do was box," quips Iceman Coolidge. Everyone laughs. Once.

NBC Sports is scheduled to originate live from the Tropicana at 3:00 P.M. Sunday, May 23. NBC Sports' broadcast day at the Tropicana gets underway at 3:00 A.M. It is at this hour that Howard Strawbridge begins his prowl. The last floor show from the Tropicana's main showroom has ended ninety minutes ago. The sequined chorus girls and the tuxedoed comics are gone now, and the only sound in the vast, draped hall is the grinding clatter of a huge elevated cubicle that the hotel's black-shirted stagehands are dragging out to the center of the floor. This is the boxing ring.

The ring will come to rest beneath a square perimeter of forty quartz lights suspended from the room's ceiling. These lights will blaze into the eyes of customers at ringside as they peer up at the fighters, turning what was historically a privileged section for the loftiest of high-status spectators into a test of the will, a migraine zone for the stars. Can't be helped; these are television lights— Howard Strawbridge's lights—and the ringsiders are used to it by now: More than a few of these customers, the women as well as the men, look as if they'd like to see the light that can make them blink.

(Veteran TV cameramen like to reminisce about the early days of telecasting fights from Madison Square Garden, in the mid-1940s. After the first few weeks of television's invasion, there began to appear vacant seats where once had reposed New York's crème de la crème of politics, show business and the underworld. It wasn't the bright lights that drove these diamond-pinkied dignitaries away, however—it was the realization that their faces were appearing on television. Right alongside their mistresses'.)

From 3:30 to 8:30 A.M., Howard Strawbridge will tinker with the forty quartz lights, standing on a stepladder, twisting each just so with his long, slender fingers, into the wee hours, until each individual beam is precisely focused and coordinated with the chroma level of the three RCA TK 760s mounted on scaffolding at the edges of the room. Then Strawbridge will turn his attention to the half-dozen smaller lights, each coated with a color gel (three orange, three blue) that hang among the quartz lights. "I like to have a little something on one shot that we can 'refer to,'" says Strawbridge, "and in this case, that happens to be the star filter that we use on our wide shots. You'll see the ring from a distance, and above it what look like these long daggers of light—orange and blue. That's done by a mesh filter we put over one of the lenses; it reflects these color gels like a prism. If you'll notice on your screen, the whole shot is darker when the star filter is in use. That's because it filters out a lot of the light that we've keyed for our normal shots."

When Strawbridge comes down off his stepladder, he will still have work to do. He must next attend to the several "foot candles" beaming upward from below the level of the ring. Without these lights, the fighters would appear to be wallowing in a waist-deep fog.

By the time he is finally finished, Strawbridge will be wallowing in a fog of his own. He will try to force himself to sleep for four or five hours in his hotel room before he must report to the truck and supervise the lighting quality for the actual telecast.

At around ten o'clock in the morning Jimmy Nottingham wanders down from his own hotel suite into the boxing area. That is Nottingham's job: to wander around. To put it bluntly, Nottingham is a snoop. His official title is "supervisor of compliance and practice." What that means is that Nottingham must maintain eternal vigilance against ushers who wear straw hats with "Tropicana" printed on the crown; for cornermen in the ring who have "Tropicana" stitched on the backs of their shirts; for large posters placed casually in the main camera's line of sight that say "Tropicana," even for the name "Tropicana" on the ring's canvas itself. Nottingham doesn't have anything in particular against the hotel Tropicana. He must ferret out similar subtle gambits of commercialism wherever the NBC Sports cameras go. It seems that while television has no inhibitions about bending sports to its own needs, television is grievously offended at the thought of being similarly used.

"It's a constant dogfight," Nottingham says with the cheerful air of a man who loves a good contest—any good contest. Not too many years ago, Nottingham was punting footballs for Yale, and he still keeps himself in athletic trim—although he says he has never *forcibly* removed anybody's Tropicana hat.

"I have to look at everything," Nottingham continues. "Here I'll check out the boxing ring's cornerpost pads, the ring mat, the fighters' *trunks* . . . Yesterday we taped a fight at another hotel in town; we wanted to have something in the can in case today's fight run short. This place, if you can believe it, had a *neon sign* spelling out the hotel name right above the main exit door. It was directly in the main camera's field of view. The hotel people told us it was a fire law requirement; it pointed out the exit. Well, I called up the fire marshal. He said it was a lie. But the sign was up, and we couldn't unhook it without short-circuiting the room's entire power supply."

So what did NBC do? Swallow its moral sense and telecast the neon sign?

Nottingham looks extremely bored. "Naw," he says. "We made an adjustment. What the hotel people don't understand is that we can make a fight look as though it is being held inside a barn in the Midwest if we want to. Plus, we instructed the announcers to not even mention the hotel name once, like we usually do."

"Compliance and practice" people are relatively new components of TV sports crews. They began cropping up not long after CBS embarrassed itself with the winner-take-all tennis series fiasco.

"But the commercialism thing is all over," says Nottingham. "Sometimes it's hard to control. Take auto racing. You've seen those cars with their oil-company stickers, their tire labels on the side, the works. How is a TV network gonna control *that*? Well, luckily for us, I guess, that problem sort of solved itself. The advertising guys at the agencies started to get smart. They realized those stickers were kind of hard to read when a car was going about 180 mph. So instead of stickers and signs, they'd just start painting the *whole car* in the color of a brand-name oil can. They counted on the public to recognize the design and make the connection, based on the TV commercials. Sort of subliminal, you know."

Shortly before 2:00 P.M. on Sunday, Mike Weisman concludes a production staff meeting in the Atlantic Room. He returns to his hotel suite and changes into a fresh pair of slacks and a clean shirt. He takes an elevator to the lobby, pushes his way through the crowds of gray-haired gamblers and through the revolving glass doors that lead to the limousine arcade. He climbs the four iron steps up to the NBC mobile van, opens the heavy cream-colored door, ducks his head and enters a small, unventilated, harshly lighted metal-gray enclave, already acrid with cigarette smoke.

This is Mobile Unit N-2's self-contained control room with its twenty TV monitor screens, its battery of telephones and its master switching unit. Seven men, sitting in three rows and facing the monitor screens, will compose the live boxing telecast from Atlantic City. They include, besides producer Weisman, a director, a technical director (who punches the buttons on the switcher an instant after being ordered to do so by the director), an associate director (who keeps track of elapsed time, down to tenths of seconds), a production assistant, a manager of sports operations, and the lighting director.

It is here that Mike Weisman, no longer the whimsical, half-cajoling young impresario of the day before, will rule like Captain Bligh for the next four hours.

Back at Rockefeller Center in New York, a functionally identical but much larger control room is filling up with its own technical crew. This is Studio 6A, the nerve center of NBC *SportsWorld*. With its shag carpeting, its spotless white walls and panel surfaces, its three graduated tiers of desks facing a wall of large monitor screens; with microphones twisting up like steel cobras on their adjustable metallic coils, and with square yards of dark audio knobs and colored video buttons, Studio 6A looks like the bunker that will someday decide the fate of the earth.

The commander-in-chief of Studio 6A is Linda Jonsson, a tall and decisive blonde woman of thirty-two. Jonsson is the coordinating producer of NBC *SportsWorld*. Connected by a direct phone line to Mike Weisman in his truck, Jonsson will exercise final authority over the product that Weisman beams in from Atlantic City. It is her job to integrate these images with commercial breaks, videotaped material, and other programing elements that will compose the finished look of *SportsWorld*.

Because of time considerations, NBC has decided to telecast the Nieto–Lockridge bout an hour before *SportsWorld* goes on the

air, under the improvised title of "Ringside." The Iceman Coolidge–
Bobby Czyz fight will be telecast within *SportsWorld*, because
Czyz is one of NBC Sports' designated stars. The network has
promoted him heavily, and is counting on him to draw a large
audience to *SportsWorld*. A taped interview of Czyz will also air
before the fight. But unlike the Iceman Collidge interview, this
one will show Dr. Ferdie Pacheco as serious, even respectful.

At twenty seconds before 3:00 P.M. on Sunday, May 23, the
associate director inside Mobile Unit N-2 calls out, "Here we go,
everybody. Have a good one." This will be the last clearly audible
remark anyone utters for the rest of the telecast.

"Ten seconds to time," says the associated director, as Mike
Weisman commands, "Cue the theme."

At 3:00 P.M., the NBC "Ringside" graphics flash across TV
screens around the United States. There is a commercial followed
by Ferdie Pacheco's whimsical word-association game with José
Nieto from the day before.

Marv Albert appears live on-screen to introduce the Nieto–
Rocky Lockridge fight (*"in what should be a brawl . . ."*) but
Weisman isn't listening. He is intent upon an off-air monitor
screen, a pan of faces at ringside.

"That's her," he shouts suddenly. "That's Rocky's wife!"

"Rocky Lockridge's wife," the director echoes into his headset
microphone. The cameraman inside the Tropicana freezes the
shot, zooms in close. If Lockridge, the heavy favorite, begins to
assume control of the fight, Weisman will order a "Quantel" of
Mrs. Lockridge: a facial closeup, electronically compressed and
then superimposed, in a corner, over the principal fight shot.

There is a commercial break ("Wait for local! Wait for local!"),
and then a long shot of the fighters at center ring, hearing the
referee's instructions under the blue-and-gold dagger points of
Harold Strawbridge's star filter.

And then the bell sounds and the Nieto–Lockridge fight
begins.

"Ready trunks," calls out the director, and the associate
director positions his fingers above a colored switcher button.

"Trunks." On-screen, a logo appears, linking the name of each
boxer to the color of his trunks.

"Lose the trunks."

The early rounds are not a howling success for José Nieto, of word-association fame. "There he stands," comes Pacheco's voice. "He's been rocked in almost every round, there he stands—he certainly hasn't taken a step backward, has he?"

"Oh, a *combination by Lockridge*," groans Albert, who sounds almost pained at the sight. Weisman leans to his right and issues a terse order to the director, who passes it along into Albert's earpiece. Weisman has decided that NBC will stay live, rather than cut to a commercial break, before round four begins.

Albert says, "Let's listen in on the corner of José Nieto between rounds." Simultaneously, in the noisy truck, the associate director is counting off the seconds to a videotape replay from the minicam at ringside. The home viewer can see Nieto, his face turned upward and his open mouth sucking air, while the clearly audible voice of his trainer screams: "How come you're gettin' hit, Joe? You gotta move to your right; as you move in, you gotta keep on movin' to your right . . ."

"I like to get audio from the losing fighter's corner," Weisman had remarked earlier in the day. "It's always more interesting."

During round four, Weisman orders the Quantel shot of Rocky Lockridge's wife. Her voice can be heard screaming, "Get that *jab* out there!" In round five, a cameraman locates Nieto's wife, Chi Chi. The closeup of her face reminds one of the women in the Atlantic Room the day before: stunned.

"And a *right* by Lockridge," Albert yells. "And an *uppercut* by Lockridge!"

In round six, Albert—with prodding from Weisman—reminds the viewers that in the word-association test, Nieto's response to the word "fear" was "none."

In round seven, NBC's ringside sound man picks up Nieto's trainer screaming, "I know you can do it! *Don't let me down!* Don't give him no space. Don't give him no damn space, Joe!"

With twenty-six seconds remaining in the eighth round, it is suddenly over. Nieto is still on his feet, but he has collapsed against the referee's chest. "Nieto had *no idea* where he was," Marv Albert bawls. Inside the Mobile Unit N-2, there is suddenly a bedlam of shouting voices. But the commotion has nothing to do with the fortunes of José Nieto, yesterday's Atlantic-Room darling.

"Think about the clock!" comes Weisman's voice, rising above the others. He orders several videotape replays of Rocky Lockridge's decisive flurry against Nieto. The associate director begins counting down to the videotape as Weisman continues to scream commands.

Weisman changes his mind. "We don't need any videotape!" he shouts. The associate director reflexively continues count a beat or two. *"Lissen to me!"* Weisman screams. *"Gimme a freeze-frame!"* His voice lowers. "Just trust us," he says. Then another impulse seizes him. "Get a closeup of Carolyn Lockridge!" A cameraman isolates the winner's wife. She looks pleased.

The associate director, John Filippelli, looks at his stopwatch and recommends a thirteen-second summation of the fight from Marv Albert, to be heard under the freeze-frame, and the director orders it. Outside, Albert at once begins to improvise remarks covering exactly thirteen seconds, while voices from the truck ring in his earpiece.

"No commercial," Weisman barks, over the voice of the director. "Think about the clock! Think about time!" As Weisman shouts, his voice mingles with that of the director, who is shouting for Pacheco to begin his interview with Lockridge. "We'll go directly to the undercard!" shouts Weisman. The assistant director begins to compute the time lengths of various subsidiary bouts that had been videotaped earlier for use in just such an emergency.

Inside the ring, the victorious Rocky Lockridge babbles happily away to Ferdie Pacheco's questions. José Nieto is nowhere in sight. Lockridge never mentions him by name; neither does Pacheco. It is as though Nieto already belongs to another time.

Back in Studio 6A in NBC Rockefeller Center, Linda Jonsson is dividing her attention between the monitor screens and the clock. She is thinking about time. Her own exercise in anxiety will commence at four o'clock. Exactly two hours later, with complete indifference to her best or worst timing efforts, *Weekend News* will replace *SportsWorld* on the NBC airwaves. If every one of Jonsson's programing decisions in those two hours is correct, *SportsWorld's* final credit will fall from the screen within a tenth of a second of 5:58 P.M., leaving exactly two minutes for commercials before the news.

Iceman Coolidge's test against Bobby Czyz will be the featured event in this day's *SportsWorld*. But while the fight represents a seminal event in the life of Coolidge, and perhaps in that of Czyz as well, for Linda Jonsson it represents only irritation. The fight will be the only live event on *SportsWorld*. It could last ten rounds, or it could last ten seconds. What that means is that Jonsson and her staff will have to add or delete videotaped segments according to the fight's length. That is, they will edit *SportsWorld* even as the show unfolds, constantly subtracting elapsed time and trimming the videotaped events to fit the remaining time. This harrowing skill is known as "collapsing." Among the components on Linda Jonsson's videotape reels are the interviews with Iceman Coolidge and Bobby Czyz, some sumo wrestling bouts from Tokyo, and highlights from the World Invitational Mixed Pairs Body Building Championships from Las Vegas.

But the fight will be irritating for Jonsson in still another way. After every three-minute round, she must decide whether to cut to a commercial or stay live at ringside. Commercial breaks are moments of crisis in network strategy. Viewers use them as opportunities to flick from channel to channel with their remote-control switches. Every three minutes, Jonsson must risk losing most of her audience to CBS *Sports Sunday* or to ABC's *Wide World of Sports*. To minimize this risk, she must monitor the programing developments on those competing programs, as well as keep abreast of the ticking clock—trying to time her own breaks to coincide with flat moments on the competing channels. And to add the final measure of irritation that Linda Jonsson must deal with during the Iceman–Czyz match, she knows that even as she monitors CBS and ABC, CBS and ABC are monitoring her.

At 4:30 P.M., the ring announcer in Atlantic City announces the featured Czyz–Coolidge fight. The core of tension, both in Mobile Unit N-2 and in Studio 6A, is about to be plumbed. The opening bell sounds. Iceman Coolidge, NBC's remaining aspirant to star status in boxing, dances out to center ring—to be met by the shattering right hand of Bobby Czyz.

"Iceman Coolidge apparently stunned by that right hand of Czyz," comes Pacheco's voice.

A moment later: "Already a nick under the eye of Iceman . . ."

A moment later: "Oh, Iceman is *rocked* . . ."

With less than a minute remaining in the first round, Marv Albert screams that "Coolidge is just looking to last the round." It is sadly true. The Iceman's face is a sponge of blood and welts. A few seconds later, Pacheco's voice exclaims: "Coolidge is fighting back, but boy, what punishment he is taking—"

In the truck, Mike Weisman stiffens. He grabs a headset phone. "Don't be afraid to criticize if Iceman looks bad, Ferdie, you gotta do it!" Weisman shouts. Later, Weisman would explain that he wanted to restrain the Fight Doctor from pretending that the fight was even. No amount of euphemism, however, can conceal the fact that something horrible is happening here. As the bell ending round one sounds, Czyz has battered Coolidge so badly that the Iceman wobbles off toward the wrong corner. The assistant director has already begun counting down to commercial.

In New York, Linda Jonsson makes an instant decision.

"I said no goddamn way we go to commercial," Jonsson recalled later. (On CBS, the basketball game was approaching halftime.) "The fight may not last any longer. Why throw away a commercial? We refused to allow the truck to count down."

Instead, Weisman—who is communicating with Jonsson by phone—now screams at the director: "*Go to the corner!*"

Out at ringside the minicam crew rushes to a vantage point below Coolidge's stool. As Iceman's bloodstreaked face fills the screen, America hears the following exchange:

"You know who you are?"

"Yeah."

"Who am I?"

"You're Morgan?"

"*Get the name up! Get the name up!*" Weisman is shouting inside the truck. An associate finally locates the graphic of Jim Morgan, Coolidge's trainer. A moment later it flashes on-screen.

"How do you feel?"

"I feel fine."

"You wanna continue?"

"Yeah."

Round two begins.

"And they did nothing for him!" Ferdie Pacheco is declaring. "The corner did nothing for Iceman. There was only one man working on his eye, there was no ice—nothing to revive him!" No ice for the Iceman. There is the stuff of poetry here, or at least one of those four-alarm ironic allusions that television seems to treasure so dearly. Twenty-four hours earlier, Mike Weisman might even have built a sketch around the idea. But now, Weisman doesn't even indicate that he heard Pacheco; he is talking into his headset mike. The time for conferring identity upon the boxers is past. Now, at least to the NBC Sports production crew in the truck, the boxers are merely expressions of digital time.

The second round ends, and the third, and the fourth. Coolidge's face is a mat of blood. Weisman instructs Pacheco to be ready to rush up into the ring for the postfight interview. "Be very, very fast," he advises.

In New York, Linda Jonsson faces a hard choice. She is already one commercial break behind, but she can see that this fight might end at any moment. She takes a chance and orders a commercial. Her misjudgment provides the one moment of grace that Iceman Coolidge, the cooperative straight man, receives from NBC television: it is under the cover of an ad for Old Spice aftershave that his corner throws in the towel.

In New York, a week or so after the fights, I visited Mike Weisman in his office at NBC Rockefeller Center. I asked him whether, in all honesty, he didn't think that José Nieto and Iceman Coolidge had been used as props—spear-carriers in the service of NBC's competitive needs vis-à-vis CBS and ABC. I was not assuming deliberate *mismatches*. Nieto, after all, did last nearly eight rounds with Lockridge, and Coolidge's record coming into the Czyz fight was a respectable 20–2–1. Still—

"Yes," said Weisman after a long moment's thought. "They *were* spear-carriers." I waited for more. "But once the telecast started," Weisman continued, "I couldn't even think of them as spear-carriers. In my telephone conversations with Linda, we weren't even thinking of subject matter. We were thinking of time."

"What will happen to Nieto and Lockridge?" I asked. I was curious to learn something about the career decisions faced by fighters who have been soundly outclassed in their weight divisions.

Mike Weisman shrugged. His telephone was ringing and he wanted to pick it up. "They'll never box on NBC again," he said.

from *White Town Drowsing: Journeys to Hannibal*

For the past quarter-century I have clandestinely carried a town inside my memory—a town, and a fragment of river, and a bridge. These images glow and fade in my consciousness like distant signals in a radio tube, and in fact the remembered town takes on the ensemble bedlam sometimes of an old radio show, the sort of show my father would dial into and then abandon, dial and abandon, as he searched the airwaves for evidence of larger universes, better times.

But the town was no cathode fantasy. It was real. I was born in this town and lived there virtually until the last moment of my boyhood, which occurred on a morning in June of 1959, when I was seventeen and my father, who was the town's Fuller Brush man, packed the family into two Studebakers and headed us west across Missouri toward the state capital and better times.

We reached the state capital. There, my father continued to sell his Fuller Brushes at an imperceptibly diminishing rate until he died twenty-five years later, in September, in a hospital room with the radio on, in the heat of the National League pennant race, having reported taxable income for the previous year of just under one thousand Fuller Brush dollars. That was the destiny of my father, who had always dreamed of leaving the river town.

I, who had always dreamed of staying, found the better times. I enrolled in a university that I would never have dared to consider had we remained in the river town with its beguiling, illusory systems of growth and education and commerce—and its Baptist junior college. I thought I would become a journalist. I wanted to meet all the famous people whose voices had floated into the river town on the radio airwaves, and I wanted to live in the larger universe they inhabited. All this on behalf of my father, who cared terribly about these voices, and memorized their jokes and their hidy-hidy-ho signature lives and made bets on their salaries with men in saloons.

So I did. I learned journalism and blindly practiced it in a broken path of cities tending north and east, the cities growing brighter and stranger as the town receded. And I met them, the famous images, and the newer, colder images of television. And I became an image on television. But the town rushed at me in dreams. And one day when I was reporting back to my transplanted father on how it was to live and work among the famous voices, he interrupted, shyly, cupping the deaf ear, to ask me to refresh him on the name of the newspaper I worked for.

He remembered details of the people with the famous voices better than he remembered the details of my life. It had been the jokes and signature lives that were real to my father all along, back in the river town; things in themselves; not symbols of personal possibility.

And then my father died, and the blind weight of a quarter-century descended, and now I was both fatherless and estranged from the river town. And a son arrived, and then another son, and I saw that it was imperative on their behalf as well as my own that I begin going back.

I had always believed that I could go back. Going back to the river town and reentering my life there had remained as plausible an option, at least in my clandestine communings, as advancing my career with a better job in a larger city. I had visited the town a few times in the first years after the family left—I brought squinting, eye-shading girlfriends; we inspected scenic sites and points of historic interest—but the visits decreased as my urban path tacked north and eastward, and at some point the visits ceased. But the idea of going back, like the intact presence of the 1959 town inside my memory, never diminished. The idea was as necessary to my subsistence as drawing breath.

Long before I knew that the town enjoyed my fame beyond the fame I conferred on it as a young child from my grandfather's front porch on the top of Union Street Hill; before I understood that the river was something greater than an interesting shard that supported barge traffic between its two framing bluffs in the

daylight and lay invisible as evil beneath the winking bridgelights at night; before the bridge came to represent in my dreams
the skeletal conduit to flight and the even more horrifying orifice
of return—before I knew all this, I knew that the town and the
river and the bridge were indivisible from one another and from
me. As I grew older I sensed that they established my moral
coordinates, and in some vague way defined my expectations of
the world. Their permanence seemed a precondition of my own.
The town and the river and the bridge formed a triptych that
forestalled the intrusion of change, decay, death.

Not that I seriously resisted. Not that I could rid my memory
of this glowing and fading image even if I wanted to. The town's
hagiography of street names (I was born in a family house on
Lamb Avenue, passed my early childhood on a street called St.
Mary's; my parents moved next to Sunnyside and finally to
Pleasant Street, where we lived next to a family named Paradise),
the bridge's phantasmic geometry, the river's seditious and
constant subtraction of time—these are the fixed evidences of my
own being, necessary as shadows.

The Mississippi flows due south to Hannibal until it bumps
against the limestone bluffs beneath Riverview Park. Deflected, it
slants southeasterly along the town's old railroad yards until it
disappears beyond a brutal, transfixing high tooth of limestone
called Lover's Leap.

The Mississippi River flows through nearly every remembered
picture I have of Hannibal. It is visible from all the hilltops that
ring the old central business district, including the top of Union
Street Hill, where my maternal grandparents lived. More than a
visual memory, though, the Mississippi asserts itself in my thoughts
as an almost sentient presence of weight and movement—a
savvy channel out there on the innocent prairie, profound with
some secret intelligence, or at least the sort of volition associated
with lifeblood.

The river lent animation to the town; the river blessed and
cursed Hannibal with animation in much the same way that
Mark Twain blessed and cursed Hannibal with his legacy. The
blessing lay in the river's usefulness as a marketing conduit, and
in its beauty, and in its irresistible metaphor as memory; Hanni-

bal has forever been dreamily in love with its unrequiting past. The curse lay in flooding. Six or seven times a century, the Mississippi River would swell up out of its channel and drown the very epicenter of commerce (railroads, hotels, restaurants, shops and stores) that its animating force had coaxed to the riverbanks. Hannibal's most peculiar trait has been its susceptibility to ruination from its assets.

The Mississippi worked on the deeper instincts. Its soundless summer-say shimmerings, its deadpan placidity and friendly lappings in nonflooding times, only sharpened its intimation of sentient weight and movement, and lent the river a patina of terror—the kind of terror felt not so much when one was gazing at the river and astonished by its daylight majesty, but later, at night, and forever, in one's dreams.

I remember—I have dreamed—sitting in my grandfather's black Packard on Third Street, facing south toward Bear Creek, which bisected our route to Union Street Hill on its flow to the Mississippi, and watching oilskinned men in flat-bottom boats heap sandbags around the Admiral Coontz Armory. In 1947, my sixth year, the spring floodwaters submerged the railroad tracks and the sidewalks and pavement of Third Street virtually up to the wheels of the stopped Packard. I remember pleading with my grandfather to back the Packard up, turn it around, and get us away from the alien plane that had obliterated this part of Hannibal's surface by a power I did not yet understand. The dark floodwaters gave the familiar buildings an amputated look; disconnected them from any unifying context. They unfixed my universe and caused it to float apart; it was as if my identity, so dependent on the town's permanence, were dissolving.

This was the terrible duality of the Mississippi: its capacity both to define my location in the world and to suddenly deny it, by some capricious swelling of its weight and movement.

And yet, like the town, I was a fool for the river. The river satisfied what limited need we felt for connection to the nation. The river carried traffic down to us—past us—from Minneapolis and up from Memphis and New Orleans. Even when no grain-bearing barge, its connected scows lying low and tricky in the channel; or excursion steamer; or fishing skiff; or parading amphibious tank from the late Pacific theater happened to be passing our levee, we Hannibal people (we *Hannibalians*) received the Mississippi as my father received the airwaves: as connoisseurs of information. We knew that the waves and currents and driftwood themselves, the catfish and turtles, the winter's ice floes, all nature's bulletins, were reaching us from Clinton and Muscatine and Rock Island. St. Louis, that snob of a city to the south, would have to wait for this particular news. Hannibal had it first.

This Ptolemaic sense of the river—that the small curving shard visible from the town was somehow the Mississippi's center, if not the universe's—allowed us to forgive the river its terrors. Besides, it was gorgeous. Not many people born and reared in Hannibal ever had much experience with great landscape that they might compare with the Mississippi; and still the river struck us as a judgment against all other displays of natural beauty.

From the vantage point of my grandfather's front porch the river, now a mile in the blue distance and safely below me, formed the unifying line in a great dioramic composition.

My grandparents' house was at the foot of Booker Street, on the crest of Union Street Hill on the South Side of town. Jasper Toalson's was the bottommost house on a short, down-sloping block that ended at the precipice of a reinforced embankment. A Jonathan apple orchard began at the foot of the embankment and slanted down Union Street Hill toward the town until it gave way to bungalow backyards. I could sit, in summer, on my grandfather's green porch swing facing south, turn my face to the breeze rising from the east, and let my gaze widen upward from hollyhocks to Illinois. The hollyhocks grew wild at the top of the embankment, across a small graveled lane bordering the yard, where my grandfather parked his black Packard. Below the hollyhocks the apple-tree branches floated in the wind; below the trees lay the rooftops and church steeples of Hannibal, and the railroad roundhouse, from where the distant thunder of boxcars coupling at night commingled deliciously with voices on the radio. At the town's eastern border flowed the Mississippi, framed in my vision by two opposing bluffs—Cardiff Hill with its centennial lighthouse on the left, or upstream side, and Lover's Leap with its inspirational myths of Indian suicide awaiting downstream. The Mark Twain Bridge arched over the half-mile river channel from the foot of Cardiff Hill to the blue-green Illinois flatland on the far side. My perspective from Jasper Toalson's front porch revealed the entire bridge's southernmost flank. At night the winking bridgelights and the headlights of crossing automobiles cut the blackness like purposeful comets. Bing Crosby sang "Did You Ever Sail Across the Sea to Ireland" on my grandfather's console Zenith radio in the darkened living room, and in my child's mind, Ireland became the mound of pinpoint streetlights on the hill beyond the orchard valley, the hill of Lover's Leap. I looked out my grandparents' living-room window toward the invisible bridge, waiting sleepily for the tiny headlights I somehow could always identify as belonging to my parents' Nash, coming back to Hannibal after a mild jukebox evening in Illinois, coming to reclaim me from the best house on the best hill I ever knew, until later in my childhood I would walk into a house on another hill, the house of my great friend Dulany Winkler.

My father met my mother on the doorstep of Jasper Toalson's house at 1503 Booker Street, not three paces from where I later would pass time in the green porch swing, gazing out at the Mississippi. The year was 1937. He had driven his brakeless Ford up Union Street Hill to sell his Fuller Brushes. I imagine pompadoured Paul Powers rapping on the doorjamb of the Toalsons' small white frame house, then backing up two steps as prescribed in the Fuller Brush sales manual (to dispel the housewife's fears), then extending his arm to offer the bait, the "free gift"—a wire brush or plastic comb that the salesmen were required to purchase with their own money. And falling, by the manual, in love.

There is a verse in the 1939 edition of *Fuller Songs*, the official company songbook, intended to be sung to the tune of "The Man on the Flying Trapeze." My mother used to croon it to me when I was very small:

> Oh, he comes to my door with the finest of aids,
> That charming young man of the Fuller brigades.
> His manner so pleasing, his brushes so fine,
> My cares he is taking away.

That, in its outline at least, almost eerily sums up Paul Powers's courtship of Elvadine Toalson. But to think of my father *precisely* as "charming," in the manner of, say, Trevor Howard pursuing Celia Johnson in *Brief Encounter*, would be to seriously overstate the case. My father was a shy man. That fact alone would not have set him apart from his fellow Fuller recruits of the 1930s. The company legend virtually depended on the romantic image of manly but laconic young self-starters in two-tone shoes, reinventing themselves and breaking the Depression's stranglehold by summoning up their pluck at the nation's screen doors.

But even within this abashed pantheon, Paul Powers merited some special niche. He took his shyness seriously; he burnished it until it approached the status of charm. His early brakeless second-hand Ford is good evidence of this. Broke, brakeless, and a stranger when he first tooled into Hannibal, and too withdrawn to impose on some service-station grease monkey for repairs on credit, my father solved the considerable problem of navigating Hannibal's omnipresent hills by easing down them in zigzag patterns (I imagine his fedora at just the right rakish tilt, his babyface deadpan), relying on low gear, telephone poles, and the kindness of strangers to see him and his dust mops safely to the bottom. Not long ago my uncle Aubrey, Dad's brother-in-law, happened across a townsman in his eighties, an ancient customer of my father's, while strolling on the riverfront. "I'll never forget the first thing he ever said to me," the old friend told my uncle. " 'I'll give you *aaaanything* to get me down off this hill.' " If my father was in anything like his usual form that day, he accepted whatever help the man offered him. And sold him a brush. My father and the town shared some central characteristics: a certain opacity of temperament that was often hard to distinguish from passivity; that talent for converting curses to blessings—and vice versa; a dreamy indifference to time and change, as if the worthwhile life lay somewhere within, inexpressible and darkly sublime. Although my father was not born in Hannibal, the people of the town understood him at once as he shrank back on their doorsteps. They found his deference charming, and bought his brushes. He never should have left.

But perhaps Hannibal never really struck him as home. My

father was a southern Illinois farm boy set adrift by the Depression. He was hired into the Fuller company by his lifelong friend Bill Helm, an unvarnished specimen as primordial and single-faceted as his name. Bill Helm had escaped a life working the dry bean fields himself by taking an iron grip on the fabled Fuller Brush sample case, a grip he would not loosen for the next half-century. By 1934 Bill Helm was already a sophisticated two-tone shoe man, a sporter of white shirts on weekdays, and the latest in hand-painted ties, a driver of coupes. All these bounties flowed from Bill Helm's absolute and almost terrifying surrender to the Sales Gospel According to Alfred C. Fuller.

Bill Helm passed these verities along to my father. He was still passing them along when I was a child listening to them at our kitchen table at night, the ball game on the radio; he even tried to pass them along to me at my father's funeral, but I had long since memorized the cadences; I knew the strategy of getting the lady to reach for the big twelve-ounce size.

"When the lady of the house comes to the door, you say, 'Hello there,' or 'Hi,' if she's a young lady, your age," Bill Helm would instruct, leaning to press my father's arm. They would be drinking beer out of beaded bottles. I would be sitting silently, looking at their arms, looking at the lines where the suntans ended and the flesh turned white as a boy's.

" 'I'm your *Fuller Brush boy,*' " Bill Helm would recite, his eyes closing as the litany took his spirit, " 'and I have a *free gift* for you.' " (Here Helm would shoot an arm into the air.) " 'Which one would you like?' And you hold up three: Vegetable brush. Pastry brush. Spatula."

"And she'll have to make a choice," my father would put in, shutting his own eyes and pursing his lips to sip.

"And *she'll have to make a choice,*" Bill Helm would inform my father. "And then you say, '*May I step in and get it out of the case?*' After you get in the house, then you try to rub some of that witch hazel on her. Women love that witch hazel. Then, why, you've got her where you want her."

Bill Helm was in fact an absurdly successful sweet-talker of housewives, especially considering a couple of built-in handicaps—a certain low-grade reflexive raciness coupled with his life-long inability to make the *th* sound due to severe overbite.

(As the years went by and Bill Helm rose in the ranks, destined for his fifty-year desk lamp, his salesmen never tired of imagining their erstwhile field manager setting up as assignation: "I'll meet you at free-furty on Fursday.")

But the only Fuller Brush romance that Bill Helm ever instigated was consummated by my father, and it led to my arrival in the world. Helm's role was to assign my father to Hannibal, where he came, with the finest of aids, to the Toalson door opened by red-haired Elvadine, just four years graduated from Hannibal High School and ready for destiny's next whim. Elvadine was an aspiring pianist, an aspiring practical nurse— and just at the particular moment working as a heel-trimmer at the International Shoe Company. She was one of eight children— six survived into adulthood—of Jasper and Tracy Toalson, the Baptist baker and his dreamy, superstitious, hallucinating Catholic wife.

Paul and Elvadine were married in 1938. Bill Helm personally drove them to St. Louis for their honeymoon—out of concern, possibly, for my father's brakes. I was the first of their three children; I arrived three weeks before Pearl Harbor in 1941. My brother, Jim, was born at World War II's end (my father did not serve; his arches were fallen), and my sister, Joyce, arrived at the threshold of the 1950s.

I grew up in a town that seemed less a town to me than a kingdom. Its hills turned neighborhoods into discrete principalities and lent its modest area a bogus sense of vastness—the South Side, with its peeling bungalows and steeply angled vegetable gardens and tire swings depending from front-yard sycamores, was as culturally separate from stolid, plumb-level St. Mary's Avenue as Portugal from Spain. Hannibal regathered itself, transformed itself as the light of day shifted its intensity on familiar surfaces; as the universe of one fenceless backyard merged almost imperceptibly into the similar and utterly distinct adjoining backyard; as the myriad possibilities and aromas contained within a dark carless garage, opening onto a sunlit back alley, yielded to an equally rich profusion suggested by a lightly traveled neighborhood street, two fielder's gloves, a hardball, and the good right arm of Bobby Schweitzer; as the presence of night, and silence, conferred a different sort of feeling—unaccountably tragic—on the railroad yards than had the mundane day.

(But if Hannibal was a kingdom, who was king? The question never presented itself in my childhood. The town did not seem to require authority. It ran on invisible allegiances, or allegiances whose objects were less visible than the forty-eight-starred flag whose allegiance we pledged every morning at Mark Twain School, and to the republic for which it stood. The allegiances seemed founded on order, on cycle, on some unresisted sense of duty—my father, driving a sturdy beetle-shaped Nash now, threading and rethreading the finite itinerary of Hannibal streets on his Fuller rounds, the Nash perfumed by the disinfectant scent of new dust mops; my humpnecked grandfather, rising at half past four each week-day morning for years and generations to eat his Shredded Wheat with banana slices and then drive his black Packard down Union Street Hill to Zimmerman's bakery, returning to the house on Booker Street at midafternoon with flour to his elbows, the hump at the back of his neck a condition of his lifting sacks of flour for years and generations. These men understood obligation, understood allegiance, and I thought I understood as well. Perhaps if I had been asked who was king, I might have suggested the shadowy late author with the white mustache whose inescapable image the town seemed to worship, and whose image I tended to confuse with God's. Perhaps I would have been correct. And a terrible authority this king would yet prove to be; in some respects a despot.)

Hannibal's architecture reinforced its aura of fantastic exemption from mere municipality. Our police station at Fourth and Church streets was a child's confection of minarets. It had parapet gables and a three-story octagonal tower whose ogee dome was taken off one day by a tornado. (Before 1903, it had served as the City Hall.) The police station's most glamorous denizen—and, save for ministers, the town's single living icon of authority—was Officer Floyd Capp. Officer Capp was a motorcycle patrolman. That was the bureaucratic way of putting it; that was the job description. Officer Capp elevated that role to the genus of cavalry; there was a Prussian fatalism about the way he spearheaded a funeral caravan or directed church traffic on Sundays. Officer Capp never revealed himself beyond the police station's meringue girdlings in anything less heroic than a wardrobe whose principal details remain as vivid and unwavering to me as my Sunday-school tenets of virtue: a pair of obsidian sunglasses, a polished Sam Browne belt lashed to his fat middle by a diagonal strap the width of a pot roast, and riding jodhpurs festooned with yellow stripes, tucked into knee-high leather boots that were laced as tightly about his calves as puttees. Appareled thus, Officer Capp loved to burst unannounced through the doors of our grade-school classrooms, where he would stand in front of the blackboard, rocking sidewise from booted heel to booted hell, and recite the Five W's of Traffic Safety. When he had finished, he would spin about and take French leave, the teacher hastily bidding us rise in a collective *so long*, and there would be a bright hole in the air where Officer Capp had been.

The storefronts and hotels along the main commercial streets sustained Hannibal's abiding air of kingdom, of sovereign idiom impervious to fashion's whim. These buildings stood, and stand today, along the T formed by lower Broadway, which points directly at the riverfront, and Main Street, which parallels it. Mark Twain was at work on *Huckleberry Finn* in Elmira, New York, when the bulk of these buildings went up in the 1870s: two- and three-story brick structures with flat roofs, mainly Italianate vernacular in design but punctuated by a few Victorian specimens, with their low-relief friezes and cornices; an occasional stab at neoclassical (the Orpheum, later the Tom Sawyer Theater) or Egyptian revival (the BPOE Hall at Fourth Street and Central Park).

These were the first implantations of serious wealth in Hannibal—they and the pretentious pilastered mansions that arose during the same building boom on the high bluffs above the town's center. They sprang from Hannibal's golden age, the lumber age, the age in which men with names like Pettibone and Cruikshank and Dulany began to amass great entrepreneurial fortunes by lumberjacking the white-pine forests of Wisconsin and Minnesota. These men arranged to float the masses of felled timber down the Mississippi to Hannibal, where their company roustabouts hauled the logs out of the river and fed them into the sawmills that lined the banks of Bear Creek. The finished lumber was loaded onto freight trains for shipment to the pullulating neighborhoods of Oklahoma, Nebraska, Kansas, Texas, and the Dakotas.

It was the town's only age of grand gesture, of imperial presumption. For a couple of decades in the late nineteenth century, Hannibal actually mattered to the nation, and for reasons that had nothing to do with the accident of Samuel Clemens's legacy. The town was the fourth-largest lumber center in America; twelve lumber mills processed two hundred million feet of wood in the 1870s. The new aristocracy showed promise of an interesting talent for profligacy. In 1877 a lumberman named Sumner McKnight decorated the crest of a prominent Hannibal hill with an imperial two-story residence. If featured five giant bay windows on its front and three on each side. Its mansard roof, elaborate cornices, and graceful staircases were the standard of town fashion for years. McKnight eventually moved away, but his creation remained—to endure a brutally crushing snub. In 1898 Hannibal's greatest lumber baron, John J. Cruikshank, decided to build an even more imperial mansion—neoclassical, in beige brick with wood trim and a grand central cupola. Since the McKnight mansion disturbed Cruikshank's prospective view of the Mississippi, Cruikshank had it moved two hundred feet to the west.

By 1904, two years after Mark Twain's final visit to Hannibal (he addressed three hundred prominent citizens at the Cruikshank mansion), the town seemed impossibly graced with hope and good fortune, a town of destiny. Its population stood at 18,000, an increase of nearly 50 percent over the 12,790 recorded in 1900. The assessed valuation stood at $4 million. There were four banks, three shoe factories, a newly opened public library, the largest Portland cement plant in the world, twelve cigar factories, two breweries, one hundred twelve factories, a streetcar system. Four thousand Hannibalians worked for factories and railroads; the town handled fifty-six passenger trains and thirty-four freight trains a day. The Mississippi flowed down like milk—twenty million gallons a day, someone estimated. "Two thousand miles of river transportation," the Chamber of Commerce boasted, "to all parts of the world." The horseless carriage had appeared in town; a man drove his through a store window and entered local history. One hundred businessmen purchased stock in a prospective new hotel, a centerpiece for conventions and civic luncheons and fashionable dining. They chose a site on South Main Street, a few falsely prudent blocks from the river. They called the hotel the Mark Twain. In 1904 Hannibal could still salute its most famous son and make the gesture seen gallant, inclusive: the town sweeping the famous son along in its triumphant ascension to the zenith.

In 1904 Hannibal, booming, dreaming, was already a husk. The white-pine forests of Wisconsin and Minnesota were nearly depleted. The sawmills along Bear Creek were producing far below capacity. In 1901 the lumber-pulling season had closed early because the Mississippi had dropped to a low ebb—a symbolic beginning of Hannibal's demise, and an eerie counterpoint to the river's virulent ravages later in the century.

The full piper-paying consequence of this inevitable cessation in Hannibal's lifeline, this prefigured termination of boom, was concealed, cushioned for several decades. The railroads and the shoe factories sustained the town's transition into its smokestack years, while the great lumber families played out their charades of aristocracy in their gilded dreamhouses on the green hilltops. If the lumberless Mississippi was beginning to isolate Hannibal from the nation's growth patterns, the Great Depression arrived to camouflage that trend; it absorbed Hannibal's inertia into the country's.

And even in the Depression Hannibal seemed especially favored, protected by destiny. The very avatar of American regeneration himself, President Franklin Delano Roosevelt, intervened personally in Hannibal's fortunes on two occasions. On the night of January 15, 1935, President Roosevelt touched a gold key in the White House and ignited the beacon atop a twenty-foot memorial lighthouse on Cardiff Hill—the ceremonial beginning of the Mark Twain Centennial, the one hundredth anniversary of the author's birth and the symbolic beginning of Hannibal's planned regenesis from hard times. On September 3 of the following year, Roosevelt appeared in Hannibal in person to sever the silk ribbon formally opening the new, million-dollar

Mark Twain Bridge across the Mississippi, consummating an integral link in a continental route known in more lyric times as the Pikes Peak Ocean-to-Ocean Highway and more lately designated Route 36.

(One of my father's most sustaining personal memories was that he had appeared in the *Hannibal Courier-Post*'s front-page photograph of Roosevelt at the bridge: a face in a crowd of seventy-five thousand. I grew up believing this. But as the occasion for verifying my father's claim began to take on a kind of inevitability—as I began to pore through the newspaper's back issues for the daily record of the town's past—I began to dread the discovery; a certain pattern of doomed imaginings had long since, by then, revealed itself in my father's life. My fears proved legitimate enough. My father's face is nowhere visible in any of the newspaper's photographs of the Roosevelt motorcade. But then, in an odd manner of thinking about it, neither is Hannibal's.)

The Mark Twain Bridge supplemented an earlier, smaller upstream bridge built mainly for train traffic; it only incidentally accommodated wagons, pedestrians, and a few cars. Hannibal's city fathers quite naturally hoped that the new bridge would prove a conduit for motoring tourists from the East—people with money to spend in the boyhood town of America's greatest humorist (for that is how Mark Twain is inevitably regarded in Hannibal—as a humorist). And for a few years, that was indeed true. Typical of Hannibal's fortunes in the matter of harnessing Mark Twain's commercial legacy, however, the bridge was completed a year after the Mark Twain Centennial had closed down.

Mark Twain recalled Hannibal as a white town drowsing in the sunshine of a summer's morning, the streets empty or pretty nearly so. My own boyish memories are pretty nearly the opposite, and yet I sense that the town's elemental claim on reverie must be essentially the same for anyone who lived here as a child. I remember a town teeming with life and voices—my wild-eyed grandmother's voice in her darkened living room as she spun Germanic fairy tales at night; the voice of toothless Old Lady Collins, behind hollyhocks across the back alley from my grandparents, shrieking the melody of "Jesus Loves Me" in precise wordless syllables; the voices of my father's fellow Fuller men singing, half in parody, their company songs over beer in the kitchen of the house on St. Mary's; the voices of all the straw-hatted shoppers on North and South Main and inside the rows of stores—the Woolworth's, the Penney's, the Famous, and the Eagle—and the grown men's voices inside the scale-scented fishmarket on the river's edge or the blood-scented poultry house where my father took me on Sundays after church; all these voices of public movement and commerce, the grown-ups fulfilling Hannibal's apparently limitless logic of exchanges and growth (although it must have been hollowing out even then, in those early postwar years, the logs no longer floating down the river); and I remember the voices on the radio, always the radio—Jack Benny and Amos 'n' Andy and *The Shadow* of course, not to mention Harry Caray doing the play-by-play of the St. Louis Cardinals through all my boyhood summers, but also our own radio voices: Genial Gene Hoenes, KHMO's Man on the Street, there at Main and Broadway at noon with his baton of a hand mile and his Question of the Day; the Reverend Johnny Golden, "The Old Ridge-Runner," beckoning me sonorously from sleep each morning from my mother's kitchen . . .

> And so we come through the rest of the night
> To look once again through the Window of Light
> With ears to hear and eyes to see
> What today has in store for you and for me.

. . . The Window of Light serving, in my dream-shedding first wakefulness, as the conduit for the aroma of skillet-fried eggs and percolating coffee. Johnny Golden's sermon would be followed by a local commercial, certifying our town's mercantile preeminence: *Yates-and-Hagens-as-you-all-know-is-just-the-place-for-you-to-go-for-shirts-and-shoes-and-ties-and-slacks-we-have-'em-ON-OUR-RACKS!*

And yet my abiding image of Hannibal is nocturnal. Twain recalled empty streets in the sun; I remember a town bursting with humanity but nearly always in the night. Perhaps I am coming back to town in my father's old Nash after a nighttime baseball game in St. Louis in one of those soft-consonant summers of my boyhood—Nash, Hannibal, night, never. Never grow up. I grew up and left Hannibal. Not out of choice, but I left nonetheless, and the town and the river and the bridge kept the account. The boy in me would dream his way back home forever afterward, but he would never make it. Perhaps he would make it as far as the top of the Mark Twain Bridge, crawling across the superstructure. Always, waking, he fell.

A quarter-century after I left Hannibal, I began to enact that dream. I began to reenter the town.

The year was overwrought with anniversaries, Nineteen-eighty-five marked the one hundred fiftieth year of Samuel Clemens's birth, and the hundredth anniversary of the American publication of his greatest work, *The Adventures of Huckleberry Finn.* Somewhere out beyond Jupiter, Halley's Comet was speeding on its seventy-five-year orbit toward the interior of the solar system and its eight-month loop around the sun. The last approach of Halley's Comet had occurred as Mark Twain lay dying in 1910; its visit previous to that had attended the author's birth.

And here I was in middle age, launching a fugitive summer of quick trips back halfway across the continent to a place I hadn't really known for more than half my life. I had planned it carefully: weekends stolen from my small boys, vacation time at my wife's expense.

And for what? For hanging out in a small town that most of my friends and relatives had departed, through death or the quest for better times; to ask questions I had not yet formulated of strangers who had no reason to trust my motives and even less reason to comprehend my essential, half-coherent reason for being there:

To try to reenter the last system of life that had ever made sense to me; to regain an old quotidian passion for the ordinary, and to see whether the town, the river, and the bridge still held their power as guardians of the old moral coordinates—the values and assumptions that cast Hannibal as an extension of my own identity.

Reasons enough, I decided, and I started going back.

Part Three

"SHA-DA-BOOM!" (A STORY)

I probably wrote this in about 1970, just after I had become the TV critic for the *Chicago Sun-Times*. Unpublished, it keeps surfacing from the depths of my files like some linear Loch Ness Monster, the sightings always reminding me what fun it was to be young and a newspaper columnist in that city, where one didn't even have to go looking for outlandish characters to write about—chances were, they'd step off the fifth-floor elevator outside the city room and audition for a line o' type or two in one's column!

Probably someone a little, or a lot, like Jack E. Gatz made that pilgrimage one day; probably I was delegated to step outside and listen to his spiel. I honestly don't remember.

Rereading this, I notice that the point-of-view shifts a couple of times. To my Bread Loaf colleagues in fiction: sorry. I just didn't know.

On the other hand, I wonder whether, in my wised-up middle years, I'll ever again be capable of writing anything like "tiptoes tapping as they touched the floor," or, "Fleck, suffering from after-shave . . ."

Sha-da-BOOM!

(A Story)

The trouble with Chicago in the weekday morning is that nobody auditions, Jack E. Gatz thought. Bowed under hemorrhoid ads, the people ride the brown buses down the brown chrome avenues of toil, trying not to touch their neighbor's pantied skirted coated hip. No one on the buses is trying out material, thought Jack E. Gatz, no trio in the aisles is doing a number in the style made famous by the Impressions. No businessman is working on his batting stance on those buses; no lipstick-sunglass shopper wants it known that she can sing like Jeanette McDonald. There is not one good shoeshine. MAN IS DOG'S BEST FRIEND, proclaim the morning photo captions, and the passengers, that jolly company, all doggedly agree. Everyone is thinking of slip covers; nobody seems to realize that there are graveyards near.

Jack E. Gatz was waiting in the yellow newspaper lobby when Fleck came to work. He was perched on a yellow sofa facing a yellow wall; arms folded, tiptoes tapping as they touched the floor. Fleck, suffering from after-shave, thought at first that the little man must be a savant or a Bible-peddler; he reeked a furtive clerical composte of old hair oil and shoe polish.

Fleck wondered whether the distracted religion editor might be the beneficiary of this morning apostle. (But never send to know for whom the guest lolls; he lolls for thee.)

Jack E. Gatz slid off the sofa as Fleck strode through the lobby for the city room. "I saw your column," he called in a tone that Fleck instantly catalogued as Eastern Public Relations in E flat major. "About the lack of humor among comedians on TV. Very informative."

Fleck had written a column a few days ago mocking certain

comics on television for their tired material, their rote delivery, their unabashed begging for laughs.

Usually, after such a column, Fleck would receive letters— letters signed "A Reader," and "Mrs. No Name," that invited him to get up off his so-and-so and change channels if he didn't like what he saw, and questioning his patriotism, and featuring two different colors of ball-point ink. Seldom a reader in person. He reached for the city-room door, but Jack E. Gatz moved like a nightclub shortstop between him and the door.

From somewhere in the lining of a shiny but sharply tailored green suitcoat, the little man had produced a business card. He thrust it at Fleck. It said:

JACK E. GATZ

GAGWRITER

MONOLOGUES   TV SKITS

IDEAS   PLOTS   SLOGANS

The card smelled of hair oil. Fitch. "I am a free-lance writer," announced Jack E. Gatz and stood his ground. He seemed to be waiting to see how Fleck would take that news. When it became apparent that Fleck would keep his astonishment under control, Jack E. Gatz added: "And I am a good critic when it comes to judging good comedy on TV."

Fleck told Jack E. Gatz that was real fine, but he didn't intend to pursue the matter of TV comedy in future columns, so he didn't see any point in—

"It's the same old sales pitch," said Jack E. Gatz, his eyes darting. Fleck saw that he had a little smooth vanilla face; skin the color of his light sideburns. The kind of face favored in living-room family portraits. The eyes were drawn a little opulent and lopsided. "Once a comic has been established in the public eye, he becomes an idol," Jack E. Gatz was saying quickly. "Not to me, of course. But he becomes an idol. He depends on his name."

The after-shave still irritated his neck, and Fleck was wondering whether the coffee machine was accepting quarters this morning. He told Jack E. Gatz that that was the way it was, all right. But the little man still guarded the door.

"Well, them days are gone forever," he was saying, and the public-relations voice had become strident show-business. "The viewers are hip to all the horny-corny repetitive shows and programs. Right? Too many eyesores. Too many aggravating characters appearing on TV shows. I'll start with my list of a few no-nos."

Fleck's impulse was to politely push the little vanilla portrait-face against the yellow wall and go get his coffee; open his ball-point no-name mail.

But years ago, in another city, after Fleck had written a newspaper article about country-western music, an aging cowboy had showed up outside the city room with glossy photos of himself, and a lariat. He had proceeded to do slow, painful stunts with the lariat. He had worn a shirt of silver spangles, with fringe, that had cost him three hundred dollars. He had referred to himself as "talent." Fleck had told the old cowboy, midway through his stunts, that there were no story possibilities. The old cowboy had gathered his glossies, looped his lariat, given Fleck the finger and walked off into the orange glow of the elevator "down" button; a beaten old good guy in a silver shirt. Fleck had felt badly.

He had a few minutes for Jack E. Gatz.

"No-nos," Fleck repeated.

"Right," snapped Jack E. Gatz, businesslike. He had planted his feet and spread his palms. "The who-wants-em-on-TV comedians." His voice became staccato; he looked level at Fleck with his lop-sided eyes.

"Jack Carter," he said. "A loud mouth. Makes more noises than a zoo. Joey Bishop. Belongs in a nightclub. Has no personality.

"Jackie Vernon, Jack E. Leonard, Buddy Hackett. One big large barge, loaded with risqué material. Mechanical dialogue that sounds like a broken record."

Jack E. Gatz paused a fraction of a beat. Fleck had the wild sensation that he had missed a laugh cue. Jack E. Gatz was moving his hands around a little, pivoting on his hips. A sly furtive look had come over his face. The man was auditioning!

"And Merv Griffin," said Jack E. Gatz. He threw a pointed

finger at Fleck. "Merv Griffin. Looks like a fowdy dowdy old lady playing patty-cake in high-heeled shoes. He has Roman eyes—on all the female guests on his program."

Fleck squinted, and Jack E. Gatz became apotheosized. He was in Living Color, on Prime Time, wearing a tuxedo and black bow tie. Behind him were Ed Sullivan's spangled curtains. Fleck's mind supplied a studio audience and a snare drummer who beat out a snappy "Sha-da-BOOM!" after every Jack E. Gatz wisecrack.

"Henny Youngman!" snapped Jack E. Gatz, glancing right and left. "Corbet Monica! Shelly Berman! (He really had them going now.) Mort Sahl! Alan King! Soupy Sales! (Soupy Sales? Sha-da-BOOM!) Totie Fields, what a mess, the same old routine I've heard before. They copy each other like kids in kindergarten. (Sha-da-BOOM!) Lots of guts, but that's about all."

Fleck felt pained. "Look, Mr. Gatz," he said, "if you don't mind I really have to—"

"HOSS CARTWRIGHT!" screamed Jack E. Gatz. He rolled his eyes in comic fright. "Hoss Cartwright of Bonanza, with that 10-gallon hat, looks like a pregnant totem pole. (Sha-da-BOOM!) And Joe Cartwright's silly laugh—he sounds like he swallowed a Jewish harp.

"George Sanders sounds like he swallowed a mouthful of marbles and his pants are loaded when he walks! (Sha-da-BOOM! and TISH! TISH! TISH! on the cymbals. Applause.)

"David Frost squirms around and gets excited in his chair like a little kid that got two lollipops from the barber where his bald-headed father got a trim only! (Sha-da-BOOM! and much laughter and applause from the audience. Fleck sensed that William Saroyan was out there in the audience somewhere, having the time of his life. And Willie Loman, smiling above his shoeshine. All the people in Jack E. Gatz's audience are going through life on a smile and a shoeshine. Stand up, Willie. WILLIE LOMAN, ladies and gentlemen!)

"Ed Sullivan!" says Jack E. Gatz. "Sounds like he's reciting the Gettysburg Address with a mouthful of crackers in front of an electric fan. He can't read the idiot cards right, and he's a *columnist?*" (Sha-da-BOOM! and a shriek of laughter from a fat lady. You know who the fat lady is, buddy? It's Jesus Christ. Jesus Christ, buddy . . .)

"Steve Allen," says Jack E. Gatz. "Steve Allen. Steve sounds like a salesman in a 5 & 10 store, he talks too much, sounds like a duck when he laughs and is always plugging his songs. He's not the only songwriter around," says Jack E. Gatz, and his voice breaks. (Not now, snaredrummer.) "I'm just as good as he is, and I can prove it . . ."

(Ladies and gentlemen, Fleck thought, Jack E. Gatz seems unable to continue! He's wiping his eyes on his tuxedo sleeve, ladies and gentlemen! Ladies and gentlemen, we'll be right back—*right after this!*

(Whatsa matter, Jack? You were knocking them dead out there. You had 'em eating out of the palm of your— "I know, I know, I'll be okay, Johnny. Just a—a speck of sand in my eye. Get me back on after the station break, Johnny. I'm okay."

(Back once again, ladies and gentlemen, with our guest, Jack E. Gatz. And Jack, you were talking about the various comedians on TV.)

Gatz (in open-collar shirt, now, by Bill Miller, Shirtmaker to the Stars; just back from a booking in Vegas): "Right, Johnny. Let's talk about Dick *Cavity* . . . (laughter) . . . can we do that on the air? Your rival, Johnny, Dick Cavity. Dick confuses his guests and asks too many dippity impersonal questions; doesn't keep the show motivated. He has no humility, and should do something about his hair; his features don't agree with his disposition. And all those anecdotes. Put 'em all together and they couldn't make me one good Mickey Mouse. (Sha-da-BOOM!) They're amateurish, ignorant, repetitious; they're gold bricks that have no talent. They look silly most of the time."

(Leaves falling from a calendar; closeup—Fleck thought—of a crack train streaking across Willie Loman America; a spinning Front Page that freezes full-screen, with the banner headline: JACK E. GATZ TO APPEAR ON CAVETT SHOW!)

"Well, Dick (double-breasted blazer by Pucci now), it's good of you to have me here, it's nice to be here, it's nice to be workin' with a real good sport. Now, Johnny Carson, Dick—Johnny looks like a giraffe when he stretches his neck and grabs his tie. (Sha-da-BOOM!) He wears the wrong clothes; they look like they're glued to him, 'cause he's sort of skinny. He should play it a little cooler, treat every guest alike. He has too many favorites and is corny at times. That phony laugh of Ed McMahon's. He laughs at anything that Carson says, after all Carson isn't that funny always. (Laughter) Most of the time his guests entertain themselves. At times, they're bombed; the public is tired of hearing their petty troubles about their kids and how hard they work for two years and how faithful they are to their wives—and *others*? (Sha-da-BOOM! and a round of applause. Cut—Fleck thought—to Cavett, who looks pained; back to Phil, rolling his eyes and tamping an imaginary cigar.)

"And Don Rickles! (An anticipatory ripple of applause; scattered "Ooooooohs.") Rickles is a nice guy—*to be away from!* (Sha-da-BOOM! and a delighted burst of laughter and applause.) His face reminds me of a pumpkin with acne! (Sha-da-BOOM!) It's colder than a hard-boiled egg in a blizzard! (Sha-da-BOOM!) He reminds me of a tobacco auctioneer with laryngitis; what a blabbermouth; he'd make a good candidate for the Lib Movement! (Sha-da-BOOM! and heavy cheering at this topical reference.)

"Flip, it's great to be on your show, it's nice to be here. Let me say this about David Susskind. David Susskind doesn't know what the word 'ain't' means. He sounds like he invented the dictionary. (Sha-da-BOOM!) I'd like to see him dig a ditch; I'll bet he'd get lost in it. (Sha-da-BOOM! cut to Flip Wilson breaking up.) He has no appeal, likes to chew people up. In my book he'd be a lost page with question marks. (Sha-da-BOOM!)

"As far as Red Skelton's program, it's corny, but don't blame him. The writers are to blame. I know that guy (addressing the camera now, Fleck thought); he has humility and honesty. I tried sending some good material to him, but since all the writers—stuck—together—(Jack E. Gatz collapses on the yellow sofa outside the city room; a sudden musk of hair oil fills the air) and kiss—each other's—fanny—they wouldn't let me—get in the clique—and I'm a damn good writer—

(Ladies and gentlemen, Fleck thought, Jack E. Gatz is sobbing now.)

"—As for Bob Hope, he expects everyone to laugh at anything he says (bitter sobs)—he's self-centered, an egotist and a great sorehead—he *had* Good Motivation and Audience Appeal, but we're (sobs) catching onto his—routine—(drags a green sleeve across the lopsided eyes)—he's getting stale like Dean Martin—(are you leaving, Mr. Saroyan? Fleck thought. Mr. Loman? Do stay—)

"After all, they aren't the only ones around (Sha-da-BOOM!)—and those broads that appear with him are looking for an easy pick and some of their legs (sobs) look like piano stools—

"I know what goes on behind the scenes—I was in Hollywood—and seen enough—that's why I (sob) hate Hollywood, it's a plan where you ruin your reputation and gain a famous name—"

Jack E. Gatz looked up at Fleck with wet vanilla displaced eyes. Very quietly, almost prayerfully (a savant?) he said:

"Would you like to write a book with me? And be my ghost writer?"

Fleck told Jack E. Gatz there were no story possibilities.

"Thanks for listening," said Jack E. Gatz, and left. He went out of the yellowed newspaper building and over to Michigan Avenue, where, as far as he could see in either direction, north and south, there were still no people auditioning.

Jack E. Gatz boarded a 153 bus, northbound; one that he was reasonably sure was free of businessmen practicing their batting stances. He deposited the exact fare. "Move to the rear of the bus," said the driver.

Jack E. Gatz faced the brown passengers, bowed under the hemorrhoid ads. He planted his polished shoes and spread his hands.

"I am a free-lance writer," he announced.

Part Four

TV CRITICISM

From 1983 until 1990, I wrote the TV column for *GQ Magazine*—all right, it's not as if I *modeled* for *GQ Magazine*. (Come to think of it, I did pose for *Playboy* once, and got published; but this is a respectable New England academic press, and I'm not at liberty to say any more about that particular subject now.

(All right, it was for a photo spread showing some Chicago newspapermen holding their favorite drinks.

(And the one they made me hold, I'd never even heard of.)

About these television pieces, then.

The column was enjoyable. It gave me a monthly chance to keep alive that wicked pop-cult satirical voice that I'd developed while writing *Face Value*, which proved a welcome counterpoint to the more sobersided books and reviews I was working on at the same time.

It also gave me the chance to close a certain loop in my career and reactivate certain reportorial skills that I'd developed decades earlier in St. Louis and Chicago. My principal mandate was to review and comment on upcoming TV shows and series; but frequently I extended that mandate by venturing out to observe certain TV personalities in their habitat.

A few of my favorite columns follow—a fitting closure, I think, to a collection of pieces that are, as I stated earlier, the work of a journalist.

The Cool, Dark Telegenius
of Robert Pittman

The man who brought you MTV and Morton Downey Jr.
has tapped into a culture's soul, if not his own

Child of Television. Bodeful title. It has been applied, at various times, to nearly every young programmer born into the video era. It is meant to suggest an extraordinary intuitive grasp of the medium's inner dynamics, possibilities—its Weltanschauung.

To the best of my knowledge, Television has spawned only one child, a son. His name is Bob Pittman. He may yet prove to be the medium's father as well.

Childhood is a fascinating motif among television executives. Walk into almost any of their offices and you enter a temple to lost childhood. Amid the memos and the Maalox, sprigs of kid winsomeness poke through like landscaping in a mall. The catcher's mitts. The filched traffic signs. The candy stash. The rock posters. The little figurines from Disney World. Rosebud Central! The trinkets seem to tinkle, "I may come on like a bastard, but what a *tyke* I am at heart."

Bob Pittman's office at Quantum Media in New York City is shadowed and nearly featureless, except for a terrifying piece of prophetic art that dominates one wall. It is a painting, by David Deutsch, of a male figure gazing out serenely at a lyric landscape. The jarring element in the composition is the figure's head. It is a television set.

"Somewhat appropriate," acknowledges Bob Pittman dryly.

Bob Pittman's childhood was interrupted, altered, the first time around. But that's all right. He is redesigning American television—and, to a large extent, American popular culture—so that we can all experience it on his terms this time.

His conventional childhood ended at age six, when he was thrown from a horse during a family Thanksgiving gathering in Mississippi. His parents—his father is a Methodist minister—looked on helplessly from behind a window. He lost his right eye. The doctors gave him a glass one.

He watched television and absorbed a kind of education for ten years. Then he came out of the small-town South, gaunt, with a beard and a hippie ponytail, to take hold of broadcasting. The year was 1971. His first stop was a Milwaukee radio station.

He was seventeen when he began programming music for a station in Detroit. He was eighteen when he took a Pittsburgh station from nowhere to the leading teenage draw in the market. He was twenty when he went to Chicago in 1974 and master-minded one of the legendary radio turnarounds in broadcast history. He was twenty-seven when he invented MTV and introduced America to its new defining popular-culture sensibility, that of the Antiauthoritarian Child.

He was thirty-three when he created *The Morton Downey Jr. Show* (The Antiauthoritarian Child as adult; public affairs as MTV); when his firm, Quantum Media, attempted to take over the J. Walter Thompson advertising company; and when he started to be mentioned as a possible future president of CBS.

He was thirty-four when he devised an action-adventure format (his cinema verité of Newark cops, *The Street*) that broke down the authoritarian "proscenium" barrier of television drama and allowed the child-viewer into the epicenter of the action. (His only setback so far, the show was dropped from syndication after last year's screenwriters' strike stopped the supply of scripts.) The same year, he also joined the steering committee of an American presidential candidate.

Bob Pittman is thirty-five now. He has yet to finish college. But apparently he has decided it is time to do something with his life. A few weeks ago, he began exploring a new partnership with an old collaborator, the legendary advertising maverick George Lois. Their combined vision is a political-advertising firm. Their first goal will be to elect a mayor of New York. Then they will look for serious work.

One of Lois's most famous advertising campaigns was "I WANT MY MAYPO," which he later adapted for client Bob Pittman as "I WANT MY MTV."

The signs suggest this is the onset of Pittman's next logical enterprise: to redesign American electoral politics. In the image of the Antiauthoritarian Child.

"Television prob'ly showed me more of the world than my parents did," Bob Pittman says in his office. "I can't get enough of television. I accept it."

The remark is pure Pittman: an innocuous-seeming observation, uttered in an innocuous soft drawl—a throwaway line, on the surface, until you begin to prod at it a little and grasp that it is, in fact, a fiercely compressed and apocalyptic little piece of haiku, a glimpse as deep into Pittman's inner cosmos as it may be possible to penetrate.

It is this aura of serene mysticism—an almost childlike simplicity and absence of guile—that has consolidated his reputation within the industry as a genius of the medium, perhaps its prophet. Greater than Arledge, greater than Silverman, a more transitional force than anyone, perhaps, since Paley. It is Pittman and Quantum that are considered the cutting edge of television as it will be defined in the early twenty-first century.

"They said to me, when I started MTV, 'You're violating the contract you have with the viewers,'" he murmurs softly. "They said, 'People want a beginning, a middle and an end to their television.' And I said, 'There is no beginning, middle and end. It's all ebb and flow.'"

He sits in his office beneath the brooding canvas, almost an extension of it—his face expressionless, awaiting questions. It is hard to find the southern child in him, the minister's son. The hippie denim has long since given way to elegant Italian weaves; the ponytail yielded to a razored coif. A trace of his roots survives in his posture: knees splayed apart, ankles pressed together, hands clasped in his lap—the pose of a gentleman caller on a front porch on a Sunday afternoon.

But the surviving eye is not the eye of a man clutching jonquils. It is scanning private frequencies. Bob Pittman has been called aloof, arrogant. Perhaps he is only thinking about something else. In any event, his preternatural surface blandness recalls another childlike sojourner from obscure places: Warhol, whose pop-cult legacy—visual hypersaturation cut with moral numbness—has become the identifying content of Pittman's new video forms. (Warhol starred, for a time, in his own program on MTV.)

"I do attitude-based programming," Bob Pittman says in his dreamy southern voice. "It's all attitude. The attitude is: Nothing is sacred. We're all having a rilly good time. We're all in on something everybody else doesn't get. We're special 'cause we're keeping everybody else out."

Whatever else Bob Pittman may or may not achieve in his life, he has done this: He has deconstructed American television and, via that accomplishment, much of the American popular culture, and not a little of the American political process. His MTV, the first truly original application of the cable-TV revolution, did more than liberate itself from the look and the meaning of orthodox television. It liberated television itself from derived, orthodox meaning. The meaning of time, for instance, or narrative. Or paradox. Or necessity, cause and effect. Or of the sacred (the symbols of Judeo-Christian worship) or of the profane (Nazi regalia). Or of authority, as represented by schoolteachers, policemen, clergy. And parents.

"This is a non-narrative generation," says Pittman. "You communicate to them via sense-impressions. There are two groups of people in this world: those who grew up with television and those who didn't grow up with sense-impressions."

In this vacuum of narrative obligation, music videos installed the aesthetic of the perpetual child: the self as star of the universe, appetite as the locus of endeavor, consumption as art, advertising as education, the grotesque as amusement, defiance as moral vision.

Arriving as it did in 1981, at the outset of a sociopolitical transformation based on greed and assertion, MTV gave definition to a new self-concept in American life. MTV's idiom of feckless, pointless montage—its ebb and flow—replicated itself in the culture like a computer virus: in movies; in advertising; in mainstream television drama (and television news); in fashion; in newspapers, magazines and book publishing; in history itself (someone turned the Vietnam War into a music video). It even transformed the style and content of political campaigning on television—and thus the style and content of political candidates.

MTV was the LSD of the Reagan Revolution.

Bob Pittman explains it more cryptically. "The key to MTV, from day one," he says, "was our logo. We had a logo that changed colors and shapes and positions. That goes against the grain of what logos are supposed to do. But what we wanted it to do was tell our audience that MTV was change."

Message received.

Pittman left MTV at the beginning of 1987 to become president and chief executive officer of Quantum Media, Inc., a firm half-owned by MCA. One of his first acts was to yank out of obscurity a fringe entertainer and Chicago talk-radio man, Morton Downey Jr., and plant his act on the New Jersey superstation WWOR, also an MCA entity.

"We invented the kind of show that Mort does before we found Mort," Pittman says. (Indeed, at one time G. Gordon Liddy was looked at as a possible host.) "We wanted a certain trashing of the boundaries of politeness in television. We wanted an antiauthority figure. When we called Mort to invite him to audition, his first words to our guy were 'Lissen, you sonovabitch, I don't do auditions for anyone!' Then he hung up. I said, 'That's our guy.'"

The fiftyish Downey quickly became a national synonym for grossness by behaving, in essence, like an MTV cartoon version of the Acceptable Adult: strutting, chain-smoking, a mouth-off artist and a gang-protected bully—that is to say, like an antiauthoritarian child. Downey triggered a rush of imitation similar to that of MTV itself. Within a year Geraldo Rivera (who had begun *his* new talk show imitating Phil Donahue) got his nose famously busted in an onstage brawl.

"Everyone trashes Mort," Pittman says, betraying not the slightest trace of anxiety over that fact. "To a great degree, you've got a herd mentality there. No one goes below the surface to analyze why Mort is working."

And what is below the surface? Bob Pittman shrugs.

"This generation doesn't respond well to authority figures," he says softly. "They don't respond to critics, for instance. My parents might go to a movie and say it wasn't a good movie because some critic said it wasn't. Kids don't think that way. What we're discovering is that the younger generation does not like the pontificating style of traditional authority figures."

Pittman reflects for a moment and then adds, with a slight smile, "That's why Ronald Reagan was so popular. He wasn't cut-and-dried. He cracked jokes about stuff. He said people were idiotic when they were. Toward the end of his campaign, George Bush began to embrace some of that. George Bush became a little like Morton Downey.

"Mort, I think," he says, "is the wave of the future in television." When I ask whether Mort is the future in politics as well—this was before the news broke regarding George Lois and a political-advertising firm—Pittman chuckles, as if I were making a joke.

Bob Pittman has a habit—almost a tic—in interviews of citing his parents as points of contrast to his present world. "That works well for my parents, but not for us," he was quoted as saying recently, explaining why Downey did not interview civilized professors instead of, say, protofascist demagogues. "My parents are used to finishing one train of thought before starting another. I can carry on two conversations while I'm reading my mail," he confided in print. "Television prob'ly showed me more of the world than my parents did" is how he put it to me.

I decided to go and visit the parents of Television's Child.

The stop signs in Brookhaven, Mississippi, are right out in the middle of the neighborhood intersections—four to an intersection, fastened to the sides of a barrel-shaped stand. An old railroad line runs along the town's spine; cars have to stop when the freight comes through. Sycamore and magnolia trees still drip their foliage over the sidewalks in late autumn. And now comes the frame where Twisted Sister leaps into this deceptive idyll: The high school directly adjoins a cemetery.

Brookhaven is where Bob Pittman and his older brother, Tom, went to high school. I stopped there first and talked to Thomas E. Sasser. Twenty years ago, the red-haired, boyish Tommy Sasser was Bob Pittman's chemistry teacher.

"I guess the most memorable thing I have about Bob," Sasser told me, grinning a sociable grin, "is the first time I ever had to paddle him. He was a junior. Tenth-grade or a junior, I'm not sure. It was probably my second or third year here. He had a glass ah. And the first lick I hit him with a paddle, he popped that glass ah out. There I was, a young teacher. I thought I had knocked his ah out. Scared me to death."

(Bob Pittman chuckles when I ask him about this later. "Prob'ly apocryphal," he murmurs. "But I did used to put a straight pin through an eraser of a pencil and tap my eye with it until the teacher noticed I was sticking a pin in my eye.")

Pittman's parents now live in Jackson, fifty-five miles north of Brookhaven, where they returned after the boys graduated from high school. Warren Pittman has served in the Methodist ministry for forty years.

Lanita Pittman was not at home when I went to see them—she was baby-sitting for the Tom Pittmans up in Tupelo—so Warren greeted me alone at the door of their beige-colored house, a modest but immaculate bungalow with shutters and a flower bed in the front yard. It was a rainy Sunday, after church. Warren Pittman wore a dignified starched white shirt, a gray-and-burgundy tie, Sansabelt gray slacks and laced-up cordovan wing tips that gleamed like polished hardwood.

"A typical kid," the father responded carefully when I asked about Bob as a boy. "As far as going, you know, farther than just a typical kid, you know, I wouldn't say that he was any more than typical in this, that and the other."

Any particular images?

Warren Pittman reflected. "Bob was a night kid," he said. "Tom would get up early. Bob hated to get up early. But he'd stay up half the night."

What would he do?

"Study. Watch TV. Or if he was in photography, maybe work in the darkroom, and all these sort of things. Oh, he was in a little band, too, one time. That was one of the things he went through for a while. Several of 'em in the Brookhaven band."

("I think back to the Sixties," Bob Pittman tells me quietly in New York. "I sat in my room with a red light bulb on, listening to Doors records. My parents thought it was corrupting. But rock and roll is just the music of people making the transition from childhood to adulthood.")

Did Bob's accident result in any sort of personality change? I asked his father.

Warren Pittman thought about that. "It's hard to tell, at that young age; it's really hard to tell. I would say, offhand, not necessarily. But . . ." He let the thought trail off.

"I think one of the defining things about Bob was the accident where he lost his eye." The speaker is Tom Pittman, Bob's older brother by three years. I met him the following day in Tupelo, about three hours north of Jackson. Tom is editor of *The Tupelo Daily Journal*. Like his father, he is an ordained Methodist minister—a warm and thoughtful man who might be Bob's twin, except for the patches of gray beginning to appear in his thick dark head of hair.

"Bob's reaction to that accident was to try to prove that he could be just as good, or do anything that anybody else could do with two eyes," said Tom. "I think it made him competitive and show that he didn't have to be handicapped."

Tom recalled one other shaping influence on himself and his brother: As a Methodist minister's sons, they were always moving. "We were always the newcomers," he said. "Monticello, Centreville, Forest Hill, Hattiesburg, Forest, Jackson, Brookhaven. Bob was always the youngest kid in his class. The youngest kid, and late-growing. And a newcomer, with one eye.

"That's all a big disadvantage—but it also gives you some vantage point on society. When you're an outsider, you can see people more clearly in some ways. You listen. You pay attention. You figure out where the power is, who the leaders are. What their values are. Bob did that. He learned very early in life to live by his wits. How to get along with kids so they wouldn't beat him up. How to have some identity apart from that formed by being the strongest, the fastest, the best-football-player kind of identity."

("I tend not to be interested in what other people are doing," Bob Pittman insists when I ask him about his competition among the newer television programmers. "I tend not to play competitive sports. I tend to be interested in consumers. In politics. In what's going on with people's morals.")

The small, handicapped outsider, the perpetual newcomer, took refuge in his records, his hobbies—and in watching television. Tom Pittman remembered that before they moved to Brookhaven—before Bob was ten—Jackson, Mississippi, was the site of an experiment in a new and generally unheralded form of TV.

"We grew up with *cable* TV," he said. "Gosh, we had that in elementary school. That's because we were so rural. In Hattiesburg, they erected a huge antenna to pick up distant signals. You know, later, when HBO started, it got tested simultaneously in two places—West Palm Beach and Jackson, Mississippi. So Mississippi has always been in the forefront of cable TV."

And so the child Bob was among the first to experience television as the present generation experiences it: as self-edited montage, as interruption of sequence, of narrative, of context— the viewer as (watch . . . *click* . . . watch . . . *click* . . . watch . . . *click* . . .) the authoritarian. The very mode that became the identified look of Bob Pittman's cable breakthrough, MTV, with its seductive appeal to the very kinds of kids Bob Pittman could never really join: the strong, the fast, the best-football-player types—the anti-intellectual, antiauthoritarian children.

Recalling Warren Pittman's assurance that his younger son was "just a typical kid," I asked Tom whether he thought his own childhood aspirations were any different from his brother's.

"Bob always wanted to be rich and famous," Tom responded without a beat of hesitation. "That was clear. He wanted to be rich and famous."

How did Tom know?

"Well, he said so."

Pittman's entry into broadcasting was apparently as circumstantial, as casually intuitive, as any of his other boyhood hobbies. Like several of his classmates, he did a little part-time DJ-ing on the local FM station, WCHJ. The next thing anyone knew, he was in Jackson. Then Milwaukee. Then Detroit. Then Pittsburgh, where he joined forces with an older and perhaps only marginally less shrewd version of himself, Charlie Warner.

"He's a small-town boy that has an incredible brain," says Warner. "It's just one of those rare things that comes along—somebody that was born with a big bucket. He has one of those very rare minds that is both analytical and creative."

Warner is now a faculty member at the University of Missouri School of Journalism. Through the 1970s, he was an outrageously successful—and successfully outrageous—manager of radio stations in Pittsburgh, Chicago, and New York. At each stop, Pittman was his program director and protégé. Charlie Warner may know Bob Pittman better than anyone.

"When he came to work for me at WPEZ in Pittsburgh, he was eighteen," Warner recalls. "It was 1972. He had a long beard, long hair—but he was very mature, even then. *I don't think he ever had a childhood.* He was a grown-up program director. Just like he is now. Very controlled.

"And even then, he knew how to win. He knew more about ratings than anybody at the station. He knew that in radio, you don't program to people—*you program to people with ratings books.* If you're gonna give away a thousand dollars in one call-in, you do it on a Wednesday, because that's when people fill in their ratings books.

"He took that station from zero to a leader in the market."

When Charlie Warner was rewarded in 1974 with the general managership of a failing NBC-owned radio station in Chicago, he made sure to take his prize protégé along with him.

The result was the Miracle of WMAQ. It took Bob Pittman exactly one ratings period to bring the station from twenty-second in the market to third. His formula was country-western music and cash-giveaway telephone promotions: endless local television commercials in which an extremely fat woman shrieked, "WMAQ's GONNA MAKE ME RICH!!!" followed by a shower of dollar bills and a graphic showing the station's telephone number. Local critics began to write columns to the effect that WMAQ was buying a listenership. Meanwhile, "MAKE ME RICH!!!" calls to the station reached such a volume that at certain hours of the day it was impossible to dial into the area's *entire telephone exchange.*

"He didn't even *like* country music," says Warner. "He *hated* it. Nobody else in the world knew that. I knew it. But he knew what to do. He was an execution *freak.*"

An example of Pittman's execution style involved a disc jockey at the station named Ellie Hellman. "The name was sort of nowhere," says Warner. "Bob asked her what name she'd *like* to be. She said she liked Bob Dylan. Bob said, 'Okay, you be Ellie Dylan.' Bob took her and trained her, as a mentor. She became one of the first big-time DJs in country music."

In 1977, Warner, Pittman, and Ellie Dylan all went skipping down the yellow brick road to Oz: to New York and the NBC flagship station, WNBC. Their mission: replicate their fabulous adventure at WMAQ. The task proved far more formidable; radio competition in New York was tougher, more sophisticated than it was in Chicago.

Using a contemporary-hits format, Pittman tried to make a star of Ellie Dylan, with whom he was, by then, romantically involved. But within a few months it was apparent that Dylan's soft, southern nighttime voice was unequal to the strident daylight demands of the Apple.

Charlie Warner recalls the denouement: "I called him into my office and said, 'Bob, it's not working in the morning.' He said, 'I know.' I said, 'I'm gonna fire Ellie today. I will do it. I will go over to her house and fire her.' He said, 'Thank you.' And I went and did it."

Pittman's distraction vis-à-vis Ellie Dylan was an aberration. His prodigious objectivity had never before yielded to emotion. ("Bob is always in total control," says Charlie Warner. "I've never heard him express great emotion, either sadness or joy. Always complete and total control.") It is not likely to yield again. He is settled now. A few years ago, he met a chic young fashion editor named Sandy Hill on an airplane. It was mutual compatibility at first sight. Sandy, now Mrs. Bob Pittman, recalled the encounter for me via cellular telephone from her limo en route to Kennedy not long ago.

"I was thrilled with my across-the-aisle mate," she briefed me. "I gathered my strategy together as to how to talk to him. I did what I always do: I started to read a magazine. I had every title under the sun in my bag. I thought I'd better not take out certain magazines. If I took out *House & Garden*, he'd think I was married. If I took out *Cosmo*, he'd think I was a Cosmo girl. I took out *The New Yorker*, 'cause that says a lot about a person. I was looking at the jokes and laughing self-consciously. He turned to me and said, 'You must be reading *The New Yorker*.'"

I asked Sandy if she could remember exactly what it was about Bob that caught her fancy.

"I just thought he was so cute." she said. "He had great style, he was extremely handsome. And we had the same haircut."

Pittman romanced her with roses for a month. "I had what looked like a funeral home" was the way Sandy affectionately put it. A couple months after that they were married. They now have a rustic house in Connecticut, a Cessna 340 that Bob flies as a hobby and a helicopter for Sandy. "I'm not much interested in flying fixed-wing," she explained.

They also have a child, a 5-year-old son named Robert Thomas—Bo. This of course makes Pittman the very sort of creature lampooned so successfully on MTV and by Morton Downey Jr.: a parent. An authority figure.

But Bob Pittman has spared Bo from authoritarianism as surely as he is sparing the generation that consumes his brand of television: So far, the child has backpacked in the Grand Tetons, skied in Aspen and logged a half hour of flight instruction in the family helicopter.

It was Charlie Warner who finally steered Pittman into his natural destiny, television.

Among Warner's New York media pals was John Lack, then a young executive with Warner Amex. Charlie Warner helped persuade Lack to hire Pittman as program director for a fledgling cable competitor to HBO and Showtime called the Movie Channel. Lack had some other vague concepts floating around the office as well—an all-game channel, an all-music channel. . . .

"I went over to Bob's office one day," Warner recalls. "This was early 1981, I guess. And he showed me some music videos that the record companies had sent over." Warner's comment was worthy of Neville Chamberlain himself:

"I said, 'That's great—but aren't people gonna get tired of watching 'em?'

"But I'd forgotten the hallmark of Bob Pittman, *Execution*. The real secret of MTV's secret was the way Bob *created the image*. He said, 'The one thing we want to communicate to our audience is, we don't look like the networks!' "

"John Lack had already had the idea of a cable channel devoted entirely to music," Pittman says. "But even though John is a brilliant guy, he was thinking in conventional-television terms. He envisioned a whole series of *programs*. What I brought to it was the whole concept of what is a music channel."

Ebb and flow.

It must be reported that not all of the MTV insiders bought the image, the perception, of Bob Pittman, champion of the Antiauthoritarian child.

"What struck me," says one longtime MTV staffer, "was his complete callousness toward the consumer of the product. Bob was sort of a chameleon in a way. He chose a field—rock and roll—to make his fortune. Rock and roll attracts a lot of people who are star-struck, fame-struck and hip-struck, if that's a word. Bob hid behind the trappings of hip to exploit the consumer in a way as thoroughgoing as any show-business person has ever done."

Asked to elaborate, this staffer says, "I don't think Bob had any feel for the music whatever" (an echo of Charlie Warner's "He didn't even *like* country music. He *hated* it").

"But," the staffer goes on, "he knows the young and adolescent mind. He knows it is very easily led. It's very turned off by adult figures, but if you can look hip, you can pick every penny out of their pockets."

How has MTV done that?

"Look at the idea—a station that runs commercials [the videos, as promos for performing groups] twenty-four hours a day. The choice of artists was always dictated by who was willing to provide videos. Bob said, 'Everything we do, we do for nothing.' And the outlandish contests, the giveaways. A weekend with Van Halen. Get to be Bruce Springsteen's roadie. Be in a David Bowie movie." (Echoes, all, of "WMAQ'S GONNA MAKE ME RICH!!!")

"Genius?" says this insider. "I don't think of him as a genius. Every production-value decision he has ever made is based on budget; then he tries to pass it off as aesthetics. Hey, he's a real

Eighties guy, Pittman. A real Reagan rock and roller. A guy in a suit and a Learjet."

Well, to be fair, not exactly. A Cessna.

Since Television's Child never hesitates to cite his parents as points of contrast to the culture he is helping to create, I was eager to learn whether they—and his brother—see his work as a contrast to their own culture and values.

In Jackson, I asked the Methodist minister Warren Pittman whether the social and moral messages transmitted over his son's brainchild cable system ever troubled him. Warren Pittman shifted in his chair. "I—as far as I'm concerned, the jury's still out on how much impact, and values, that MTV really . . . it may reinforce certain values. It probably reinforces more than it establishes values." He thought some more. "I don't see it as a corrupter of values, things of that sort.

"How *impressed* I am with it is a good question, you know."

The next day, in Tupelo, I posed the same question to Tom Pittman—who had told me he'd chosen to remain in Mississippi "because I felt like I was equipped to make life better in this place."

"It's a *medium*" was Tom's careful answer. "Bob created, in essence, a new *medium*, by combining some preexisting elements. And then the way that medium's used, I mean, you know, that's another decision. Whereas to create a new medium is a morally neutral act, I'd say. What kind of content you put on that medium would be the ethical question, I'd say."

That the content of MTV has raised moral and ethical questions is one of the better-known pop-cultural facts of the decade. One of the most vociferous opponents of certain rock albums and videos, based on their sexual and antisocial content, has been Tipper Gore, the wife of Senator Albert Gore, who campaigned last year for the Democratic presidential nomination. Ms. Gore endured a great deal of hostility, not to say public ridicule, from the firmament of MTV stars and their defenders as she pressed her case.

Yet when the New York steering committee for Senator Gore's campaign was announced last summer, one name on it was that of Bob Pittman. I ask Pittman whether he would care to unravel that particular paradox.

"I understand what Tipper is saying," he replies. "I understand her feelings. I think she's wrong."

And now Bob Pittman is in the process of forming a political-advertising apparatus that might advance candidates, such as Tipper Gore's husband (Pittman and George Lois are both Democrats), through an application of the very techniques he perfected on MTV.

"None of the current political advertising is geared for my generation of viewers," Pittman acknowledges when I ask him about this. "It has no credibility. They don't understand how to create an image with a whole attitude."

In the 57-year-old Lois—an aggressive and often profane Madison Avenue warrior—Pittman feels he has the consummate ally. Lois has created campaign ads for many politicians over the years, including Robert Kennedy in the sixties, and he has a long history with Pittman and MTV.

"We understand how to communicate in this day and age, using the options available," says Pittman. "Look at George Bush. Here's a man who used the tools. George Lois and I have worked together a long time. I used him for almost everything. He'll come up with a great ad for you."

Just all sorts of things are cooking at Quantum Media. Children—real children, Bo-sized ones—are to be the next beneficiaries of its special vision. The company has produced two episodes of a kids' game show "with a high-tech new look," says Pittman. A pilot is also in the works with Fox Television. There is a series commitment with CBS, which has also bought a special from Quantum.

Pittman is silent on the details of every project that has not yet aired—with one exception: a home-video feature that he mentions in the context of what he calls "social trends." The subject of the home video is golf.

"Golf is a major growth sport," he says, his voice taking on some animation. "We've come across a man with a plan. He's looked at the physiology of the body as it relates to golf. The body doesn't produce power in the ways that have been traditionally assumed. [I half-expect him to add "by my parents."] He's developed a new system for teaching golf, and we're producing a home video on that."

A home video on golf. It seems a peculiar passion for the man who has built an empire reshaping American culture in the image of the unleashed, antiauthoritarian child. (Pittman himself does not play golf.) But when you begin to add it up, so did country-western music. So did rock and roll. So—for a softspoken son of a southern minister—did Morton Downey Jr. So did the candidacy of Albert Gore. So does the partnership with George Lois.

One of the most consistent and noticeable features about Bob Pittman (aside from his extraordinary intelligence) happens also to be an overarching characteristic of television itself: an utter absence of a consciousness of paradox.

The video consciousness is a consciousness of the *moment*—isolated from past and future, disconnected from cause and effect. And absolved, therefore, from such tedious linear considerations as paradox. Or irony. Or consistency, logic, coherence, memory. Or moral accountability.

It's just ebb and flow.

These are among the traits that behaviorists and social critics are beginning to identify as central to the personality being shaped by the onrushing environment of a video culture. These are the traits of that creature of the right-brain hemisphere, Analogic Man: intuitive, nonlinguistic, image-sensitive, but disinvolved from sequential reasoning, linear logic, context, narrative—artifacts, all, of downcast Digital Man, the debased and dustbinned creature of the left-brain hemisphere. Of typography.

"I've never lost anyone any money," says the Child of Television in his office, beneath the portrait of the man with a TV set for a head.

Not the most ringing of epitaphs, perhaps. But this is an age of logos, not epitaphs. Barely anyone remembers epitaphs anymore. Or axioms, or proverbs—such as the one relating to who shall rule, in the land of the blind.

Joe "the Living Legend" Franklin Is a Very Lovely Guy. We've Got Proof!

The venerable talk-show host loved the Forties so much he decided he'd stay there

I am going to answer the telephone," Joe Franklin's voice is saying on the other end of the telephone line—to someone else in his office; Joe Franklin hasn't yet quite got his mouth to the receiver. Joe Franklin takes all his own calls.

And then, upon hearing my request:

"You are hitting me at a *crest*, my friend. I am on a *roll*. This is the *right time* for me to do a slick interview. I will give you stuff that will get on page *one*, that will get on page *four*, all over the world. I got my *doctor* here, spraying my throat. I will see you at eleven-thirty Friday. I love your vitality."

My *vitality*? It has been a long time since anyone has complimented me on my vitality. And Joe Franklin has never even met me. Already I am liking Joe Franklin's vitality. So at several minutes before 11:30 A.M. on Friday, I am killing time in the rain below his office—perhaps his suite of offices—at 42nd Street and Broadway, in Manhattan's famed Times Square district.

Joe Franklin. Mister Memory Lane. The longest-running television-talk-show host in history—thirty-six years—he entered the *Guinness Book of World Records* with broadcast No. 21,050 on WOR in New York on June 1, 1985. Joe Franklin. A man whose guests over the years have included the likes of Woody Allen, Barbra Streisand, and (in his *Death Valley Days*) Ronald Reagan. The likes of "Weird Al" Yankovic, they have included. And Jerry Vale and

Margaret Whiting and Lou Jacobi. A man who has earned the plaudits of the critics ("A kind of weird reverse charisma," enthuses Wayne Robins of *Newsday*) and even his own publicity ("Joe Franklin, I salute you, your fans salute you, and the world of TV and radio salutes you," wound up an emotional Joe Franklin press release of a few years ago). A man who has had the distinction of being parodied by Mister Billy Crystal, ladies and gentlemen! A Living Legend!

No chrome-and-glass aerie for this legend. No Scandinavian, no Donald Trump. Brick. Honest brick, and cornices. The address scribbled on my scrap of paper corresponds to the number above a small lobby entrance cheek by jowl with S&L Tuxedos (second floor) and Times Square AC (boxing). Across 42nd Street is the famed Les Gals 25¢ Live Revue XXX Movies, plus a second-story window bearing the identification "New York School of Lock-smithing."

I take the automatic push-button elevator to the fourth floor and step into a lost era. Bare tile floors. Hardwood molding. Office doors with frosted-glass windows. *Good evening, ladies and gentlemen of the radio audience. Coast to coast, border to border.* A cardboard arrow taped to one wall announces: "Chinese Acu-puncture rm 408 ." Wrong era. My man is in 417.

I stride past the open doorway, glimpsing what I think must be the maintenance man's cubbyhole, before I realize that this . . . *is . . . it.* A hand-lettered sign directs the eye: "Memory Lane."

"Eugene McCarthy's doing my show; yeah, he's a great friend of mine, and Roger Williams, the great pianist. You work at CBS? Larry Tisch is a fan, a fan-*natical* fan, my God. Oh, he calls me. We have dinner together. I never follow through; I got too much on my mind. I've written twenty-three books, this one you're gonna love." Joe Franklin presses a soft-cover edition, still in the original cellophane, into my hand. I have not yet introduced myself. A telephone rings; Franklin bends down to scrabble for it amid some stacks of papers on the floor. My trench coat is not fully off. I examine the book's title: *Joe Franklin's Show Biz Memorabilia.* The author is listed as Sandra Andacht. I do a pretty good double take. And then I begin to gain awareness of where I am.

In the center of what might once have been a root-canal

specialist's waiting room, I face a small and somewhat waxen man who is perched on the edge of a frayed sofa talking into a black dial telephone. "Hello? Speaking," says Joe Franklin. Another telephone, muffled and invisible, is ringing. The small man is dwarfed—nearly engulfed—by the vertical silage of his belongings; this office is a fallout shelter of show-biz detritus, a time capsule of glitz.

There are stacked cardboard boxes bursting at the seams with press releases, glossies, photocopies of notices. There are industrial gray metal shelves bent under cubic yards of old LPs—78s. "I gotta lotta good news for ya, Ben," says Joe Franklin into one of two phones he's holding. "Today's gonna be the best day of your life, okay? I got my doctor here, spraying my throat. I'll talk to ya." Other shelves groan under canisters of film reels. There are old Sunday newspapers, complete with comics. A fragment of wooden cabinet tilts against the venetian blinds. I turn to look behind me. On the wall, half-hidden by another cabinet, is a gigantic tinted photograph of a platinum blonde, a satin doll. A page of sheet music is pasted to the open cabinet door. Its title reads: "Joe Franklin's Televising in Secaucus."

Secaucus, New Jersey, is the home of WOR's television studios. I would never have dreamt that people would gather around to sing about it. But in this room anything seems possible.

"I dunno how to say it without bragging," I hear Joe Franklin say, and I realize he is talking to me, "but I'm really hot with the campus crowd. Letters? Can't count 'em. Can't count 'em. Can't count 'em. Can't count 'em."

Both telephones ring again, and he dives for them. It is then that I notice the suits.

The suits are wadded into a mound of worsted and garbadine on the other half of the sofa where Joe Franklin is sitting. Houndstooth arms splay; natural shoulders lie crushed. It is as though a tour bus of empty suits has crashed and rolled on his couch. These must be the clothes he wears on *The Joe Franklin Show*. But what—? Why—?

I begin to form a question—but now Franklin is passing me one of the phones. "It's Irving Fields, the greatest pianist in the world," he tells me. "Talk to him. See what he says about the experience of being on my show."

I put the receiver to my ear. Irving Fields tells me he's at the Plaza and I should come over for a drink sometime. "Ah," I say. "Ah . . . I guess you've been on *The Joe Franklin Show*—a lot." Fields tells me he's been on about 400 times "in the last 400 years." He seems to feel that a quote is called for, as do I. "Stamina," Irving Fields says at last. "I guess that's what keeps him going."

I thank him and hand the receiver back to Franklin. He passes me the other one. This time it's another frequent guest, Judi Jourdan. Judi Jourdan of the Shower Singers.

"We get people from all walks of life," she explains to me. "We do cabaret; we also teach a course." There is a silence. "All walks of life," says Judi Jourdan. "The best get on Shower Singers. Wonderful things happen to them. One of our girls was up for the lead in a Broadway show."

"Talk to him for thirty seconds," Joe Franklin is saying into the other receiver. "Tell him why I pulled for that beauty cream." I find myself talking now to a sponsor, a pharmaceutical man named Henry. Henry is speaking for the record. "To some people, he's like avuncular," he says. "Like an uncle, you know. He's a tower of strength, on a macho basis. He, uh—" Henry is groping. "He covers all bases and crosses all boundaries."

Joe Franklin is wearing suit pants—windowpane pattern on navy blue—a red-and-gray-striped shirt and a pink-and-brown necktie with crossed tennis racquets. We are talking now about the secrets of his success. "I got one great thing going for me," Joe Franklin is saying. He gives it a beat. "I'm not tall. If I was tall, like you, I couldn't walk in the street. People wouldn't leave me alone."

From the hallway have been coming the notes of somebody running the scales on a trumpet. Now Franklin's thought is totally interrupted by an intruder in the tiny and bulging office. "It's the fire marshal," explains a small elderly Hispanic man named Hector, who may be Franklin's assistant. I turn. Sure enough, there is a man in a white uniform shirt, holding a clipboard. Franklin stares, suddenly at a loss.

"He wants your autograph," says Hector. The fire marshal, a young man, grins and nods, pushing forward his clipboard. "My name's Lieutenant Joe Amadeo," he says.

Franklin has recovered his wits. " 'Joe,' same as me," he points out graciously. "Joe, you are a great man."

"Oh, thank you," says Joe. After he has left, Franklin says, "That's a funny bit. I thought he was comin' here to give me a summons. Hector, you're a lovely guy."

He picks up the thread. "I'm the last of the organics," he explains. "The last of the organics in a world where it's gotten very, very plastic. Joe Franklin doesn't change. He symbolizes something solid. With the jacket and tie. I say, 'Good morning, ladies and gentlemen. . . .' " Something clicks in his mind. "You read that certain stars, the great ones, wouldn't do television talk shows. I've got proof." He glances upward significantly, at the canisters. "Ronald Reagan, *five times*. Charlie Chaplin—the great ones. You read that Cary Grant, Elvis, Gary Cooper never did a talk show. *I've got proof.*"

His age shocks. He is 58, three years younger than Johnny Carson. He seems older—not so much in appearance as in the context of his career span (he's been in broadcasting for forty years) and his inner calendar: He communes with an era defined by the Second World War. (The platinum blonde on his wall is Dolores Moran, he says, a third lead for Warner Bros. of that time. Asked whether he knew her, Franklin shakes his head, shrugs. "She typifies the Forties," he explains.)

He drives over to Secaucus Tuesdays and Thursdays to tape his five daily *Joe Franklin Shows*. The shows are aired at 1 A.M. on WOR in New York, and they get out around the country on cable. A recent ratings survey estimated his New York viewership at over 50,000 households a night. Yet his sense of being hot with the campus crowd may be accurate, in a weird sort of way: A fairly heavy collegiate sampling shows up in his demographics. It has been suggested, not entirely kindly, that viewers wised up on David Letterman's show-biz ironies regard Joe Franklin as a kind of field assignment in camp. And there was that Billy Crystal thing. Of which more later.

In addition to the television show, Joe Franklin does a weekly stint, *Joe Franklin's Memory Lane*, on WOR's sister radio station. This marathon of swing and big-band nostalgia is accomplished in two heroic shifts: Franklin is on the air from 7 until 10 P.M., and again from midnight until 5 A.M. "They want me to do it every night," he says with typical modesty, "but I'm going to start phasing out. In a couple of years, I wanna go behind the scenes, produce." (Later, going through his press clippings, I notice he has said exactly the same thing to an interviewer a couple of years ago.)

Radio is his true medium, just as fin de siècle is his true moment in time. Perhaps they are interwoven. Although his television career has spanned more than three decades, it was radio that first enchanted the young man who worshiped Eddie Cantor, and followed him through the streets of New York, and sat in NBC Studio 8H for every one of Cantor's nine-o'clock Wednesday broadcasts of *Time to Smile*. "I was very, very close with him," Franklin says. "I worked with him. After the Golden Age of Radio was over, in the Fifties, he had another show, *Ask Eddie Cantor*. Eddie would respond to letters from listeners." Joe Franklin pauses a beat, leans forward, his voice swelling a little. *"I wrote the letters!"*

I am again conscious of a presence behind me; another visitor. "I am nerviss," says a voice. "Believe me, I am nerviss." I turn. A young black man is standing there, staring at Joe Franklin. His name is George; he is an "impressionist." "I watched you since I was a kid," George tells Franklin. "I watched you with Woody and with Cosby." "Boy, this guy's got a memory, God bless him," Franklin tells me. I am sitting in the middle of a force field; I'm an impediment between George and his Lourdes.

"I gotta get things working," George says, almost under his breath. "I need some exposure. I got chills," he says, staring again at Franklin. He looks at me. "This man is an institution," he says. *"Forget* about it. *Forget* about it. *Forget* it."

George launches into some voices. "Hul-*lo* a-gain ev-ree-*body*, this is *How*-wud Coss-*ssell*." The voice goes all soft and raspy: "Ah'm *fazz*'t. Ah'm *preddy*. Ah'm *the Greatisss'*." For some reason I glance down at the man's shoes. The yellowish soft-leather tips are wet from rainwater.

Joe Franklin is rummaging around him. "Do you see a blue datebook?" he asks me. I rummage, too, and find it on a chair under a stack of photocopied news stories, which slide to the floor as I extract the book.

"Leave it, don't worry about it," says Franklin, reaching for the datebook. "Lis-sen," he says, riffling the pages. "I'm gonna make up a cabaret show. George, give me your number; I'll call you tonight between five and seven. My word of honor." George is fairly jiggling with happiness. "Very good, very good," he says.

After George has left, I ask Joe Franklin about The Parody: Billy Crystal's on *Saturday Night Live*. It is a topic I have not been eager to raise. Crystal's evocation of Franklin had been brilliant and wicked; a merciless send-up of a doddering, past-addled talk-show host nattering on self-importantly with his menagerie of show business's misbegotten.

I expect Franklin's response to be grandly dismissive, perhaps even wounded—anger seems truly foreign to his soul. I am surprised at the directness of his answer.

"Billy Crystal made me a superstar," he says flatly. He considers. "I'm great now, but I was very, very, *very* hot when he was doing me. I'd give anything to get him back on that show."

I look at Franklin; he looks at me. A moment passes. "But you know," says Franklin, leaning forward on the sofa as the phone rings, "he was doing a *satire of a satire*. 'Cause I'm putting the world on. That's something only a select few can see."

The phone keeps ringing. "I'm very, very close with my audience out there," Joe Franklin says. "They can read between the lines. They know my moods. The critics say he's bland, he's neutral—my audience can read between the lines. They *know* I'm not bland or neutral.

"They meet me; they say, 'Joe, you gave that guy a zinger last night; I'm proud of you, Joe.'" He reaches down, feels for the phone, picks it up. "Hello? Speaking. Yes, my dear . . . I promise . . . if it means anything, I'm a personal friend of the governor."

Real (Sick) People

In his quest to go Hollywood, former news whiz Van Gordon Sauter discovers that patients are a virtue

Van Gordon Sauter remembers the exact moment it hit him: There were dollars to be made in diseases! A fortune in phlebitis, riches in rickets, megabucks in mastoiditis—Gold in Them Thar Ills.

"It was June 1987," says Sauter, speaking of a time not yet a year after he himself had been surgically removed, like a rejected organ, from the presidency of CBS News. "I was giving a speech to the American Medical Association's annual broadcast meeting at Rancho Mirage, California. You know how it gets after you give so many of those things. I was just standing up there, flapping my arms like some robot at Disneyland—when suddenly I realized that *I was looking at a whole roomful of Judge Wapners!*"

Leaping lymph nodes! Judge Wapner . . . *People's Court* . . . AMA doctors . . . *People's Pancreatectomy*, right? Before you could hum two verses of "(It Ain't Hard to Get Along With) Somebody Else's Troubles," Sauter had mentally memo'd himself a high-concept premise: a strip-syndicated early-fringe vehicle in which viewers would be allowed to gape and listen, *for the first time on TV*, inside the examination rooms, the labs and the offices of actual, working, *good-looking* physicians as they dished out heaps of bad news to their patients.

Give it to me straight, Doc—how long is your option?

And thus was conceived *Group One Medical*, a Sauter-Piller-Percelay production in association with MGM/UA Telecommunications, Inc., scheduled to begin operating October 3, five days a week, in upward of eighty-five American cities.

It's an inspirational story in itself, really—worthy of a treatment for a TV movie: Sauter, flamboyant and controversial network news mogul, former wunderkind; career in ashes following series of disastrous management decisions at CBS News; suddenly reborn at the relatively advanced age of 53 as a Hollywood-entertainment impresario.

Van Gordon Sauter, the Grand Mal Moses of reality programming.

Ah, yes. Reality programming. That heaven-sent antidote to the writers' strike and its aftermath, not to mention the long-delayed answered prayer of the unknown network president, who shrieked in the sweet long ago, *"There's not even enough mediocrity to go around!"*

He was talking about *scripted* mediocrity, of course, and he was right. And that was even before cable, before superstations, before Siskel and Ebert. But those days are over. With the recent advent of reality programming—controlled real-life situations in which the misfortunes of actual people are presented as edifying entertainment—there is now plenty of mediocrity to go around. More than plenty, if you count reality programming's inevitable and almost instantaneous offshot: scripted-, or simulated-, reality programming.

Give it to me straight, Doc—are you a doc?

Did I say "recent"? Can *People's Court* be eight years old already? Can it have been 1980—the outset of that Rancho Mirage of a decade—that a retired judge named Joseph Wapner began hearing small-claims-settlement eases in a studio-courtroom toward the greater glory of American jurisprudence and Ralph Edwards/Stu Billett Productions?

Yes, it can. And the purveyors of reality programming have learned quite a lot since that big bang, that spontaneous combustion of a genre. They have learned, for instance, how to cover their asses.

Back in 1980 the concept of "entertainment" hadn't quite attained the all-embracing holiness that it enjoys today. Close, mind you, but not quite all-embracing. The *People's Court* people,

for instance, never thought to promote their new concept as a
kind of pop-cult-equivalent experience for Harvard Law School;
they offered it up as standard honest voyeurism. And took a
terrific drubbing from certain critics, who were shocked at this
arrant mongrelizing of entertainment and the august sanctity of
the courts.

But, boy, Your Honor, did the show mop up on the bottom line.
Big ratings in the late afternoon, but, just as important, *People's
Court* ran on an almost-invisible budget. Reality proved not only
popular but cheap. Real plaintiffs didn't drag down soap-opera
salaries. Not even Judge Wapner himself required the care and
feeding of, say, a Redd Foxx.

Give it to me straight, Judge—how much do you make?

And so within a very few years, the early-evening pre-local
news hours were filled with this sort of stuff. Ordinary people,
caught on the barbed wire of life's little torments, thrashing to get
loose for the titillation of the folks at home. And always under the
legitimizing gaze of a robed authority figure.

Superior Court. Divorce Court. The Judge. Americans couldn't get
enough of watching old men whack their gavels. And every one
of these offshoots shared an interesting quality: They were
scripted. Even as Edwards/Billett was selling reality as entertainment, its imitators had turned it around: they were selling
entertainment as reality.

Or quasi-reality, anyway. Although the simulation disclaimer
was pretty fine-print stuff in the credits, the make-believe-judge
shows were not falsely presented. Still, they needed a rationale,
some high-sounding claim of Redeeming Social Value, to justify
the fake-documentary look.

And so the marketing concept took hold that these entertain-
ments were *good for you!* And what's more, it didn't even hurt:
That even as you salivated over the slit-skirted slut on the witness
stand and wondered whether she'd get nailed for sleeping with
her husband's sister's tax accountant, you were learning some
valuable case law, real insider stuff that would come in handy if
your own slut—oh, never mind.

That was the evolving strategy of reality programming out of
Hollywood in the early Eighties—the high-water-mark era of the

docudrama, the predawn of Morning Again in America, you may recall. That was the genesis of the form that has lately decayed into such morbid freak shows as *America's Most Wanted*, the noxious Fox Television series that dramatically re-creates violent crimes—actorish bodies twitching and jumping as bullet after simulated bullet sinks wetly into them—and then flashes the likeness of the real-life at-large perpetrator. *America's Most Wanted* has led to a couple of dozen capital-case arrests and has contributed to the cultural acceptance of gunplay as spectator sport. It's a measure of this country, and these anesthetized times, that the series has been praised as a public service.

But meanwhile, back in the early Eighties, by one of those fascinating coincidences, a similar "reality" strategy was starting to manifest itself on the other side of the country—in the network news citadels of New York City. Its mastermind was one Van Gordon Sauter, the president of CBS News, who had come to believe that, hell, *reality* needed some reality programming.

Sauter began to tear apart the philosophical foundations of CBS News—information selected on the basis of public interest and presented concisely, without dramatization. In the ruins of these foundations, Sauter erected his philosophy of "moments"—trends and political currents as refracted in the glimpsed lives of ordinary people (farmers, laid-off factory workers) who were "experiencing" these currents.

It was in those moments, and not at the moment of Sauter's speech to the AMA, that *Group One Medical* began to be born.

"It was easy for me, when Van talked about *People's Court* as a prototype entity, easy for me to get a sense of his interest in creating a reality medical show. I said I'd be quite pleased in working with him. I was invited to be part of the creative process."

That's Ron Pion talking. *Doctor* Ron, ob-gyn, a 57-year-old state-of-the-art California medico-media smoothy who attended that Rancho Mirage confab, did lunch with Van and Van's people at Scandia afterward and, après Scandia, rang up some pertinent MGM/UA people on his car phone to say he was coming in with a concept.

Dr. Ron, a former NBC News medical correspondent, became

Group One Medical's technical consultant. ("Initially, there was some thought of my being on-camera.") Dr. Ron was put in charge of coming up with talent—doctor talent and patient talent. Since nearly everyone in Southern California is an actual or an aspiring talent anyway, this did not prove to be the problem it might seem.

"I started by looking through a California AMA picture book of active members," Dr. Ron says. "Then the MGM people and I started to highlight those people who *had a look*. Then—"

What *kind* of look? I rudely interrupt, fascinated. Reality always fascinates me.

"The look kept changing," says Dr. Ron. "Some people on the creative team wanted a man, some wanted a woman; some voted young, some old; some voted a look of confidence, some a look of caring. . . ."

The creative team finally voted on three doctors: one with a look of Tom Selleck, one with a look of Jessica Walter, and one with a look of Lou Gossett Jr. The three would more or less play themselves on-camera, listening to patients describe their complaints, providing diagnoses, and just plain *relating* with them in a caring but confident sort of way. At the end of each program the three doctors would huddle for a few "moments" and do a little cross-talk about the day's horror sto—excuse me, the day's cases, just like those "real correspondents" on CBS News' *West 57th*.

And the patient talent? A slightly larger order, but no problem, really, for Dr. Ron.

"I wrote a 'Dear Editor' letter to *Los Angeles County Medical Association Physician* magazine," says Pion, "asking colleagues to loan us their patients. I wanted our doctors to be able to borrow these patients in a continuing-care arrangement. It's similar to what we doctors call teaching rounds, or case presentations, in which permission is obtained for the patient to be presented to a body of professionals for the purpose of teaching."

Ah! Teaching! Glad Dr. Ron brought that up! *Teaching*, of course, is the hortatory cornerstone of *Group One Medical*—its mission, its raison d'être type of thing. What! You thought this was some kind of *entertainment show*? Just listen to Dr. Ron.

"Look up the word 'entertain' in your dictionary," he prescribes. "You'll find it says 'to hold in the mind.' [I did. The doc had given it to me straight.] The ultimate purpose of this show is that, truly, someone may be assisted. I believe the American public is desirous of having more health information. My own bias has been that it would be nice if patients with similar conditions tuned in."

Now, *that* would take one hell of a lot of "Dear *TV Guide*" letters from Dr. Ron, but who's to say? Meanwhile, let's get down to cases—the sorts of cases *Group One Medical* will be depicting for the theoretical edification of its viewers.

"First of all, it's all real-time conversation," Dr. Ron assures me. "Edited down, of course. But no rehearsals, no retakes except for technical problems."

But the patients' reactions to bad news, I press. Isn't it a little exploitive for a camera to be on someone—even if he's volunteered and is getting a token fee—at the moment of a life-shattering discovery?

"No. On our program, *nobody ever learns anything before the camera*," the doctor says. "That's too exploitive. No way in the world will the patient-physician confidentiality be broken. It will always be *last week* that they've learned that they have cancer, learned they have AIDS. What you will see is the patients as they *continue to experience* the diagnosis."

I have no reason to doubt Dr. Ron's word, and yet his choices of examples are interesting. On the promotional "vignette" tape that MGM/UA has released to stations and potential sponsors, there is one exceedingly memorable tight-focus vignette—a "moment," if you will—of a middle-aged man raising his expressive dark eyebrows and mouthing with incredulity, "*Cancer?*"

Another "moment" on the tape shows the Selleck-type doctor saying to a patient, "First of all, let me ask you your sexual preference." The patient responds that he is gay. It's not clear to me how either of these moments can be fit retroactively into the "continuing to experience" rubric. (The gay patient learns to his evident surprise just moments later that his previous visits to other doctors may not have resulted in adequate tests for the HIV virus.) But I'm willing to believe that some explanation exists.

What I am considerably less willing to believe is that *Group One Medical*, or its soon-to-be-burgeoning imitators (something called *Family Medical Center*, a scripted medical show taped by documentary-style hand-held cameras, was set for fall syndication by Lorimar Television), will deepen any lay viewer's comprehension of medical theory beyond a few useful palliatives.

In fact, I am deeply convinced that *Group One Medical*, like most other self-justifying programs of its genre, is running counter to the old Hippocratic admonition to "first do no harm."

The harm done by reality programming is doubtless unintentional, but it is harm just the same: the harm of falsely suggesting to the culture that there are no distinctions between entertainment and education—or entertainment and specialized knowledge, or entertainment and heightened citizenship (or, in the case of the fading televangelists, between entertainment and sacredness). The magnitude of this passive lie can be grasped if one imagines prelaw or premedical students actually studying for their professions by hunkering down, notepads in hand, before fringe-time broadcasts of *People's Court* or *Group One Medical*.

It is monstrous—and pitiful—to imagine what calamities await an individual, or a culture, who believes himself to be "experiencing" the process of education through entertainment television. As social critic Neil Postman, among others, has argued, nearly everything that defines entertainment is inimical to education, and vice versa.

This video-generated myth of learning by entertainment, or learning stripped of rigor and discipline and incentive, is worse than banal. It is insidious and is helping to make respectable a growing national contempt for literacy and learning. The result? A widening gulf between unspecialized consumeroid Americans and a new, paternalistic managerial and technocratic elite. As suggested, the consequences of this rift—a passive, depoliticized, credulous body politic—are unlovely to imagine.

Give it to us straight, Doc—how long have we got?

It Came from New Jersey

The beast is loose, and it's helping make Morton
Downey Jr. *the most horrifying show of the Eighties*

The elevator doors slide open on the studio floor of the
television center. Morton Downey Jr.'s piscine eyes bulge left,
then right.

"Oh, shit," Downey mutters. "The audience is here." He says
it with the unconvincing moue of a Washington hostess murmuring, "Oh, shit. The secretary of defense has just arrived."

Downey bounds from the elevator, skipping on the balls of his
feet, which are snuggled in Italian tasseled loafers. It is more than
an hour before tonight's taping of *The Morton Downey Jr. Show* on
Superstation WWOR-TV in Secaucus, New Jersey. But already
the audience has come in from the boroughs and the industrial
darkness. Already it has coalesced into the shape and the mood
of a sentient animal, an elongated beast lying patiently outside
the studio door.

Downey sprints alongside the flank of the beast, high-fiving its
several hundred hands. Lots of black leather. Football jerseys.
Chains. And the guys look tough, too. The beast stirs: It recog-
nizes its master. Its many eyes are already filmed over with a kind
of erotic lust for the theater of abuse to follow. It commences a
tremendous guttural bark: "*Mort! Mort! Mort! Mort!*"

Many Americans are not yet aware, my friends—as Downey
would doubtless put it—*not yet aware* that there is any such thing
as a *Morton Downey Jr. Show*. LIKE HELL THERE ISN'T! And I'll
tellya—wait, lemme finish, you'll get your turn, little guy—I'll
tellya something else! A lot of those *bubbleheads* and *squeaky-faced*

wimps who *have* seen it since it went on the air last October—
they're saying. "HEY! DOWNEY'S NOTHING MORE THAN A *THROW-
BACK*! Like Joe Pyne in the Sixties! First-in-the-mouth television.
Right?" WELL LEMME TELLYA! THEY CAN *KISS MY BUTT*! BECAUSE
THAT'S *BULLCRAP*!

No. Downey is exactly what his publicity claims him to be: the
talk-show host who will take the genre into the twenty-first
century. A frighteningly accurate assertion.

The secret ingredient is Downey's audience. Not the pasty-faced
matrons of Donahue and Oprah but . . . kids. Working class.
Trans-Am owners, pro-football fans. They come to *rock and roll*.
They've seen the show. They know what's expected of them: to
cheer when Downey screams "SHUT UP, FLESH-FACE!" at a guest
who starts to disrupt his trade with a coherent debating point. To
whoop and dance when Downey literally wraps himself in an
American flag and offers a Tehran-born student the opportunity
to kiss his ass. To bellow frothing invective as Downey lavishes
such hateful ad hominem sarcasm on a panel of porno actresses
or robed Ku Klux Klanspeople that he inadvertently confers a
kind of dignity on their helplessness.

It is the audience-as-attack-dog that transforms Downey's
cretinous vulgarities into a sort of performance art—a sulfurous
music video without the music. *Exactly.* How could it be otherwise? The producer of the *Downey Show* (along with MCA, the
new corporate owner of WWOR) is Quantum Media, Inc. The
president of Quantum is Robert Pittman, the man who invented
MTV.

Downey dashes into the makeup room, where he peels down
to his boxer shorts and socks, indifferent to the presence of the
WWOR anchorwoman in the hairstylist's chair. "*Very* strong, *very*
strong demos [demographics] with the kids," he is saying to his
own reflection in the mirror. He slides on a pair of brown slacks,
notches the Gucci belt. He wears lots of gold. "This is the first
young people's talk show. These kids keep getting told in school,
in their jobs: Keep your lips buttoned; don't get out of line; don't
talk back. Well, my friend—they come to *this* show, and here's
someone who's *doing* it . . . and *getting away with it* . . . and
letting them do it!"

His face, at 55, looks like two profiles stitched together, but badly—the watery blue eyes aligned too far to the outside, the chins overlapping to form a point like the bottom of a valentine heart. The hair, brushed up and back Bobby Darin–style, is jet-black. But what really dominates Morton Downey's features is the teeth. Rows and rows of them, pure and blinding porcelain, welded into his mouth like piano keys. It is these teeth, which flash horribly when he speaks (*the canines!*), that signal an affinity between Downey and the audience-beast.

He was a radio man for five years. This is his first television show. The dossier on his peculiar career is by now fairly well known to his cult fans: son of the late beloved Irish Tenor Morton Downey Sr. and the actress Barbara Bennett. Former rock-and-roll singer and songwriter (he coproduced the Sixties classic "Wipeout"). Adventurer and hero (he claims to have smuggled starving Ibo tribesmen out of Nigeria during the Biafran war). Former vice-president of the Canteen Corp. A cofounder of the American Basketball Association. Presidential candidate in 1980 for the American Independent Party.

As of this night in early November, *Downey* is available five nights a week to about 10 million American households, 11 percent of the viewing public. That could change soon; syndication plans are a possibility. Meanwhile, the low profile might be working to the program's advantage. Its producers are still booking guests who are innocent of what they're getting into.

Tonight's guests, for example: Two distinguished academics will debate each other (*or so they think!*) on whether a national policy should be established for withdrawing health care for old and hopelessly sick people. Or, as Downey will frame it at the top of the show, "I wonder whether we're still CIVILIZED tonight, my friends! I wonder whether the GOVERNMENT . . . has the RIGHT . . . to END A PERSON'S LIFE!"

Half an hour before showtime, the beast is released into the studio.

It is impossible to sense the full adrenaline frenzy of a *Downey* audience by watching it on TV. Only inside the studio can one feel the hunger for action—the hysteria—like a kind of barometric pressure on one's skin.

They file in, looking around, cracking gum, fiddling with their neck chains, and fill up the bleachers, where they sit gaping down at the lighted but empty set. And what a deceptively bland-looking little instrument of terror that set is: a dais of chrome and fiberboard. A chair for Downey, chairs for the guests. But Mort's chair is adjusted several inches higher than the others. The guests' chairs whip back and forth, but—subtle designer touch—Downey's chair swivels, the guests' chairs don't. (The production staff has bolted them solid.) Meanwhile, the main camera on Downey is positioned low, near ground level, to emphasize his domineering presence over his guests. It's amazing how docile people become on that set.

Downey is killing time by pacing around the runway behind the bleachers, beneath a bevy of butts. I decide this is as good a time as any to ask him where the rage comes from.

The answer seems surprisingly disarming. "I was disciplined hard as a kid," he says. "Military school at 11. Jesuits."

But—but wasn't he the son of the beloved Irish tenor Morton Downey Sr., the darling of radio's Golden Age?

"My father," says Downey, and shows a few dozen teeth. "I only saw him every three weeks, when he came in off the road. We lived on Park Avenue and in Connecticut. My parents were divorced. I never saw my mom from age 7 till age 21. My grandmother would watch us while Dad was gone. She'd make a list of all the things we'd done, all the misbehaving. Dad would read that list. Then he'd take us up to his room, where he kept this elephant tusk carved into a long shoehorn sort of thing— Paul Whiteman had given it to him. He'd take that shoehorn and he'd beat us with it."

Showtime.

The theme music—a kick-ass hard-rock riff—lashes out at top decibel. A floor director whips the beast into an orgiastic tumult of whistles and applause.

"MORT! MORT! MORT! MORT!"

Downey makes his patented entrance. Tracked by a long-range camera, he comes hustling down the same runway where he'd been killing time. Now he's flanked by two assistants. He seems to be studying some blue note cards. Just as he reaches the rim of the set, he flips a card to each assistant, then breaks into a full sprint for the dais. This is a bit of performance kitsch that Downey cooked up—"It makes me look like I'm getting information right up to the last second," he told me. In the context of what usually follows, it makes him look more like a gang leader getting an escort by his bodyguards to the killing field.

The show's first segment is deceptively calm. The guest is a man named Sydney Rosoff, chairman of the Society for the Right to Die. Rosoff says that everyone should have the right to terminate his or her life-support system if recovery seems hopeless.

The beast isn't sure how to feel about this. It gives off some ruffs and woofs, waiting for the attack cue from its master. Downey, a lighted cigarette between his fingers, has slid off his chair and now towers over Rosoff. The beast growls in its throat. Rosoff shrinks in a bit, a suddenly naked and alone man.

"How about *this*," Downey snarls. "I see this as a *progression*, to the *government* having this right."

woof! woof! grumps the beast.

But the segment ends with no ripped flesh. Rosoff climbs out of his chair, a dopey grin on his face. He's a man who has looked into the *jaws*—and survived! Back after this.

Now Dr. Daniel Callahan is in the chair. He is chairman of the Institute of Social Ethics and Life Sciences and wrote *Setting the Limits: Medical Goals in an Aging Society*. The book argues for an age limit on technological life-support systems. Grrrrrr. woof! But Downey is the picture of suave solicitation.

"If we set the age limit up here [hand at eye level] today," he asks reasonably, "who's to say tomorrow it isn't set here . . . and lower . . . and lower?"

Downey offers Callahan two minutes to state his case without interruption. "I don't want to be a bully"—the porcelain teeth flash like knives; the beast stirs—"*do I look like a bully to you, Doctor?*" Downey turns, teeth still bared in a grin, to the audience. "*My gang is not a gang of bullies, either.*"

Knowing chuckles from the awakening crowd.

Callahan, an earnest, curly-haired man in glasses, launches into his case: Americans enjoy a wealth of high-technology life-extension care . . . it costs a lot of money . . . thirty years from now, 50 percent of the federal budget will go toward health care for the elderly . . . we have to rethink . . . there will have to be an age cutoff eventually . . . the late seventies or early eighties. . . .

And then Callahan carelessly bares a slice of throat. "I'm really very impressed by the British system," he says. "They provide no access to dialysis or expensive heart surgery, but their overall health care is terrific."

Downey is upon him before his last syllable dies away. "Their system says if you're 55 and need dialysis, you can't get it." "Right," says Callahan, "but I wouldn't—" "Well, the British did, and you just said you *ad-miiiiiiirrrred* their system!"

Olé! The bedlam from the bleacher seats is deafening. The beast senses attack; its forest of arms shoots into the air. Over the din Morton Downey suddenly screams into Callahan's face, "FIFTY-FIVE YEARS OLD . . . LEMME TELLYA, PAL, I'LL BE 55 IN THREE WEEKS AND *NOBODY'S GONNA CROAK ME!*" Whoops, howls fill the air.

"I said the late seventies—" begins Callahan.

"THIS IS THE SAME CRAPPOLA — ALL THE POPULATION EXPERTS STATE 80 YEARS. SO YOU START THERE! THEN THE *NEXT* JERK WHO INTERPRETS THE LAW SAYS 70! THEN YOU GET SOME *OTHER BUBBLE-HEAD* IN THERE. AND *HE* SAYS 60! AWRIGHT, HOW CAN YOU BE SURE IT'LL STAY AT 80? *HOW DO YOU KNOW?*"

"We don't—"

Downey thrusts his lighted cigarette toward the camera. "UNCLE GEORGE, YOU WATCHING TONIGHT? YOU WERE 93 YEARS OLD LAST WEEK. WHADDAYA SAY TO THIS GUY. HE WANTS YOU CROAKED RIGHT NOW BECAUSE IT'S *COSTING TOO MUCH MONEY TO KEEP YOU ALIVE!*"

Screams! Taunts! A waterfall of mockery from the seats!

"Excuse me. I *didn't* say I want him croaked—"

From the beast: "YOU'RE A ROACH!" "GO TO RUSSIA!"

Station break. Don't go way. We'll be right back.

Now Dr. Richard L. Rubenstein has joined Callahan on the set. Rubenstein is president of the Washington Institute of Values in Public Policy. Under normal circumstances, he would be an opponent of Callahan's; he disagrees that age should be a criterion for terminating health care. But in this arena, this pit, such nuances seem laughable, the fine distinctions of life on another planet. The two men draw together, wary and grim.

Rubenstein has a go at the pretense of debate: Yes, limits must be set. But targeting age groups runs the risk of the "bureaucratic possibility" that such groups would be considered "surplus." In a time of national crisis, such groups might be eliminated.

Downey isn't listening. Rubenstein doesn't exist. Downey has targeted his own victim for the evening. Turning back to Callahan, he asks him offhandedly, "Your mom and dad alive, or are they dead now?"

There is a long, tense moment before Callahan replies evenly. "They're both dead."

"Would you have cut off medical care to let them die?"

WOOF! CHUFF! CHORTLE!

Callahan draws a breath. Then he says, "I should make one thing clear: We need decades of discussion and dialogue on this—"

"You're safe, Uncle George, you're safe. . . . He's not gonna killya tonight. . . . Nazi Germany started the same way. They wanted to take some time to build it up, didn't they?"

"I reject the analogy!" Callahan, twisting in his fixed seat, has finally risen to the bait. *"I won't call you the Dr. Goebbels of the media, and you don't accuse me of Nazism!"*

The beast is quivering with vilent glee—"GO! GO! GO! GO!"— but Downey prowls calmly. "You can call me the Dr. Goebbels of the media; that's quite all right . . . *and I will, whether you do or not, refer to you as the Nazi in medicine."*

Amid the thunderous riot of joyful bays and war whoops comes a sound so singular, so anguished and pure, that it remains in the consciousness long after all the other sounds of this grotesque hour have congealed. It is the cry of a surprised and wounded man: "OH, NO-O!" The beast hears it and bellows louder.

But now Rubenstein is on his feet. *A guest has left the low, unswiveling chair!* The beast loves it: "GO! GO! GO! GO!"

Rubenstein stands there, this white-haired man in a gray suit, stands there until even the beast seems a little abashed. And then, pointing at Callahan, he says, "I have spent thirty years studying Nazism! I wrote three books! I know this man! I disagree with this man! But you *cannot call him anything like that! It is absolutely unfair!*"

Downey has backed up to the rim of his audience. He shrugs. "The doctor is entitled to his opinion, I'm entitled to mine—"

"When it comes to a man who has worked as hard as he has—"

Now the camera is on Morton Downey's face, and it is suddenly transformed into a convulsion of tics and winks. The eyes bulge, the porcelain teeth are bared.

"*ADOLF HITLER WORKED HARD TOO! ARE YOU SO DUMB? YOU WROTE A BOOK ABOUT AUSCHWITZ!*" Bedlam. Theme music. Break.

Back near the runway, one of the young rock-and-roll boys of Morton Downey's production staff is gazing at Rubenstein's image on a monitor screen. There is something like love-light in the kid's eyes; his face is a mask of beatific awe.

"It's great television," he croons, to himself as much as anyone. "You can see the sweat on the top of his head. . . ."

On the morning of the day I drove over to Secaucus to watch the taping of *The Morton Downey Jr. Show*, a magazine had come in the mail. It was a commemorative issue of *The Quill*, a professional journalist's monthly, and in it were reprinted some articles written decades ago.

One of them in particular had caught my attention. It was from the late 1940s, the very dawn of television—about the time of Morton Downey Sr.'s great national fame.

The article was full of the stentorian phrases of the time—"the vast and unlimited potential of this new medium," and so forth. But what really fascinated me was the accompanying photograph. It showed a pioneer television cameraman—shooting 16-mm film—perched on top of a station wagon in the Chicago Loop. Below him on the bright sidewalk, a group of passersby had paused to glance upward—men with wide ties, women in pillbox hats. Their faces told it all: those smiles of arrested curiosity, the delight and inclusive pride just starting to spread, that are the special and irretrievable qualities of faces from that era.

I did not see any such faces leaving the WWOR studios that night in Secaucus. I saw satiation; I saw the afterglow of adrenaline rush. I saw faces that were already forgetting what the excitement had been about.

I saw the face of television in the twenty-first century.

L.A. Law: D.O.A.

A new series by the creator of Hill Street Blues *has a long rap sheet of sins, including a television rarity—trying too hard*

It's the dawn of another typical workday at the high-powered, comprehensive-service L.A. law firm McKenzie, Brackman, Chaney & Kuzak. The subplots are still wandering into the story line, and the ambient confusion is just starting to rise from the sound track. But Arnie Becker, rakish, womanizing junior partner, has already figured out what the terrible smell is. It's Chaney, over in the corner office. Chaney croaked in the night, one claw still clutching his desk appointment calendar, like a blatant, ironic detail.

"He's dead," observes Arnie's secretary, slowly lowering her can of spray disinfectant.

"He is," agrees Arnie. "I had dibs on his office."

Bam! Opening titles: *L.A. Law.* Executive producer and cocreator, Steven Bochco . . .

"Creative control" used to be the Golden Fleece of prime-time entertainment—the phantom "vision" in television. If a sensitive, idealistic young screenwriter could only find some way to wrest creative control from the bad network vice-presidents, then he or she could instill *content*, could essay *dramatic shading*, might even venture a teensy step in the direction of *values*—certainly *production values*.

It was a comfortable myth; comfortable because it would never be tested. Looming like Cybil Shepherd's kneecaps in the path of such righteous impulse was an impediment of diabolic cunning:

that bureaucratic answer to the Undead known as the *writer-producer*. So long as the best TV screenwriters were rewarded with an administrative stake in their projects' ratings success, with all the incremental wealth that the "producer" mantle guaranteed, they would be highly disinclined to venture out beyond the safe, soggy boundaries of the unthreatening, the formulaic, the vanilla.

Then five years ago that comfortable myth was—aiiee!—fulfilled. *Hill Street Blues* flashed onto NBC like a meteor to wipe away the brontosaurian limits on action drama's capacity for realism, complexity, authentic dialogue, moral ambiguity—to say nothing of plausible tenderness, earned affection, humor and grief. Chief among its creators at MTM Enterprises was Steven Bochco, a brash and brilliant young producer who had risen through the ranks of salaried writing jobs at Universal Studios and NBC. At MTM, the New York–born Bochco welded the contradictory mandates of writer and producer into a seamless artistic function. He limned cops-and-lowlifes dialogue with the ear of a young Dashiell Hammett. He orchestrated interweaving subplots like William Saroyan. All the while he fought, as a producer, *on behalf of* the show's birthright—to take thematic chances, spend money.

He was personally rewarded with six Emmys (*Hill Street* won a total of twenty-six during his tenure there), a Peabody, a shower of humanitarian awards, and, more important, the Golden Fleece itself: At the age of 38, Steven Bochco, poet and protector of prime time, gained unfettered access to creative control.

What lessons are to be learned, then, from the early signs that Bochco's new *L.A. Law*, on NBC (Fridays, 10 P.M.), is a disagreeable mess, bordering on a monstrosity?

The ambient sound divides like a cell; divides again as the denizens of McKenzie, Brackman, Chaney & Kuzak (oops, make that McKenzie, Brackman & Kuzak) struggle with their responses to the death of the senior partner. Through the obligatory murmurings—"What's going on?" "Mr. Chaney's dead." "Oh, my God!"—there emerge a few wisps that hint at this law firm's prevailing regard for the moderating virtues. "One minute," a voice is heard to drawl from the gaggle, "you're hip-deep in the tax code. The next—" there is a snap, as of fingers.

"The guy's so stiff you could put him in a museum," a cop joshes, and someone else says, "His feet are, like, frozen." A jocular voice asks, "Can we have a little *reverence* here?" There is a close-up of the corpse being hauled away, lurching and yawing. "Turn him, *turn* him—no, the other way!" "Be careful, you're gonna lose him!" Wittily, Chaney's mortal remains go *clunk* against a doorjamb and sag like yesterday's enchiladas suizas to the carpet as a secretary's voice, off-camera, answers a ringing phone: "Mr. Chaney's office—no, I'm sorry, he's not available right now."

Clearly, these are not the offices of *Owen Marshall: Counselor at Law*. Perry Mason would probably flee this place in tears. But, hey, we're still just in the amenities stage of this two-hour pilot episode; we're getting *acquainted* with these people. The serious slime is still a couple of commercial breaks ahead.

A Bochco-induced sense of extremism, of set-piece scenes jacked up to their ultimate shock-value payload, quickly begins to insinuate itself. ("Spiking," this is tenderly called in the business.) We meet Kuzak, the ensemble's designated empathy figure (it helps to have a scorecard, or a press release), as he broods double-breastedly over the arrest charges filed against his thuggish, Method-actorish client in a jail cell. Kuzak is played with moist and cow-eyed passivity by the alarmingly well-groomed Harry Hamlin.

Is Kuzak's client a wrongo, a bad apple? Just listen to Kuzak, reading from the rap sheet:

"Says here she was beaten, raped—*and when her wig fell off during the assault, she was tossed into a Dumpster.*" (My italics; I love the wig part. *Quel* pathos.)

The client is somehow unmoved by this remembrance of things past. Twisting his mouth into a sneer the approximate shape of an L.A. freeway cloverleaf, he avers that it wasn't that way at all. "She followed me outta a liquor store," he leers. "Sez she'll do the three of us for fifty bucks." As the hisses and catcalls begin to cascade from America's living rooms ("Minimum wage! Minimum wage!"), the wastrel sinks deeper into perfidy: "You talked to my *father* yet? For a thousand bucks she'll fold like a deck chair."

"That's doubtful," ripostes Kuzak, with icy civility. "She has . . . *acute leukemia!*"

Yowee! This is better than Martina versus Chris Evert Lloyd. Just when our necks are starting to get sore from all this back-and-forth swiveling, this ground-stroke rally of one-downmanship, we are mercifully whisked back to the plush offices of McKenzie, Brackman & Kuzak, where a working luncheon has been convened to indulge a little trendy cynicism.

A secretary (need one bother to say "comely"?) passes a wrapped sandwich to Arnie (Corbin Bernsen), he of the upwardly mobile nostrils. "This is *tongue*, honey," cracks Arnie over his shoulder. "Are you trying to tell me something?"

More subplots rush, like so many white blood cells, into the story line. In a courtroom, a flinty judge summons the bickering prosecutor (female) and public defender (male) to his bench to ask the legalistic question, "You two hot for each other, or what?" (Spike No. 1.) "I'm mad 'cause I lowered my standards," retorts the prosecutor. (Spike No. 2.) "Yeah," snorts the defender, "along with your skirt." (Spike No. 3, but don't start counting your pulse rate yet—the judge is about to announce that he needs a potty break.)

Lawyers (Kuzak included) spin deals over drinks, furtive as Florentine courtiers. The patriarch of the law firm, Leland McKenzie (Richard Dysart), nudges Kuzak to see to the defense needs of the millionaire's son turned wig snatcher and Dumpster tosser. Kuzak is a silent (but acquiescing) partner to a brutal courtroom cross-examination of the thug's victim—who, it turns out, not only was raped, beaten, de-wigged, Dumpsterized, and leukemia-ridden but is *black.* (Spike!) Kuzak's associates seek to portray the woman as a terminal thrill-seeker—"Gather ye rosebuds while ye may, Miss Moore!" (Spike!)

And meanwhile, the viewer's sensibilities scan this sordid little universe of preeners, posturers, viperous shysters and zomboid exploiters for—a hero. Or, absent a "hero" (quaint term!), a locus of sympathy, some avatar of hope. If not Othello, then at least Daniel J. Travanti. And scan and scan, but no such figure emerges from the sulfur. *L.A. Law* seems truly a vision of urban, professional America as unremitting hell.

Instead of finding hope, we get relief from the mendacity in the form of black humor—or what Bochco apparently flatters himself is black humor. Arnie and his hired private investigator, a punk-cropped Valley toughie in a satin tank top that delineates some Serious Prime-Time Nipple, are perusing some covert photographs of a divorce-seeking woman's husband and his doxy.

"And here's the pièce de résistance," snickers the gal gumshoe, handing over a glossy. "George and his honey poolside on a chaise lounge, engaged in a sex act usually described by a two-digit number." (Spike! Spike!)

A moment later, the femme fosdick has turned philosophical. As Arnie prepares for lunch with his soon-to-be-devastated client, she probes the ineffable: "I swear I don't understand you, Arnie. You take this poor woman to some snitzy restaurant. You slap *these* on the table. She goes into the ladies' room and ralphs up fifty bucks worth of lunch all over the velvet wallpaper. What's the point?"

It is a question that must have occurred to more than a few viewers by this time. Is Bochco asking us to take these dreadful people seriously or for laughs? The tone veers drunkenly between the two attitudes. In the two-hour episode's most gratuitous and painfully off-key scene—Chaney's funeral—one colleague ends his groping eulogy with the archly written line, "If I had to describe him in one word, it would be—'fiduciary.'" The succeeding eulogist, a newly hired secretary, reveals herself to be . . . a transvestite. She met Chaney in a gay bar. *L.A. Law* is at this point trafficking in what someone considerably to the left of the late Meese Commission—the oversigned, for example—might unflinchingly term "smut."

Black humor, properly sustained, artfully rendered, is a welcome device for a prime-time series. But it is a testimony to this pilot episode's ultimate soullessness that the satiric tone is contradicted—subverted—by a recurring streak of white-knuckled Liberal Oblige. This violent mood shift occurs mainly when the Women of the Firm are on-screen. Jill Eikenberry as counselor Ann Kelsey gets to declaim a lot of feminist-idealist sentiments on the order of "I am not against earning a buck, Leland, as long as we don't sell off our humanity in the process." (Meanwhile, the

episode's "little" women—Amie's divorce client, for instance—
have to content themselves with more plebian sentiments, such
as "Chew on those numbers, you impotent piece of snot.") The
I-Am-Woman fugues are no doubt traceable to Bochco's cocreator
on *L.A. Law*, Terry Louise Fisher, a veteran of *Cagney and Lacey*
and no stranger herself to the delights of creative control.

So benumbed was I at the end of this two-hour crawl through the
swamps of hip cynicism—and so put off by the facile last-minute
anointing of the schlemiel-like Kuzak as a Really Good Guy at
Heart—that I reached into antiquity for possible parallels. I
flipped on a cassette of the original episode of *Hill Street Blues* to
see whether Bochco had suffered similar catastrophes in the early
stages of his great masterwork.

I found no such problems. True, certain Bochco tendencies had
not yet been smoothed into their eventual subtlety—characters
took turns hogging center stage for long set-piece turns, as when
Belker complained that he had not been allowed to bite a suspect
on the leg. There was the now-famous vignette of unbridled
horror, the stark shotgunning of two highly sympathetic officers.
There were oversimplifications of personality.

But at the center of that first *Hill Street* stood Daniel J. Travanti
as Captain Frank Furillo, an unmistakable rock of benign authority and (dare I write it? It's the *d* word) decency, and, however
compromised he was by the frailties of the flesh, duty. And
around Furillo swarmed a myriad of grubby, irritable, violent,
tender and comical people—citizens of, and vulnerable to, a
society that was both monstrous and radiant. In *L.A. Law*, by
contrast, the monsters have taken over—both on the outside and
in the inner circles of the ensemble cast.

What has changed in the five years between the premieres of *Hill
Street Blues* and *L.A. Law*? Is it possible that Steven Bochco, with
his undisputed ear for the rhythms of American life, is respond-
ing to some wrenching downdraft in the country's capacity for
redemption? Has he thus created a greater—if infinitely darker—
masterpiece than the series that won him fame? (And if so: Is he
accountable, even granting his genius, for the act of pandering to
the dark appetites?)

Or is the explanation for *L.A. Law* more limited, more narrowly behavioristic in scope? Is it a simple testimony that *too much* creative control, even in an industry as rudderless as network television, results in a tarnishing orgy of hubris? A tendency to reach ever more wantonly for the next spike?

It's hard to say for sure. But in either case—to borrow from the eloquence of Kuzak's client-thug when he heard that Miss Moore had leukemia—that's too bad.

Trivial Pursuits

Despite lofty aims, ABC's thirtysomething *is really aboutnothing*

Welcome to totally rull life. ABC's precious pasta-link of a series designer-labeled *thirtysomething* (alternative title: *skinnywhitepeoplefromhell*) is pouting its way toward the triumphal windup of its first season. Like its success-clenched characters, the program can find, perversely, plenty to pout about.

'Cause, see, it's got IT ALL! Rully! Ratings, critical prestige, the thanks of a grateful baby boom—POUT CITY! As Michael himself might huskily verbalize it, asked hyperanalytically by Hope why he can't enjoy the things he has, " *'Cause I might lose them.*"

Well, hey. Not rully. Not if the people meters and the popcult press can help it. So far, *thirtysomething* has rully, like, MADE IT! Quickly renewed for '88! Awesome numbers and demos! Great "buzz" factor! (People are talking about it.) *thirtysomething* has won everything but the Overachievers' Citation for Uncommon Narcissism with radicchio cluster.

Isn't this what we fought the Battle of Grenada for? So that the next generation could be totally free to deal with the concept of preweaning?

Let us not minimize the achievement of creators Edward Zwick and Marshall Herskovitz: With *thirtysomething*, they have accomplished the nearly impossible task of flattering the least flatterable generation in American history. (Not entirely beside the point, it is also the most desirable generation in the history of television audiences.) The subtlety of this accomplishment has not been properly appreciated.

Let us now praise famous yuppies.

The characters in *thirtysomething*'s ensemble are a markedly waspish lot—in all senses of that term. Even the Jewish characters. Their abiding petulance has been owned up to, often uneasily, even by the show's most breathless boosters. Camera shots track across vast geographies of listless (but great!) bodies, to settle upon angst-ridden faces gazing pensively into the Zeitgeist. Sensitive guitar music accompanies a wife's tearful revelation that she's *cleaned house three times today!* ("I don't want to hear this," her best friend from college is sure to pipe up—"it's too hurtful.")

Unmarried women in wine bars wonder if they should have arguments with someone who wears polyester shirts. ("They're not even blends?" their companions ask, incredulous.) There is much talk of sex ("Total stress!"); there is some modified upscale stripping (down past the Princeton sweatshirt); there is upscale kissing. The kissing scenes are augmented by a sound effect suggestive of, say, a 1967 Château de Fargues being s-l-o-w-l-y uncorked. Children appear, children named Ethan and Brittany. A site must be found for Brittany's theme birthday party. The republic holds its breath.

In its thematic concerns, at least, *thirtysomething* is scarcely the breakthrough concept that some have credited it with being. It is to some extent the old *Dick Van Dyke Show* as rewritten by the Ephron sisters. This is scarcely a critical flaw. The denizens of Ephronland cannot consume enough anthropology about themselves, as Diane Keaton and the nonfiction bestseller list will attest.

Michael and Hope Steadman, *thirtysomething*'s central couple, are the sort of black-belt strivers who can seamlessly free-associate the killing of a cockroach into an ototoververbalized referendum on their entire domestic financial structure:

She [*stalking the insect*]: There's a baby in this house! I will not have these disgusting, disease-ridden invertebrates running through her apricots and tapioca—HA! [*Smash!*]

He: Aaah, my racquetball shoe! [*They kiss*] Listen, I'll call the exterminator tomorrow, they'll spray the place with carcinogens.

She: They'll come back with mutant strains.

He: So we'll spray again.

She: Janey will grow up stunted.

He: So we'll move.

She: We can't afford to move.

He: We can't afford to live here; what's the difference?

Try introducing a neutral topic to the Steadmans over the baked Brie at the next gallery opening.

Michael, played with snail-buttered sincerity by Ken Olin, is a young advertising executive. (A master touch, since advertising is the semiotic that unifies the characters' essential concerns with those of its target audience.) He wears kick-ass raw-silk jackets to show he's Arrived and adorable canvas sneakers to show he hasn't forgotten his Values, and he speaks in this eensy-teensy little Sincere Voice in which every hand-stitched sentence ends in a gasp of angst-laden air.

Michael's wife, Hope (played by the scarcely less adorably named Mel Harris—don't these people ever LET UP?), is the kind of woman whose genetic fate is to be Rully Nifty, so why fight it? Aerobicized to within an inch of her skeletal structure (*no raisin bread!*), blessed with a brave crooked grin that only enhances her snookums good looks, tossing off ironies like disposable diapers, Hope is the June Allyson of the junk-bond age. Don't take her lightly; she has an outlaw streak a mile wide. ("Who's dealing with dinner, 'cuz . . . *I'm not dealing with it!*") But overall, she exists to psychoanalyze her and Michael's way through the thicket of upscale America's Big Issues: Is backpacking viable without a good baby-sitter? Is wallboarding the sun-room rully worth $5,000? Should one nuzzle one's spouse's hair after mousse has been applied?

Orbiting Michael and Hope's mortgaged milieu is an assortment of case histories who seem to have bolted en masse from an Oprah Winfrey panel on white anomie. There's Elliot (Timothy Busfield), Michael's adorable but hypermasculine creative partner, who spends his time at the office dream-sequencing about his impending divorce and twirling a Nerf basketball the same shade of orange as his hair and beard (no symbolic comparisons implied, surely). There's Elliot's neglected wife, Nancy (Patricia Wettig), a Joan Kennedy look-alike, who must amuse herself with brittle bons mots in posh bistros. ("I'm not gonna eat any animal where I have to eat its house too," she announces, disdaining the soft-shell crab.) There's Melissa (Melanie Mayron), the screwed-up single gal. ("How'm I ever gonna have a baby? I'm *dating* babies.") And—let's rully hear it, you gals in the audience—how about a big welcome for Gary, the de rigueur Peter Pan Bachelor Guy, portrayed with such shoulder-ringleted infantile perfection by Peter Horton that you start looking for the little green slippers and the gossamer wings.

Tickled into dramaturgic action, what these various types do mostly is behave—and speak—prototypically. (Since behavior, for this particular demographic pool, is virtually indistinguishable from speech, the *thirtysomething* crowd tends to speak *quite a lot*.) "I blew off the Teller account," Michael is likely to whisper as he pecks the missus in the evening, a refreshing Eighties variation on the old Van Dykean "Hi, honey, I'm home!" To which Hope might well respond, "Why do you have that look on your face?" Which will prompt Michael to huskily aver, "I *don't* have a look on my face," and so on, into the very abyss of transactional analysis.

All of which is accurate and contemporary—*rully* accurate and contemporary, let us hasten to acknowledge—but it veers frequently into unwitting Feifferesque excess. Creators Zwick and Herskovitz, in their zeal to render a video verbal vertié, may have triggered the next prime-time megacrisis: gratuitous dialogue. Imagine Crockett and Tubbs this coming fall, in the midst of a perfectly respectable firefight, pausing to deal with their commitment to their total relationship. Imagine the *Tour of Duty* gang forming a male encounter group.

Frankly, a little hyperverbalism in prime time is just what the analyst ordered, from one's retrograde linear point of view, anyway. In palmier moments, one likes to imagine *thirtysomething* as the long-awaited antibody to the MTV virus.

But there's a flaw built into *thirtysomething*, and it is, regrettably, the obvious one: The show's famous "little moment" situations— the microprocessed plots—simply do not support all the wonderful grace notes, the dead-on scripting and the menus and the clothes. Although the characters display tons of fashionable irony, the show itself seldom risks ironic distance from the characters.

To put it most brutally, their pathologically petty self-absorptions—Gary's horror of "commitment," Nancy's shattered dream of illustrating children's books, Michael's goddamned wallboard fixation—are presented at face value. Almost never is there more than the subtlest whisper of satiric edge. It is in this sense that *thirtysomething* shamelessly flatters the legendary narcissism of its thirtysomething core audience.

One can expect some argument on this score. Didn't *Newsweek* hit the mark in its rhapsodic review last December when it paused to worry that the show's "mirror" reflects something "by and large remarkably unflattering to the very viewers it most wants to win over?

Naaaaaaaah! Au contraire, as they say down at the Rolex repair shop. Those viewers GOTTA LOVE IT! *thirtysomething* is the culmination of the yuppie civil-rights movement. At last, the mass media is portraying their grievances seriously. When Michael puts his chinny-chin-chin on his hands and gurgles, "I'm depressed about everything in life not ever being exactly the way you want 'em to be," the huddled masses out there in their condos aren't hurling sun-dried tomatoes at the screen; they're shouting, "RIGHT ON!" Michael has been to the montaintop! And skied down it! Can I get a rully neat *hallelujah?*

Here's how the program calibrates its scale of values to the prevailing mood of the times: In the first episode, the overmastering issue seems to be whether Michael and Hope can find a suitable baby-sitter in time to go backpacking with Gary and his ex-girlfriend. (Trust me.) There is a lots and lots and lots of oververbalizing on this matter, and a funny little set-piece spoof of the baby-sitter interview.

Weaving among the many subplots, meanwhile, is a moral dilemma confronting Michael back at the ad agency. Elliot has designed a campaign for an important client—a rip-off of a currently successful campaign. Needless to say, the client loves Elliot's approach.

Michael is *sincerely* troubled by this. "What are we doing here?" he asks Elliot huskily. "Why did we start this business?"

"To do our thing," Elliot husks back. And then: "We won't always have to deal with sleazeballs like this. [*Pause*] Someday we'll be dealing with a higher class of sleazeball. [*Pause*] We'll come back to it [viz.: the moral issue] another day. Right now, we've got two wives, three kids, four cars, two mortgages and a payroll." Elliot sits back: "That's life, pal."

And bango, as they say. So much for *that* little distraction. Rationalized in their compromise, the guys return to more pressing considerations—Michael's choice of sleeping bags, Elliot's secret choice of sleeping partners. As for the work-place (which is as close as any of the *thirtysomething* crew gets to public life—politics and civic affairs being total abstractions, mere fodder for bons mots), well, it's the old ends-and-means game, Pal. Ciao!

Flattering to the arrested-adolescent id? A little. I'd say that if the movie *Wall Street* is an indictment of baby-boomer values, *thirtysomething* is the editorial reply. Fine; so be it. Television entertainment need not be a call to moral regeneration (not that it ever is), but let us at least be clear-eyed as to the intent here. *thirtysomething* satirizes its audience the same way the Gridiron Club satirizes the president and First Lady: ve-rrrrr-y gingerly.

And yet there is the occasional, the all-too-occasional, hint that somewhere down deep the show knows better. Toward the end of one episode, Elliot turns to Michael and remarks, apropos of nothing in particular. "Maybe our wives are secretly the same person." Then he thinks a bit and adds, "Maybe *we're* the same person." Another thoughtful beat. *"Maybe we're only leading one life."*

To which this jaded (and admittedly fortysomething) observer can only append: *Rully.*

ACKNOWLEDGMENTS

The Bread Loaf Lecture, "Don't Think of It as Art," was adapted for publication in the *Kenyon Review*, Summer 1989.

The essays in "TV Criticism" were first published in *GQ Magazine*, then included in the collection, *"The Beast, the Eunuch and the Glass-Eyed Child: Television in the 80s,"* published by Harcourt Brace Jovanovich, San Diego, New York, and London, 1990.

Face Value was first published by Delacorte Press, New York, 1979.

Toot-Toot-Tootsie, Good-Bye was published by Delacorte Press, New York, 1981.

Super Tube: the Rise of Television Sports was published by Coward-McCann, New York, 1983.

White Town Drowsing: Journeys to Hannibal was published by Atlantic Monthly Press, Boston, and New York, 1986. From *White Town Drowsing* by Ron Powers. Copyright © 1986 by Ron Powers. Used by permission of Doubleday, a division of Bantam Doubleday Dell Publishing Group, Inc.

University Press of New England publishes books under its own imprint and is the publisher for Brandeis University Press, Brown University Press, University of Connecticut, Dartmouth College, Middlebury College Press, University of New Hampshire, University of Rhode Island, Tufts University, University of Vermont, Wesleyan University Press, and Salzburg Seminar.

Library of Congress Cataloging-in-Publication Data
Powers, Ron.
   The cruel radiance : notes of a prosewriter in a visual age / Ron Powers.
      p.   cm.
   ISBN 0-87451-690-0
   1. Journalism—authorship.   I. Title.
PN4775.P645   1994
808'.06607 — dc20   94–20541
⊚